THE RESEARCH STUDENT'S GUIDE TO SUCCESS

This book

Second edition

PAT CRYER

Open University Press
Buckingham · Philadelphia

Open University Press
Celtic Court
22 Ballmoor
Buckingham
MK18 1XW

email: enquiries@openup.co.uk
world wide web: www.openup.co.uk

and

325 Chestnut Street
Philadelphia, PA 19106, USA

First Published 2000
Reprinted 2001

A catalogue record of this book is available from the British Library

ISBN 0 335 20686 7

Library of Congress Cataloging-in-Publication Data
Cryer, Pat.
    The research student's guide to success / Pat Cryer.—2nd ed.
        p. cm.
    Includes bibliographical references (p.) and index.
    ISBN 0–335–20686–7 (pbk.)
        1. Study skills—Great Britain.   2. Doctor of philosophy
degree—Great Britain.   3. Report writing—Great Britain.
4. Dissertations, Academic—Great Britain.   5. Graduate students—
Great Britain.   6. Research—Great Britain.   I. Title.

LB2395.C787   2000
378.1′70281—dc21   00–037514

Typeset by Graphicraft Limited, Hong Kong
Printed in Great Britain by Biddles Limited, www.biddles.co.uk

CONTENTS

FOREWORD TO THE SECOND EDITION

High quality postgraduate education is of central importance to the creation of the ever more highly skilled workforce that is necessary if business and industry is to flourish in an increasingly complex and competitive world. It also brings great benefit to individuals and, through them, to society as a whole. And over the past decade we have witnessed some really quite dramatic and challenging changes in the shape, nature and volume of education at this level; changes that not only support our immediate needs for the workforce and knowledge-based economy but also reflect today's remarkable and rapidly advancing technology. Of course, such changes don't come for free and I am only too well aware of the various pressures to which postgraduate education is subject, pressures that in turn impact upon staff and students alike. It is against this backdrop that I truly welcome Pat Cryer's comprehensive study guide for research students. The first edition was immensely successful, as is so evident from the world wide sales, the number of printings, a translation into Chinese, an Indian reprint, being recommended reading for many postgraduate programmes, and most notably being adopted as an Open University set book. Pat's second edition is a complete rewrite and has much wider remit, not only addressing the plethora of different types, modes and levels of postgraduate study – an issue I'm only too well aware of from the 1996 Review of Postgraduate Education that I chaired – but also the now omni-present use of IT. I'm convinced that this new edition will be even more successful than the first, successful with both postgraduate students and their supervisors. If only this book had been available when I was a research student.

Professor Sir Martin Harris
Chair of the National Review of Postgraduate Education
Vice-Chancellor, The University of Manchester
February 2000

PREFACE TO THE
SECOND EDITION

When the first edition of this book went to press, I didn't even have an email address. Since that time, less than five years ago, the use of information technology (IT) has grown at a rate that few of us could ever have imagined. It is now a mainstay of countless aspects of many walks of life, and research students have not escaped its impact. This is one reason why I felt it crucial to update this book – to help research students to capitalize on the growth of IT.

There are other reasons for a second edition. All are set against the background that the first edition proved more successful than I had ever anticipated. Letters of appreciation from students were touching, the reviews were pleasing, so were the sales. The book became set or recommended reading for a number of postgraduate programmes both in the United Kingdom and elsewhere, and a set book for an Open University masters programme in the United Kingdom. I had designed the first edition mainly with PhD students in mind, but it was clearly being found useful by students undertaking research at other levels. To meet this use, this second edition has a wider remit. Throughout, it addresses students on any postgraduate programme with a research component, anywhere where the language of instruction is English. Many such students are mature, in employment and studying part-time, and this second edition addresses their concerns much more than did the first edition.

There are two new chapters in this edition. One (Chapter 2) stems from the 1996 *Review of Postgraduate Education* (HEFCE 1996) which noted, *inter alia*, the profusion of options for postgraduate study and research. This new chapter offers guidance to help aspiring postgraduates decide on what seems best for them. The other new chapter (Chapter 15) responds to a number of high-profile calls (e.g. HEFCE 1996; National Committee of Inquiry into Higher Education 1997) in connection with key skills and employment issues for postgraduates.

A feature of this edition is that, apart from the two new chapters, all the updates have been integrated into the existing chapters. That seemed entirely right, as they need to be regarded as integral aspects of students' research programmes, not as separate entities. In consequence, this second edition is a complete revision of the entire book, which it supersedes.

I am grateful to the following colleagues for checking over various parts of the book: Dr Derek Bell of Bishop Grosseteste College, Lincoln; Professor Paul Cammack of the University of Manchester; Jamie Darwen of Warwick University's Student Union and the National Postgraduate Committee; Dr Pam Denicolo of the University of Reading; Professor Lewis Elton of University College London; Ann Tothill of the National Research Foundation of South Africa; and Mark Wainman of Sheffield Hallam University. I am also grateful to the following colleagues for advice on specific issues: Professor Paul Bridges of the University of Derby; Dr Janet Carton of the Dublin Institute of Technology; Dr Will Coppola of University College London; Professor Martin Swales of University College London; Nikolaos Tsarmpopoulos of the University of Manchester Institute of Science and Technology; and Professor Steve Wratten of Lincoln University, New Zealand. Errors are of course my own responsibility.

I enjoyed researching and writing this second edition, and I hope that it proves useful.

Pat Cryer
Research and Graduate Support Unit, University of Manchester
June 2000

1 INTRODUCTION

Fortune favours the prepared mind.
(Louis Pasteur, address given on the inauguration of the
Faculty of Science, University of Lille, 7 December 1854)

The rationale for this book

Research should be fascinating and fulfilling, packed with intellectual excitement. If this is to be your experience, you need to appreciate that ways of working which proved effective for taught courses, important as they still are, are no longer enough. New skills and strategies need to be developed. This book introduces them, as collected from students and supervisors across a range of disciplines and from a range of universities, colleges and other institutions of higher education.

Who the book is for

This book is primarily for students undertaking research for a higher (postgraduate) qualification. Perhaps you are registered on a programme in which a research component is assessed alongside taught components, or perhaps your programme is 'entirely' by research (there is more on this in Chapter 2). As a student on either, or a prospective student on either, you should find this book useful irrespective of your research topic, field of study, stage of work or institutional attachment. The book will also be useful to a lesser extent if you are working on an undergraduate project requiring a dissertation.

Some parts of this book will be more relevant for you than others. One reason is that to do its job properly, the book has to be designed for the hypothetical student who needs a great deal of guidance, help and support throughout the entire span of a lengthy research programme, and who has a very wide range of uncertainties. You are not such an individual. You bring to your work your own unique background, experience and needs, and the research component of your programme may be relatively short. Furthermore, although the advice in the book does have a wide applicability, it is not made up of absolute rights and wrongs, and there is no reason why you should not reject what does not seem likely to be helpful for you and use or adapt what does.

You may possibly assume or be persuaded that this book must be of limited use to you or anyone else because it is interdisciplinary, and the needs and requirements of each discipline are different from those of any other. To dismiss the book on this basis would be a mistake. Although it is unquestionably true that different disciplines do require different strategies and skills, the differences are often only in terminology and emphasis. Where fundamental differences do exist, the book points them out. So you should find it useful, irrespective of your discipline, provided that you continually bear in mind that your task is to interpret the advice for your own needs. Certainly this was the case for the students from a range of disciplines who worked with the first edition and the pre-published drafts of this edition.

Although the main studies on which this book is based were in the United Kingdom,* this does not necessarily limit its usefulness elsewhere. Differences do exist for students in different countries and cultures, but these too are often a matter of terminology and emphasis. For example, the terms 'postgraduate student' and 'supervisor', as generally used in the United Kingdom, are equivalent to the terms 'graduate student' and 'adviser' as used in certain other English-speaking countries. Examples of different emphases might be whether students studying part-time are permitted a formal (and cheaper) 'part-time' mode of registration as is common in the United Kingdom but not necessarily elsewhere; the various types of postgraduate programme; the nominal duration of the research components within them; the nature and extent of any associated assessed taught components; the administrative structure of supervision; and the form and even existence of the oral/viva examination. Yet the process of research is essentially the same worldwide; so is interacting effectively with people with whom researchers have to work. So, provided that you accept the task of interpreting the terminology

---

* Smaller scale studies were also carried out in Australia, Ireland, Singapore, South Africa and Sweden, and individuals from a wide range of other countries were interviewed.

and modifying the emphases, you should find the book useful irrespective of the country in which you are studying.

How the book is designed

A criticism of many study skills books is that they merely give advice. They do not help readers to adapt the advice for their own personal requirements or to internalize it so that its use becomes second nature. To overcome this criticism, this book provides frequent activities with spaces to indicate that some form of response is required. Their purpose is to help readers to apply or interpret the suggested skills and strategies for their own personal circumstances. You may prefer to do the activities in your head, or simply read through them, or even omit them altogether. Each of these options is entirely acceptable. If you would find it helpful to respond in writing, then make notes in the spaces provided. For lengthier written responses, use separate sheets of paper, which could usefully be kept together in a dedicated file.

The nature of the activities is such that there are seldom 'right' or 'wrong' answers. Where, however, certain responses may have implications that were not previously mentioned, these are discussed immediately after the activity. You will be able to do many of the activities as you come to them, but some require talking to someone who may not be there, or referring to something which may not be to hand. In these situations, think about what the responses might be and mark the pages for returning to later. Peel-off stickers of the 'post-it' type are ideal for this.

You may find it helpful to work through the book with other students. They need not be working in the same field because the skills and strategies involved are either independent of field of study or are presented in such a way as to help you to identify the norms in your own field. In fact, as later chapters will show, there are many good reasons for developing the habit of working in groups and forging links with researchers in other disciplines.

How the book is sequenced

The order of the early chapters is roughly that in which most students are likely to need them. So, whereabouts in the book you will want to start will depend on how far you are into your research programme. For example, readers who have not yet decided on a postgraduate programme will want to start at Chapter 2, whereas those close to completion may merely want to read the final chapters.

If you are a fairly new student, a good way to get the best from this book could be to study the early chapters in detail and just scan the later ones to get a feel for the type of advice in them. As your research programme progresses, your detailed requirements for later chapters will develop somewhat in parallel. Nevertheless, some later chapters will repay early study. For example, Chapters 17 and 18 on originality and creativity come fairly late because they are particularly relevant for the sorts of probationary hurdles which commonly occur some way into longer research programmes. Yet, it is never too early to start thinking about them, first because originality and creativity invariably require lengthy incubation time, and secondly because once you are used to using creative thinking techniques you will find all sorts of situations where they are helpful, even for relatively short pieces of research and in everyday life. Similarly, it is never too early to start thinking about writing your thesis, which is the subject of Chapter 20. As you study later chapters it will probably also be useful to return to earlier ones, because your developing experience will enable you to recognize and appreciate insights which were overlooked on first reading.

At the end of the book are four reference sections. The *websites* section and the *further reading* section are structured under a general interest heading followed by headings which reflect the structure of the book. The *websites* section provides quick and easy access to further information through the Internet and the *further reading* suggests some written material which you may like to consult for delving more deeply into certain topics. The *select bibliography* lists some of the more significant literature which was consulted during the preparation of the book and the *references* section gives full bibliographical details of all the material quoted in the book.

What the book does and does not do

It is important at the outset to be clear about what the book does not do:

- The book is not concerned with the sorts of work strategies and study skills which are generally accepted as helpful for students on taught courses. If you feel that you need a refresher course, there is no shortage of useful material. The *further reading* section suggests some possibilities.
- The book does not attempt to give sufficient advice to guide individuals through the design and implementation of their own

research project. Apart from the obvious limitations of length, this is for two reasons. One is that the book is for students across disciplines, and research design and practice do, for good reason, vary considerably from one field of study to another. The other is that research design, with all that ensues from it, needs to be developed and refined over time, through face-to-face discussion with people who know all the aspects and ramifications of the work and who are experienced researchers in the general discipline area. These people are, first and foremost, supervisors. They are, or should be, closest to the work of the students in their care, and their advice should always take precedence over anything in any book. Chapter 6 does, however, as a stimulus for discussion, provide some general pointers on what could contribute to good research, and the *further reading* section suggests some basic reading on research design.

- The book cannot be a manual for the various uses in research of IT. IT is developing at an enormous rate on numerous fronts, so there can be no substitute for current manuals and local technical support. The book facilitates use of these by indicating throughout the types of IT which are or may be helpful for particular purposes, so giving direction to your own enquiries. Becoming comfortable with IT is a skill in itself, and IT has become part of the lives of most professionals – so all students should aspire to proficiency with it. Yet there are individuals who are, as yet, less than comfortable with much of it. So the book tries to steer a path between the IT and the traditional ways of doing things. In places it offers both.

- Where the administrative procedures associated with working for a particular postgraduate programme shape the strategies and skills required, the book touches on them, but it does no more. Administrative procedures always vary somewhat from department to department, from institution to institution and from country to country, and they are liable to change at any time. So do not rely on this book for them. Always check the current position where you are registered.

- Finally, the book does no more than touch on topics which depend crucially on the field of study or the nature of the research, or which are subject to regular updating. Common examples are research ethics, health and safety, and intellectual property rights. Responsibilities to address these lie with supervisors and institutions.

In summary, the book is firmly and solely concerned with non-discipline-specific strategies and skills for students who are involved in research.

Developing and refining your work strategies and study skills

Understanding the need for work strategies and study skills, and knowing what they are, are the two first steps towards developing them, but they are only first steps. You need to practise them continuously, think about how well they are working for you, adapt them to suit you better and then keep on practising them. This cannot be emphasized enough.

2 EXPLORING THE OPPORTUNITIES FOR POSTGRADUATE STUDY AND RESEARCH

A door that seems to stand open must be of a person's size, or it is not the door that Providence means for that person.
(Henry Ward Becher, quoted in Tripp 1976: 649, item 2, modified for sexist language)

The profusion of options for postgraduate study

In recent years there has been a proliferation of postgraduate courses and programmes across most of the world. From their titles alone it can be by no means obvious what needs they are likely to meet, either in terms of training or educating the students who undertake them or of their value to potential employers. Hence the initiative described in Box 2.1. Quite apart from content (i.e. what the students are expected to learn), the courses and programmes can also vary in 'level', 'structure' and 'mode' of study. Most involve research of some sort. At one extreme are the relatively lengthy PhDs which are 'entirely' by research, in that any supporting taught components seldom count for the final assessment. At the other extreme are the mainly taught programmes which also contain short investigations or projects. In between there is a profusion of programmes made up of various mixes of research, taught courses and other activities, each in their own way attempting to meet the specific and individual requirements of those who undertake them.

The aim of this chapter is to help you to make effective decisions about the programme that seems likely to be most suitable for you. As departmental, faculty and institutional regulations differ widely

---

Box 2.1   The initiative to address the confusion with postgraduate provision

The 1996 HEFCE-CVCP-SCOP Review of Postgraduate Education (the Harris Review) made a number of recommendations concerning quality and standards . . . The Review recommended a national Directory, structured on a typology, and greater standardisation of nomenclature. [The task ahead] involves the development of a structured set of typological categories for the collection of information about postgraduate courses . . . to provide the basis of a national Directory of programmes . . . to improve public understanding.

(Jackson 1997, p. 3)

---

and are regularly updated, you should use the chapter merely to identify issues that could be important for you and as a stimulus for seeking out up-to-date information from appropriate sources.

'Level' of postgraduate study

The 'level' of a postgraduate award reflects both the minimum period of registration and the standards to be attained. All postgraduate levels should be such that the intellectual challenge goes beyond what is required for a first degree.

Normally 'certificates' require the shortest outlay of time (a matter of months full-time and correspondingly more part-time). 'Diplomas' require up to twice as long. Then come 'masters degrees', then 'doctorates' (about three years full-time and correspondingly more part-time, although this differs in different parts of the world). However, there is no uniformity across institutions. So you will have to enquire of the current position with each institution.

Many courses and programmes are run on a modular basis, with each module earning a certain number of credits which can be either traded in for an award or accumulated. The modular approach enables institutions to offer a remarkable variety of postgraduate courses and programmes, some of which can seem uniquely pertinent to the specific requirements of individuals. To achieve this variety, some institutions may be integrating undergraduate-level taught components with the postgraduate work, and it is important to be aware of this and to check suitability for your own requirements.

'Structure' of postgraduate study

Many postgraduate courses and programmes tend to be mixes of various activities – for example, taught modules specific to particular disciplines or professions, taught modules on research, research projects, simulations, portfolio development (documenting professional experience and achievement), plus all sorts of other learning activities which can be remarkably innovative. Structures even differ from one type of masters degree to another and from one type of doctoral degree to another. For example, the MPhil, as it is normally run in the United Kingdom (but not necessarily elsewhere) is 'entirely' by research, in that any taught courses which support it are not normally assessed for the final award. In contrast there are masters degrees that are often referred to as 'taught masters', which contain substantial taught components as well as research components, all of which are assessed for the final award. Similarly there are different types of doctorate. The PhD, or the DPhil as it is called in some institutions, like the MPhil, is normally 'entirely' by research in the United Kingdom. Elsewhere it may have assessed taught components. The so-called 'taught doctorates', 'professional doctorates' and 'practice-based doctorates' vary considerably from one field of study to another and from one institution to another, and they can, like 'taught masters' programmes, be highly innovative in structure. As they tend to have a professional orientation, the title of the award differs from one subject area to another. A DEd and a DEng, for example, are likely to be a doctorate of education and an engineering doctorate respectively, but nomenclature does vary across institutions. The PhD, on the other hand, is the same award in all disciplines and institutions, although the research topic and the research training relate to the discipline.

In addition, there are the 'higher doctorates' – for example, DSc, DLitt, etc. They are of no direct concern here because they are not awarded through courses or programmes for which students register. However, you ought to know they exist. Having one is a considerable honour.

As structure can be so confusing, it is important to check the details of a course or programme against your own requirements. Pay attention to the balance between taught and research components, what is to be taught, how the assessment works and whether academic or professional needs are primarily addressed. This book uses terms such as 'research' degree or degree 'entirely by research' for programmes for which only the research component counts towards assessment. The most common examples are the PhD and the MPhil, as they are commonly offered in the United Kingdom. The book uses terms such as 'other' to describe programmes for which the research component is assessed alongside other assessments, such as in most diplomas and masters degrees.

'Mode' of postgraduate study

Two modes of registration are common in the United Kingdom: 'full-time' and the cheaper 'part-time'. (Elsewhere these modes are not necessarily distinguished for registration or fee-paying purposes.) Other modes of registration are, for example, 'collaborative' and 'at a distance' or 'through distance learning'. The former means in association with another organization, often for its own staff development purposes, and the latter means that the work is largely conducted away from the institution. Modes may affect fees and the minimum (and maximum) time permitted for completion.

Modes of study generally have considerable implications for individuals and are a recurring theme in this book. In particular, they are returned to later in this chapter and in Chapter 4.

Fees and sources of funding

Fees for postgraduate work are not uniform across disciplines or institutions, as Box 2.2 illustrates. In fact all funding issues are complex, and funding procedures are constantly changing. It is important to familiarize yourself with the current position and to shop around. What follows is intended to stimulate your investigations.

A useful source of funding is from departments which offer bursaries, scholarships, awards, grants or studentships. These may be in return for some teaching, tutoring or assessment of undergraduates or they may be just to boost the departmental or institutional research output. If they interest you, it would be worth your while to check specifically on their availability with the department of your choice.

It is also possible to be paid to do a specified piece of research under a contract which allows the contract researcher to be registered for a research degree in parallel with the contractual work. This provides a helpful source of funding and a ready-made research topic. Before accepting contract research, however, do realize that it is not likely to last for the full duration of a doctoral degree and that it is normally to produce findings that are in the interests of the provider of the contract, which may not include original work of a

Box 2.2 The complexity of the fee structure for research degrees – the UK position*

In the UK:

* Fees for students who are British nationals and citizens of European Union (EU) member states are the same (about £2500 per year for full-time registration). Fees for part-time registration are about half of that for full-time registration.
* Some institutions vary their fees slightly from the norm, either up or down, either according to what the market will bear or to attract students, or to reflect their track records and reputations. The established research-centred universities tend to charge more than the norm, and those newer institutions which offer degrees on franchise from more established universities tend to charge less.
* Departments in which research is heavily resource-dependent charge fees to meet their additional costs.
* Fees for students from outside the EU are currently about three times the British/EU rate.

* *NB.* Fees are always under review, but the information is accurate at the time of going to press.

doctoral standard. So contract researchers, registered for a PhD, usually have to do additional work in their own time.

Another source of funding is via the collaborative mode, where a student receives a salary from an employer who may also contribute to the fees. Collaborative research is excellent from the point of view of funding, but, as the research topic is normally one which addresses a need of the employer, it is crucially important that the academic supervisor considers it suitable for the postgraduate level concerned and that supervisors from the place of employment work well as a team with the academic supervisor (see also Chapter 7).

For research degrees, major sources of funds are the research councils which are accountable to Parliament to ensure that they distribute public research funds to the best possible effect. Candidates for their awards must hold a first or upper second-class honours degree in the appropriate field. In the United Kingdom the awards are given only via those departments with completion rates for higher degrees which are deemed satisfactory, and it is to the institutions, not the research councils, that candidates must apply. After interview and/or other procedures, heads of department nominate the individual of their choice for each award.

For students based outside the United Kingdom, their government or employer may be able to provide funds to cover fees. If not, for registration within the United Kingdom, the British Council may be able to advise on alternative sources of funding.

Deciding whether postgraduate work is right for you

If you are thinking of undertaking postgraduate study, it is important to examine your motives before going ahead. Two categories can aid your thinking: reasons which are essential for success and reasons which are only supporting. Fortunately, many students who start out with motives which could be regarded as merely 'supporting' do find that the 'essential' ones develop over time as a natural outcome of trying to do the work well.

Motives such as anticipated career advancement or satisfying someone else are reasonable and common. However, they are best regarded as supporting rather than essential. Alone, they are unlikely to be enough. With a quite short research component in an otherwise taught programme, you may just get away with it. You certainly will not for a degree that is entirely by research. These degrees are seldom failed, but, not at all uncommonly, they are simply just not completed. Reasons lie either with deleterious personal circumstances (see Chapter 4) or with lack of the right motivation.

Motivations which are essential for success – certainly for degrees that are 'entirely' by research, but probably to a lesser extent also for the research components of other postgraduate programmes – are almost certainly intellectual ones: developing a trained mind; satisfying intellectual curiosity; finding a challenge when one feels 'in a rut'; experiencing an academic community; contributing to knowledge; fulfilling a lifelong ambition; etc. The extract in Box 2.3 underlines this.

If your sole aim is to get a postgraduate qualification as 'easily' as possible, you would probably be storing up trouble for yourself by going ahead.

Choosing the type of postgraduate programme

A common factor in the choice of a postgraduate programme is how it can be expected to enhance career development and earning power.

Box 2.3 Reasons for doing a PhD, as expressed by students at the 'writing up' stage

The verdict was unanimous. They did a PhD for love . . . They were doing a PhD because it made them happy. These are people who are not pretending when they say they are fascinated by [what they are doing]. Their eyes light up when the librarian brings them a big, heavy pile of dusty books . . . [In] the chemistry lab, things are, essentially, no different . . . They talk about the 'buzz of discovery' and 'loving what they do'.

(Taaffe 1998, p. vi)

Postgraduate certificates and postgraduate diplomas are normally orientated to a profession, and, being short, can be undertaken either on a part-time basis while in paid employment, or as a gap-filler between jobs. Many 'taught' masters courses are also professionally orientated. They take longer than diplomas, but are increasingly becoming an expected qualification in the professions. Professional or 'taught' doctorates are undertakings of several years, but they do provide a rounded research training pertinent to specific professions. Degrees entirely by research can also be made to support the needs of a particular profession or place of employment if they research-out answers to problems of particular concern to that profession or place of employment.

Regular 'research' degrees such as the MPhil and PhD can keep career options open, even in subject areas which do not seem to relate directly to employment (see Chapter 15). For a career in academia, they are increasingly becoming a requirement. When taken 'full-time', the lifestyle is flexible and students are very much their own bosses, which provides its own form of professional training.

Another possibility which keeps options open is the MRes (master of research) which has been gaining momentum in the United Kingdom in recent years. As its name implies, it provides a broad masters-level training in research. It also involves a wide range of activities across broadly related disciplines. Holders of MRes degrees are reported to be attractive to employers and to 'hit the ground running' where they go on to do higher research degrees.

When choosing a postgraduate programme with career prospects in mind, you need to weigh likely enhanced earning power against the costs of fees and any associated losses of earnings while studying. This is particularly important with full-time registration on the lengthier doctorates and for individuals who are not supported by an employer and who have debts accumulated from their undergraduate study. Also bear in mind that although employers in some areas like to employ holders of doctorates to work at the frontiers of knowledge (such as in academia and research units), most prefer graduates of shorter programmes. These individuals command lower salaries and the employers can then afford to provide the training themselves, customized for their own requirements.

The following activity encourages you to think about how the issues raised so far in this chapter affect you.

 ACTIVITY

What are your reasons for wanting to undertake postgraduate study? Be as specific as possible.

How do these reasons fit into the above categories of 'essential' reasons and 'supporting reasons'?

What are the financial issues that you ought to take into account when choosing a postgraduate programme?

Hence, is postgraduate study right for you? If so, what type of postgraduate programme would seem likely to suit you best?

Choosing an institution

The choice of institution is obvious for those prospective students who are fortunate enough to have an institution nearby which happens to offer the programme that they want at a price they can afford. For the less fortunate, this section suggests some factors, in no particular order, which could influence their choice.

- Where a bursary, grant, scholarsh.
  research in the field of study of on.
  ered more fully later).
- Where a group of friends or compatriot.
  sures the ongoing support of friends and
  dents from non-English-speaking countries –
  their own language. How far this may be bene.
  in Chapter 4.
- Where one did one's first degree. One knows th.
  which makes it easy to have informal exploratory disc.
  the admissions tutor and prospective supervisors, and o.
  the locality and has friends there.
- Where one can live particularly cheaply, possibly with exte.
  family or friends.
- Where a suitable programme is offered fully or partially 'at a dis
  tance', so that one can live where one pleases for much of the
  time.
- Where there are attractive extramural facilities. Theatres, museums
  and galleries, for example, are most accessible from city institutions; whereas some types of sporting activity may be more accessible from rural and coastal institutions.
- Where the department appears particularly caring towards its postgraduates. Early signs of this may show up in clear and adequate
  prospectuses and in fast and personalized responses to exploratory
  enquiries.
- Where there is an internationally renowned research group in the
  proposed field of study. Such groups can be identified by recom-
  mendation or by checking through relevant research journals.
- Where the system of supervisory support seems particularly appealing (see Chapter 3).
- Where one is already employed, so that one can take advantage of
  reduced fees for employees. This may involve being supervised by
  a close colleague, which can bring both problems and benefits –
  see Chapter 7.
- Where there is a graduate school. The existence of a graduate
  school does demonstrate that an institution has given thought
  and resources to postgraduate research, but it demonstrates little
  else. Graduate schools differ markedly in structure and responsibilities, and some excellent institutions do not have one.

The first step in choosing an institution is to think carefully about
the relative priorities of these types of consideration. If you have
access to the Internet, it is well worth checking the web, as it is a
rare institution that does not have its own website (see the *websites*

at the end of this book). Useful general information should be available in public libraries and the libraries and career of most educational establishments. Also check out advertise-s in the national press and keep an eye open for a national graduate fair coming to your area, where a large number of titutions are likely to have information stands designed for pro-ective postgraduates. Outside the United Kingdom there are local British Council offices which provide advice on studying in the United Kingdom.

Write or email for the postgraduate prospectus of a number of likely institutions.

 ACTIVITY

Bearing the above considerations in mind, what are you particularly looking for in an institution for postgraduate study?

3 LIAISING WITH INSTITUTIONS

Look before you leap.

(Proverb)

The importance of liaising effectively with the institution

Once you have identified a course or programme that appeals to you, you need to find out more information about it. Informal contact may suffice. At some stage, though, you will need to go through the procedures of making a formal application. This in no way commits you until you have signed up, but it does involve considerable processing work by staff in the institution. So it is unreasonable to do it unless your interest is serious.

There are intertwining strands to making an application for postgraduate work, some of which are best done in parallel. This chapter has to consider them in sequence, but if that sequence is not appropriate for you, just scan through to see what is here and then study each section as you need it.

Making personal contact with an institution

Ideally students should apply for admission well before the date they wish to start. Institutions in the United Kingdom normally advise prospective students from overseas to apply, if possible, a year in advance for full-time registration on the longer postgraduate programmes, and not to set out from their home countries until they have received and accepted a formal offer. Students may be invited to contact a graduate school, where one exists, or to contact faculties or departments directly. It is essential to check the instructions in the prospectus because they do vary from one institution to another. At some stage students will be required to provide certain documentation including, possibly, evidence of competence in the English language.

It is in your own interests to make all correspondence as neat and professional-looking as possible. It may get copied and circulated to those who will be making decisions about you, possibly in competition with other applicants. Emails and faxes can look scrappy and it is probably best to use them only where distance or other constraints make regular mail unreliable.

It is always worth raising the matter of funding at this stage, just in case there are untapped sources available. (For example, United Kingdom postgraduates on both taught and research programmes are eligible to apply to their institution for awards from what are known as 'Access' funds. Part-time students must be doing at least 50 per cent of a full-time programme.)

Checking out the system of supervisory support

If your interest is in a degree which is entirely by research it is important to check out the system of supervisory support before committing yourself to registering. A number of systems are in common use, and although none is necessarily any better or worse than another, you need to feel comfortable with what you eventually get. It is often said that although a research student's formal registration is with an institution, it is, for all practical purposes, with a supervisor, because effective supervision is the key to success.

If your interest is in a largely taught programme, the supervisory aspects of the research component are probably low in your priorities. You may have no option anyway. If you do, first talk to other students about their experiences of being supervised by various supervisors and scan Chapter 7, which is about interacting with a supervisor.

For programmes at doctoral level, where a supervisor has not yet supervised a doctoral student through to completion, many institutions require there to be a second experienced supervisor to keep a watchful eye on the supervision process. This individual may be overseeing a number of research students and new supervisors, and may, in some institutions, have a formal position. The term 'director of studies' is a common title.

Where a research topic is known from the outset to require the supervisory expertise of more than one individual, students may start with joint supervisors or even a team, panel or committee of supervisors, each having a particular role or responsibility. In collaborative research, for example, one supervisor is generally based with the industrial or commercial partner. Sometimes the need for joint supervisors emerges over time as unforeseen avenues open up; then additional supervisors may be appointed. There may also be external supervisors from other institutions.

Some departments provide their students with 'personal tutors' or 'peer mentors' to whom they can turn for informal advice and information. The former are normally academic staff, other than the supervisor, and the latter are more experienced students.

Another common practice is for there to be a single member of staff with general responsibility for the research students in the department. Such an individual is likely to have an interest in research; to sit on a research committee of the institution; to be the intermediary between the registry and research students; and to be responsible for any formalized group training. His or her role may be administrative and pastoral. Sometimes the role may be shared across a department or institution by members of a committee.

Some supervisors are more sensitive than others to the needs of part-time students with respect to timing and location of supervisions. There are all sorts of possibilities in this connection, but any which are at all unusual need negotiating in advance.

You should be aware that good supervisors, like all good employees, are in demand elsewhere. They may move on, and their students may or may not be able or willing to move with them.

⬛ ACTIVITY

Find out what you can about the supervisory support available in the institutions in which you are interested. If you will have commitments in parallel with your research programme, how flexible is the supervision in terms of timing and location?

Are you comfortable with the idea of working with this type of supervisory support?

What backup arrangements are in place if a supervisor has to be away for an extended period or moves on to another job?

DISCUSSION OF ACTIVITY

Chapter 7 offers advice on working with various kinds of supervisory support, and you would be well advised to scan it before committing yourself to any one kind.

Choosing and refining a research topic

How a topic for research is selected and refined is likely to vary considerably from one field of study to another, and to depend on how, if at all, it is linked to organizations outside academia.

In the arts and humanities, for example, students will probably be given a free rein with their choice of topic, subject of course to the department's ability to supervise it, and they may have to put in a considerable amount of work in the library to identify it and justify it as worthy of attention.

In natural science subjects, for example, the research may have to fit in with the availability of expensive equipment provided under a research grant and with what other members of a research group are doing. Then the research topic and the rationale for doing it are provided, and if prospective students do not like this, or think that appropriate enthusiasm is unlikely to develop, they should apply elsewhere. It is never a good idea to commit oneself to years of something uninspiring, just because of the availability of a place to work on it.

The research topic is similarly provided, at least in terms of broad area, where employers are providing the funding with the purpose of producing answers to questions of concern to themselves, or where the student is employed as a researcher under contract.

In the current climate of rapid change and resource reduction, a few departments in a few institutions may not be as careful as they might be about checking that they can provide a student with what is necessary to research a particular topic effectively. It is in your own interests to check for yourself that you have found a department that can provide a supervisor, resources and training commensurate with your personal needs and interests. Alternatively you can amend your topic to fit the department's ability to supervise it, but it is essential that you should feel comfortable about doing so. The decision should not be made lightly and it may require considerable discussion.

Refining the research topic into something which is researchable and achievable in the time available is intimately linked with developing a research proposal. This is considered in the next section.

Writing the proposal for what you want to do

Where the degree is to be entirely by research, prospective students will almost certainly be required, prior to registration, to write an outline proposal for what they want to do and why. This section should help. Students on other research programmes should tailor the section for their own needs when they need it.

The proposal should use language and terminology that is understandable to an intelligent lay person as well as to a subject expert. Formalities will differ from department to department, but prospective students will probably be required to show that the proposed work is worth researching, lends itself to being researched, is sufficiently challenging for the level of award concerned and can be completed within the appropriate time; that it can be adequately resourced; that the prospective student is suitably qualified to do it; and that no serious constraints exist. Common constraints lie in potential conflicts of interest between students, academics and those funding the research (see the next section). Other constraints may lie in ethical or political considerations.

Most departments, via their admissions tutors or prospective supervisors, do what they can to help prospective students to make their proposals as clear, detailed and precise as possible. The aim is to provide a safeguard against difficulties arising later, as could easily happen if a department were to agree to accept responsibility for a vaguely defined research topic, which subsequently proved difficult to clarify and refine; or if no suitable supervisor could be allocated; or if the methodological or ideological approaches of a supervisor and student were incompatible. As a safeguard, such a proposal is unfortunately not foolproof, because it can require prospective students to make decisions about research design before they have necessarily had any research training or read much within the subject. For this and other reasons, research as it ultimately turns out can vary considerably from what is in an initial proposal. As the difficulties with initial proposals are so well recognized, supervisors may pay scant attention to them or use them merely as discussion documents from which to develop students and progress the research. In institutions where the proposals have to pass the close scrutiny of one or more committees before registration is permitted, more flexible attitudes are usually adopted afterwards.

The development of a research proposal should generate confidence about what lies ahead. If you find, instead, that it is making you feel progressively more uneasy, you need to establish why, while there is still time to do something about it. Causes may lie in a mismatch in your implicit assumptions about the facilities available, the nature of research or the roles and responsibilities of supervisors. Chapters 5, 6 and 7 should help and are worth scanning before committing yourself to a research proposal with which you feel uncomfortable.

Agreeing work with or for an outside organization

Where the proposed research is to be conducted with or for an outside organization, there will need to be some sort of agreement between all the parties. Three issues in particular tend to cause problems if they are not openly addressed at the outset. They all concern potential conflicts of interest.

One is the issue of confidentiality, i.e. if and when the work can be published in journal articles and even in a publicly available thesis. The second concerns any financial advantages that the work may yield, as it is not uncommon for commercial partners to make considerable money on the backs of students' research, while the academics and students get nothing. The third issue concerns ensuring that a project which is of value to the outside organization is appropriate for research at the level for which the student is registered. For this, you must rely on the experience of supervisors in the academic institution. However, research is necessarily a journey into the unknown. So you may need to increase or decrease the scope of a project as it progresses, or give it a more significant or original slant. Advice on all of these is given in later chapters.

Visiting the institution

Prospective students may be invited to see the department to meet the staff and students. It is in your best interests to regard such meetings as two-way interviews. If you have not yet been asked to produce a proposal for what you want to do, you should prepare some ideas in advance. Then you can interview the departmental staff and students as much as they are interviewing you, to see whether you feel you could work productively in that research environment. Take the opportunity to check the office accommodation and other facilities available to students and – where appropriate – to judge whether there seems to be a healthy and supportive critical mass of research students and research-active staff. You may like to scan Chapter 5 to make a checklist for your enquiries.

Box 3.1   How to impress at an interview for a research studentship

The following is a checklist of what an interview panel is likely to be looking for in the successful candidate:

- ability to grasp concepts and to reason analytically;
- motivation and perseverance in achieving objectives;
- capacity for independent thought;
- organizational skills;
- independence as a learner;
- self-confidence;
- nature and extent of any relevant work experience;
- nature and extent of any previously undertaken training in research;
- likelihood of establishing a good working relationship with the allocated supervisor and others working in related areas;
- language skills, which are particularly important for overseas candidates who have never previously studied in the UK.

(Adapted from Engineering and Physical Sciences Research Council 1995, Section 5:4)

If your visit is to compete with other candidates for one of a limited number of places, you will particularly want to impress. Box 3.1 suggests some of the points that the interview panel is likely be looking for. It will pay you to study them and work on them.

Handling an offer

Once you receive an offer from an institution, it is only fair to accept or reject it relatively quickly, rather than expect it to be kept open for an indefinite period.

In most institutions, students can be admitted for research degrees at any time during the academic year. However, the beginning of the academic year (October in the United Kingdom) is the best time, so as to take advantage of any induction programmes and taught courses in related areas.

Using waiting time constructively

If there is a significant delay between accepting an offer and taking it up, you are fortunate, because you can do a great deal to make life easier for yourself later. Here are some suggestions.

If you do not already have keyboard skills, acquiring them must be an early priority. Your first task should be to learn to type quickly and accurately. You may have 'got by' until now using only two fingers, and you may continue to do so, but you would be putting yourself at an unnecessary disadvantage. If you can learn on a formal course, all the better, but there are cheap and effective alternatives which you can use in your own time. The best is probably a self-instructional tutorial, which may be bought in CD-ROM form from most computing suppliers and run on your own computer.

Word processing should be your next priority because you will be using it a great deal. Word processing packages offer a number of sophisticated features, and a highly worthwhile use of time on your hands now would be to familiarize yourself with them and, ideally, become comfortable with using them. This advice holds, irrespective of the type of word processor that you may eventually be using, as all word processing packages are broadly similar. Also useful if time permits is a basic familiarity with other computer application packages, such as databases, spreadsheets and presentation packages (e.g. Microsoft's 'PowerPoint').

If you have access to the Internet, it is also worth spending any additional spare time becoming proficient at searching the web and with the general features of email. Training on these and IT generally will almost certainly be available at your prospective institution, but it will save a great deal of valuable time later if you do some groundwork in advance. The *websites* section at the end of this book gives the addresses of some useful sites, which should, in turn, give links to further potentially useful sites. Box 3.2 suggests a way of going about searching the web, and it should get you started if up-to-date technical advice is not on hand. Don't be surprised, by the way, when the searches throw up advertisements and sites that you don't request along with those that you do.

If English is not your first language, you would also do well to spend time improving it. Spoken English is as important as written English, and the two are not always developed in parallel. It will be important for you to be able to converse freely, which includes being understood as well as being able to understand. So spend time trying to improve your pronunciation as well as acquiring new vocabulary. Perhaps you could find a native English speaker to talk to, or failing that, work with audio tapes spoken by a native English speaker.

Box 3.2 Searching the web

There is so much information on the Internet that users must exercise ingenuity to look for the simplest of facts . . . To use the web effectively, on-line investigators must become familiar with tools known as search engines . . . Some search engines allow you to seek out a specific phrase but, if not, specifying a series of words between quotation marks will usually do this automatically . . . There are well in excess of 200 separate search engines you could use . . . Variants of the search engine theme include so-called meta-search engines. These go through a number of search engines simultaneously and produce a consolidated list of hits . . . Some, such as the curiously named Dogpile (http://www.dogpile.com) search groups of search engines sequentially, inviting the user to continue the search at each stage if the required reference is not found. Metacrawler (http://www.metacrawler.com) appears choosier.

(Temple 1999: 4)

NB. Currently top of most people's list of search engines are: http://www.google.com and http://www.google.co.uk

---

If you have spent your life in a country where the culture is markedly different from a western one you would be well advised to familiarize yourself with the common practices and expectations of where you are about to study. Ways of behaving in particular circumstances do vary considerably, which can all too easily give rise to misunderstandings and bad feeling. Seek advice from those from your own culture who have spent time in a western culture, and who, where possible, have been research students in the country where you are to study. The *further reading* section at the end of the book suggests some literature which should help.

You may also like to find out more about what lies ahead. If you have access to the Internet, you can start this via websites linked to the institution's home page. Otherwise you can ask the institution to provide background papers, reading lists, registration forms, joining instructions and, where necessary, advice on living accommodation. Try to sort out banking arrangements and living accommodation well in advance. Where relevant, passports and permits are also best organized sooner rather than later.

Finally, many of the suggestions in this book require elapsed think-ing time (an incubation period) to generate the greatest benefit. So it would be a good use of time to peruse the book now. In particular, Chapters 4, 6, 15, 17 and 18 will repay early attention.

4 SETTING YOURSELF UP IN A SUPPORTIVE WAY OF LIFE: THE PERVASIVE INFLUENCES OF PERSONAL CIRCUMSTANCES

To be forewarned is to be forearmed.

(Proverb)

The importance of recognizing the need for adjustment

Undertaking a long research programme has to be a way of life, not just a job, because it cannot simply be locked away into office hours inside the institution or other place of work. Remember that research degrees are seldom failed. In general, students either pass them or drop out. Causes of dropout normally lie either in the lack of the right motivation (see Chapter 2) or in personal circumstances which do not permit the work to be given the attention that it requires.

This chapter flags up some of the more common personal circumstances that may affect the efficient and effective conduct of the work and lives of research students. Not all, if any, will apply to you. You, like everyone else, have a unique personal background, expectations, needs and responsibilities to others, and implicit assumptions about how you expect to lead your life. The aim of this chapter is to help you to recognize potential problems at an early stage so that you can head them off before they become serious.

The chapter is primarily for students on the longer research programmes, although students on shorter ones may also find it useful.

■ ACTIVITY

Tick all the circumstances in the following checklist which apply, or may apply, to you:

- Studying full-time
- Studying part-time
- Studying 'at a distance' from the institution
- Recently graduated from first degree
- Not straight from first degree
- Not comfortable with IT
- Employed in work outside academia
- English not first language
- In a 'foreign' country
- Living with parents
- Living with a partner
- Living at home
- Living away from home
- Living with other students
- Having to spend several hours travelling from home or base
- Not in the best of health
- Caring for children
- Caring for aged relatives
- Finances likely to be a problem

Now add any other of your personal circumstances which may possibly have an influence on your way of life during your programme of research.

■ DISCUSSION OF ACTIVITY

The checklist does not include items like 'lack of background or experience in research'. That is an underlying theme of the rest of the book and is not to be confused with the personal circumstances which sap one's time and energy – although there can, at times, be an overlap (see in particular Chapters 10 and 11).

The full-time/part-time divide

In the United Kingdom, more than half of all postgraduate students are studying on a part-time basis. The statistic is similar elsewhere, and it is widespread practice to categorize students according to whether they are full- or part-time. However, such a sweeping two-way divide is not particularly helpful for highlighting the adjustments that students need to make in their lifestyles, because everyone has such different reasons for wanting or needing to study full- or part-time. Part-time students may, for example, be caring for children, in which case child-minding care needs to be sought, either from the institutional nursery (where one exists), or from a relative or partner, or on a paid basis. Part-time students may be caring for elderly relatives who may require different and progressively increasing degrees of care. Part-time students may be in employment, which can provide anything from a great deal of support to none at all, and which may or may not impose restrictive office hours. Part-time students may have financial responsibilities for others. In fact, the only circumstance that all part-timers have in common is the difficulty of finding extended blocks of time for their studies. Chapters 9 and 10 should help, and useful advice for part-time students is also referenced in the *further reading* section.

The following sections consider the implications of some of the most common personal circumstances that influence the lifestyles of postgraduates, whether full- or part-time. In practice, though, no personal circumstance occurs in complete isolation from any other. Personal circumstances interact with each other in complex ways. So you will have to think carefully about the strategies you need to put into place to handle your own lifestyle as a postgraduate.

Preparing for the effects on family life

Only rare individuals undertake postgraduate study without some sort of disruption to their families. Lack of money may mean going without, quality contact time may be curtailed or even disappear, and day-to-day problems may have to be handled without the support of the now preoccupied student. It is crucial to discuss these matters with all the adults in the family and to agree in advance some form of informal agreement about what they are prepared to take on or go without, for how long and with what ultimate benefits.

There is a related matter about which this book can do no more than forewarn. It is that students on the longer research programmes, living with non-academic partners, need to be sensitive to any signs that their partners are feeling threatened or 'left behind' at not being able to keep up academically. The likelihood and significance of this cannot be overemphasized, and the fact that problems tend not to surface until some time into the research programme can produce a false sense of security.

Preparing for being a 'mature' student

An increasing number of postgraduate students have had a break between their undergraduate and postgraduate work. They may, for example, have spent time 'out' to develop themselves and make decisions about their lives; they may have set up home and started a family; and they may have started a career which they wish to run in parallel with their study or continue later.

'Mature' students are normally at an advantage in so far as they know their own strengths and weaknesses, they know what they want and they are dedicated to achieving it. Yet their greater life experience may not be directly relevant to the research and they may need time to get back into the routine of studying, and to put effort into bringing themselves up to speed with IT (see Chapter 5). Some 'mature' students may also have to come to terms with what they may perceive as a loss of prestige in being treated as a student rather than a relatively senior member of staff or an autonomous adult. If this applies to you, do realize that supervisors, too, may be uncomfortable with the situation and that you, through your own attitude, can do a lot to help (see Chapter 7).

Preparing for the influences of living accommodation

Where students live or stay has an impact on the progress of their work.

Living at home, for example, is comfortable and companionable, but skills and strategies have to be developed to cope with the distractions there. Chapters 12 and 19 offer suggestions. As mentioned above, there is also the need to negotiate a form of agreement with respect to effects on family life.

Living with other students has advantages and disadvantages. The advantages, apart from cost-sharing, lie in the easy interaction which counters loneliness and isolation. The disadvantages are being distracted from work. Chapters 10 and 12 respectively offer strategies for combating the latter and enhancing the former.

Students whose research base is away from home need to find living accommodation that is convenient and congenial. The institution may have its own accommodation on or close to campus, and there should be an accommodation office to advise on seeking private rented accommodation and formalizing tenancy agreements. Once in some sort of accommodation, a good way to find something better is to take advantage of informal networks to hear of accommodation about to be vacated.

Preparing for working in a western culture

All cultures invariably give respect where respect is due, but ways of demonstrating this respect vary from one culture to another. In particular, some cultures expect a student never to stray from giving the outward appearance that a teacher is right in all respects all of the time. These cultures tend to value deference, humility and compliance, without displays of emotion. Students from such cultures face a major readjustment when they first arrive in a western academic system where independent thinking is valued and where students, particularly research students, are expected to demonstrate this in ways which may seem alien and uncomfortable.

Some supervisors are sensitive to these issues, and help their students to handle them, but supervisors who have never worked in different cultures may not be. This puts the onus on the students. The issues will not go away. Remedies are matters for individual preference, often worked out with guidance from more experienced members of the same culture. Often all that is needed is a form of 'permission' from supervisors that academic argument and creative thinking are acceptable within the framework of the research; that this is what will in fact please supervisors; and that it will not be regarded as lack of respect. Chapter 7 suggests ways of taking initiatives with supervisors on this and various other matters.

Students from non-western cultures also need to understand that supervisors, just like everyone else, can be sufficiently insecure to feel threatened in certain situations. Some ways of handling this are also suggested in Chapter 7.

The *further reading* section lists a booklet which, although primarily designed for supervisors, should also be helpful for students who wish to gain a better understanding of the implications of cultural matters.

Preparing for working in English as a foreign language

Students who have English as a mother tongue have a head start on those who do not. The English for academic reading and writing of most postgraduates tends to be good. However, spoken English is also important. One reason concerns the benefits of being able to communicate freely and easily with supervisors and others. Another is that some institutions regard their degrees as implying possession of the skills to discuss, argue and possibly later also to teach in English. As far as language skills are concerned, a problem can be that students from other countries tend to conduct their social lives with compatriots, so that they can relax in their own culture and interact without language difficulties. While this is entirely understandable, it does nothing to develop spoken English. So, if English is not your mother tongue, do make an effort to take opportunities to include native English speakers in your social life.

Preparing for working 'at a distance'

If you are registered entirely in a 'distance' mode, you will need to set yourself up so as to make your working life as straightforward as possible. You will need somewhere quiet and comfortable to study, appropriate IT facilities (on which Chapter 5 elaborates) and access to a good library. The library at a nearby institution may, for a fee, extend membership to outsiders, or it may have a reciprocal arrangement with your institution, whereby you can use all the facilities without charge. Distance learning is on the increase and most institutions are doing what they can to help their distance students. So, if a reciprocal arrangement with the library of a local institution does not exist, it may be worth bringing this to the notice of an appropriate person in the institution where you are registered, to see if anything can be done. Alternatively your institution may be persuaded to conduct a postal service for distance students, but this is still rare. Local public and specialist libraries are likely to be worth investigating.

It is also important to do everything possible to combat isolation, which could have a seriously detrimental affect on your life and health. One way is via support groups with other students. You may like to ask your supervisor if he or she can recommend a suitable one, or you may like to set one up yourself or to link in with the email discussion group of the National Postgraduate Committee (see

Chapter 5 and the *websites* section at the end of the book). Many subject associations and professional bodies have their own email lists, some provided through the mailbase service (see the *websites* section). Some of these are specifically for postgraduates.

If you are not registered as a fully 'distance' student, you will, at times, have to travel to the institution. A certain amount of this is beneficial: to meet staff, to interact with other students and to attend formal training. However, travel can be tiring, time-wasting and expensive. So you should try to set yourself up with the home or work facilities of a fully 'distance' student (see above). Most supervisors will agree to a certain amount of supervision via email and telephone. Some, albeit fewer, are comfortable with teleconferencing, and some even agree to organize their other commitments to travel to their students rather than the other way round. It is not reasonable to expect any of these things unless specifically agreed at the time of accepting your place, but, given goodwill, a great deal can be done to minimize difficulties associated with travel.

If you have to travel in specially for supervisions and seminars which may be cancelled at short notice, contingency plans prevent wasted journeys. Such plans are part of time management skills and are considered in Chapter 10.

Preparing for working on a project in or for an outside organization

Students who are funded externally or are on contract research are under a particular set of pressures. They may be expected to produce findings that suit employers or funding agencies; they may be on the receiving end of conflicting advice from academic and work-based supervisors with differing loyalties and value systems; they may find themselves working on topics that are not readily suitable for research degrees; and they invariably find that they have to put in considerable time of their own to extend and develop a research report into a thesis which is viable at research degree level. All these issues are considered more fully later in this book, but it is worth mentioning here that if your research supports your paid work in some way, it should be possible to negotiate some measure of flexitime with your job, or time off during the day.

The *further reading* section lists two highly relevant booklets. Although designed for supervisors supervising students based in industry and public-sector organizations, they should also be enlightening for students.

Preparing for being employed by the institution

It is not at all uncommon for postgraduate students to be employed in some way by their academic institution, for example as undergraduate tutors, laboratory demonstrators or contract researchers. Even regular departmental academics may enrol on postgraduate programmes. Such dual roles can be excellent for ready access to facilities and personnel, and there are usually also beneficial financial implications. However, difficulties can arise at the boundaries between the roles. Some such difficulties are embedded in policy, such as whether the students are allowed the 'staff' or 'student' allocation of books from the institutional library and whether the students are allowed to attend staff meetings. There can also be interpersonal problems in terms of shifts where power is perceived to lie. These have to be handled with sensitivity all round.

Preparing for being on a grant

Students on grants have to make exceptionally good cases if they are to have their grants extended into extra time. So they need to settle quickly into a routine of productive work.

While on the subject of funding, Box 4.1 gives some ideas for making money go further. Although most are obvious, they may nevertheless have slipped your mind.

Box 4.1   Making your money go further

- State handouts. There are not many left! If you are a United Kingdom citizen, you may get free prescriptions, eye tests and dental check-ups. It is worth asking about them.
- Watch those transport costs. If you travel by public transport, don't just assume that buying a travel card/season ticket is the cheapest option. Often it is not if you don't have to come in every day. Don't forget that a bicycle or walking is the cheapest form of transport.
- Don't live at the Ritz. It is always worth looking to see if you can move somewhere cheaper or nearer. Halls of residence are often cheap, if you can get a place. The most important advice is to seek help from the institution's accommodation office. Finally, living with relatives may be unbearable, but it can be cheap!

- If you can get some kind of job, it will help your situation considerably. It is worth visiting the careers service on a regular basis. If you have any special talents, this is a good time to discover them.
- Shopping for bargains. Supermarket own-brand items are often considerably cheaper than branded products and often just as good. Try markets and second-hand shops for clothes and CDs.
- Managing your money. Don't put £2000 under the bed. Don't put it in a student bank account either. Put it into a high-interest building society account or (if you are brave) a unit trust (which can go down as well as up). Use credit cards to buy items like books and travel cards. Pay when you get a statement; under no circumstances pay any interest charges. Remember that heating bills are related to how much you use your heating!
- Be nice to people. You may wonder what this has to do with finance. However, it is very important – especially with parents or spouses. If you want people to support you or make sacrifices for you, you need to be nice to them. Remember birthdays and make people understand that you appreciate their help. That way they are likely to go out of their way to help you. Bank managers also appreciate being told that you want to go into overdraft before you do.
- Do they do a student discount? A surprisingly large number of places do. Don't be afraid to ask – many places do not advertise the fact. It is also worth using any money-saving vouchers you can get your hands on. If you do not have a student union card, it is worth getting one for discounts.
- Selling the family silver. Many people plead poverty but appear wealthy. Each of us has various bits and pieces we keep in a cupboard somewhere. Books are especially prone to sitting idly on bookshelves. Remember that second-hand bookshops buy as well as sell. Virtually everything can be sold for a price.

(Adapted from University College London Graduate School 1994: 4)

NB. Issue 2 of the *University College Graduate Society Newsletter* elicited responses from staff which flagged up the existence of hardship and travel funds of which postgraduates could take advantage. These were specific to University College London, but suggest that it would be worth finding out what other institutions can offer.

ACTIVITY

What issues in the previous sections seem likely to be relevant to you?

What strategies might you consider for dealing with them?

Recognizing and preparing for the influences of other personal circumstances

You may have – or imagine that you have – special circumstances which could affect your being taken seriously or fully accepted in your new academic community. You may, for example, be considerably older than the average research student and think that you could be a target for ageism; or your previous experiences could make you think that you could be the target of sexism. There are many other such '-isms', and all sorts of terms could be coined for what is imagined to cause or genuinely does cause prejudice in others. Although genuine and deep-rooted prejudice does exist, most of it is either imagined or can be negated over time by appropriate professional behaviour. If you think that an '-ism' is likely to bother you, make resolutions to get advice from others who seem to be coping well with the same 'handicap', and possibly to set up or join self-help support groups, either on campus or electronically at a distance. These groups can be as large or small, formal or informal, transient or long-lasting, as you and other members find appropriate for your own needs.

This book is not the place to advise on what to do if other personal difficulties arise. Use your judgement about how far to load supervisors with personal matters. Most institutions provide alternative sources of help (see Chapter 5).

ACTIVITY

If you think that you need skills or strategies to meet any special circumstances in which you find yourself, make a note of the problems here. Then ask around for suggestions.

The three necessities: health, motivation and support

A recurring theme of this chapter is that postgraduate students, particularly those on long research degrees, need to set themselves up in a way of life that supports their work. The chapter has made some suggestions. However, the vagaries of life affect everyone differently, and have to be handled individually as they occur. The three necessities are health (or stamina); motivation (i.e. the wish and determination to succeed); and the right sort of personal support, both financial and interpersonal (i.e. from friends, parents, partners, children, etc.).

5 SETTLING IN AS A NEW STUDENT

We were forming a group of people who'd be working together and learning together, going through similar experiences, creating together. I thought it was terrific.
(Leonard Nimoy, speaking of the original series of *Star Trek*, where he played Mr Spock, quoted in Shatner 1993: 204)

The importance of being integrated into the academic community

Once you formally start your research programme, the sooner you can settle in, the sooner you can work productively. This chapter is about speeding up the settling-in process. This involves finding out about the facilities and the people who can support you, familiarizing yourself with them and then putting yourself in a position to take advantage of them.

Responsibilities for your integration

The responsibility for your integration is a joint one, between yourself and your institution, department or supervisor. How it should best be undertaken depends on your mode of study, the nature of your programme and your point of entry in the academic year.

You may be starting with a number of other students on a 'face-to-face' programme at the beginning of the academic year. Then the department will probably run formal induction events and supply folders of useful information. Much of the responsibility for integrating yourself will thus be taken off you, and you will have little need of this chapter, although it is probably worth scanning quickly. There may, however, be few if any formal procedures for induction, perhaps because the department or group is small, because you are arriving at a time other than the beginning of the academic year or because you are working in some form of 'distance' mode. In this case, you have to take responsibility for your own integration. This chapter provides a stimulus for action, but it can do no more than that because departments and groups are so different in terms of the resources at their disposal, their management preferences, and the needs and requirements of their disparate disciplines.

If you are part-time on a degree entirely by research, this chapter is particularly for you. It is all too easy to assume that shortage of time will necessarily prevent you from availing yourself of all but the most basic of support facilities. Although it is true that the calls on your time will be severe and that you will have to identify priorities, this does not mean that you should allow decisions to be made and behaviour patterns to develop by default through lack of information. It is important for you to appreciate the types of support which are normally available to full-time research students. Then you can locate or set up alternatives which you can access more readily from home or your place of work.

If your research is a part of an otherwise taught programme, the chances are that you will already feel at home in the department before the research starts. You will know the staff and students who will want to support you, and you should feel relatively comfortable in utilizing that support. You may, nevertheless, find it helpful to scan this chapter, as there is much in it that you can adapt for your own situation.

If you are working 'at a distance', your supervisor or someone else in your institution will probably be extremely careful to provide you with support and advice on settling in. You, too, though, may like to scan this chapter as a stimulus for the sort of support that you will have to find from somewhere or set up for yourself.

Familiarizing yourself with departmental accommodation

With the best will in the world, departments vary enormously in terms of what accommodation their resources allow them to provide for their research students. The extract in Box 5.1 by a former officer of a postgraduate student union is part of an article on facilities for postgraduates, and many departments manage to achieve its recommendations for their full-time research students. It may be beyond their means to do the same for part-timers, although it is reasonable that part-timers should at least have somewhere to put their coats and books, if they are to stay longer in the department

---

Box 5.1 Space and facilities for research students

Accommodation of research students must be specialised to meet three ends. First, every research student must have an office, possibly shared, to be used as 'home base'. This will have to include certain other facilities. Second, students sharing offices will require part-time exclusive access to other departmental rooms. Third, each department above a certain size needs a common room set aside for its research students only. Common space is a valuable weapon in the war against isolation.

Each student needs a place of his/her own. The minimum acceptable provision is a desk, chair, lamp, bookcase, file drawer(s), telephone and room key.

(Gross 1994: 21)

---

than merely popping in to see supervisors and then leaving again. Laboratory and workshop space, where appropriate, should also be available, although not necessarily in the department itself.

The following activity should serve as a stimulus for finding out what accommodation is available for research students in your department. If you are asking questions outside a formal induction programme, use your judgement about who to approach, depending on who seems knowledgeable and prepared to chat. Some possibilities are supervisors, other research students, the departmental secretary and the member of staff with special responsibility for research students where one exists. Everyone is bound to be busy. Social occasions, such as coffee or lunch breaks, when people seem happy to talk, are a norm in some departments, but unheard of in others.

 ACTIVITY

What does the department provide for its research students in the way of the following?

• An office to work in

• A desk

- A locker for bags

- Somewhere to hang clothes

- Coffee-making facilities

- Laboratory and workshop space, where appropriate

- Any other accommodation

How, if at all, is the accommodation different for full-timers and part-timers or for students on different programmes involving research?

● DISCUSSION OF ACTIVITY

The extract in Box 5.2 gives a flavour of the importance of adequate office space for research students.

Box 5.2 The importance of proper accommodation for research students

The provision of better office space for all research students will have major and longlasting benefits for all interested parties. Students will be better able to proceed with their work and will feel more satisfied by their postgraduate experience. Members of staff will find that creating a cohesive body of research students will give them a readily available body of help for research, teaching, seminars and other activities. The community will be enhanced by the inclusion of its senior students. The funding bodies will also approve.

(Gross 1994: 24)

Familiarizing yourself with departmental facilities and services

Departments also vary in terms of what general facilities and services they can provide for their research students. Use the following activity as a stimulus for finding out about them.

 ACTIVITY

The following facilities may not be available in the department and, if they are, they may not be free. Find out about them, how any payment works and, where applicable, whether prices are cheaper anywhere else nearby.

• A phone for incoming and/or outgoing calls

• A photocopier

• A fax machine

• Departmental stationery, including personal business cards

• Departmental computers, printers and application packages

• Internet access, for using email and searching the web

• Specially produced in-house software

• Keys to work areas

If you do not already have access to any of these at home or in a place of regular employment:

- Is it worth the trouble and expense of buying a computer and/or modem so that you are not tied to a particular location for word processing or data processing and so that you can use email and surf the web from home or other base?

- What application packages (word processing, databases, spreadsheets, etc.) would you need to make you compatible with others in the department? Can these be bought more competitively through the department or institution than through normal sales outlets?

- What are you going to do about virus protection?

- If applicable, how is your employer or funding agency prepared to help?

What is the institution's attitude towards using its facilities and services for personal use?

With reference to Box 5.3, what is the institution's policy on security of use of the Internet?

Box 5.3 The security (or otherwise) of the Internet

One useful lesson to learn from the Clinton scandal is that emails do eventually catch up with you. Too many PC users have been lulled into a false sense of security by the 'delete' command. It is good to be able to access worldwide information and send electronic mail in seconds from a university PC, but the price of this is loss of security. Because you are accessing the internet through the university's computers and networks, details of every website visited and every email sent are stored and can be retrieved by administrators. The information is often kept on file for months or, in some cases, years.

(Times Higher Education Supplement 1999: 11)

■ DISCUSSION OF ACTIVITY

Having an email address, being able to use email frequently and being able to access the web are essential parts of modern academic and professional life, and your research will be greatly disadvantaged without them. So you should try to set yourself up with them sooner rather than later. The department, your place of employment or somewhere else may be able to meet all your IT needs, but if not you may have to acquire your own hardware. Portable computers (also known as laptops, notebooks and palmtops) are particularly versatile, and it may be possible to set costs off against tax if you have or have recently had an income. Fortunately there is no shortage of free Internet service providers (ISPs) for supporting home working. Ask around for advice on their track record on such aspects as related costs, speed and reliability. All of these are likely to be considerably inferior to institutional facilities which are generally connected via a permanent network, which is fast and free (to users). Home use has to rely on telephone lines.

Most educational institutions have licence agreements for their most commonly used computer applications (including virus protection software) which allow students to buy software at a discount. These are not always well advertised, so you may have to ask around for them. Some basic application packages can be downloaded free of charge or on a trial basis from the web.

The *websites* section at the end of the book gives the site of a provider of IT training for higher education. Even if you do not wish to use its training directly, its publicity should be a good indicator of the sorts of IT skills that are currently considered important, and you may like to discuss with your supervisor which of these you may need.

Many institutions 'turn a blind eye' to students' personal use of institutional facilities such as email and printing, provided that the use is 'limited' – a term which they do not usually define. However, some other institutions have strict restrictions. It is worth finding out what the position is in your institution, as it is not uncommon for institutions to present students with unexpected bills for unauthorized use of facilities.

Familiarizing yourself with the system of supervisory support

By the time that you formally start on your research programme, decisions will already have been made about your supervision. In particular, you will almost certainly have already met the single person, probably just called your 'supervisor', who undertakes your 'day-to-day' supervision. (This term implies 'first port of call', not necessarily that meetings will take place every day, although they may on a casual basis.) You may not, however, be fully aware of the other forms of supervisory support that may be available to you, either quite generally or if your research should change direction. Reread the section on forms of supervisory support in Chapter 3. Then try the following activity.

⬛ ACTIVITY

Find out the names and roles of everyone, in addition to your day-to-day supervisor, who has or could have a formal supervisory responsibility towards you, for example:

- A principal supervisor, who oversees supervision, but does not have a day-to-day involvement.

- A team, panel or committee of supervisors, with a joint responsibility or with each member having a unique responsibility.

- Joint supervisors, with equal responsibility towards you, but in different areas of your work.

- A collaborative supervisor, who supervises from the perspective of an outside organization or agency.

- A mentor or adviser.

- Anyone else, such as a visiting expert of some sort.

(■) DISCUSSION OF ACTIVITY

Wording to encompass all the possible forms of supervisory support would make for clumsy reading. So unless stated otherwise, the single term 'supervisor' is used from here on throughout the book for the individual academic who has day-to-day responsibility for supervising a student. Where you have additional supervisory support, you will need to adapt the terminology for your own circumstances.

Informal supervisory support can also be very important. For scientists working in a laboratory, for example, post-doctoral researchers and technicians can be a considerable help with routine matters on which students may not want to bother supervisors.

Familiarizing yourself with departmental and institutional research training and support

Departments vary in terms of what general training and support they provide for research students and the names that they use to describe it. Use the activity below as a stimulus for finding out what is available for you.

(■) ACTIVITY

Apart from the interaction between students and their supervisors, is any of the following general training offered by the department?

• An induction programme

• Weekly (or other regular) seminars

• Relevant taught courses in your subject area (possibly designed for another study programme)

• Relevant courses in research design and research methods

- Training on basic use of computers – in particular word processing, use of databases and spreadsheets, and 'PowerPoint' (computer-aided presentation)

- Training on the use of email

- Training on the use of the web – in particular, the use of browsers and search engines

- Training on the use of the institutional library

- Some form of group support

Are there any social events which bring staff and students together?

Are there any special induction events for students from other countries?

Is there a dedicated resource centre where copies of course materials and reprints of research articles can be obtained?

If there is a graduate school, does it offer any training and support in addition to or in parallel to that of the department? Or, if there is not a graduate school, is cross-departmental training provided elsewhere?

⬛ DISCUSSION OF ACTIVITY

Training in association with research can be crucially important, vaguely helpful or wastefully time-consuming, depending on its scope and the background and needs of the students concerned. In particular, there is the inevitable conflict between the need to start the research as soon as possible and the need to find out about computer applications, research design and research methods so as not to waste time doing what may turn out to be inappropriate. Your supervisor's advice is crucial in establishing what is reasonable for you.

If you are not already comfortable using basic word processing, email and the web, do take advantage of any opportunities to become so. (Chapters 8, 13, 14 and 20 indicate some of the features that are probably worth learning.) If training opportunities are not supplied, you would be well advised to make them for yourself. You can learn about more advanced applications later if your research seems to warrant it.

Familiarizing yourself with departmental staff and research groups

Each member of academic staff in the department will have his or her own personal area of research, possibly with a group of research officers, research assistants and research students working in various aspects of that area. The research areas of some staff may be so closely related that they and their students together form a research group, which may or may not extend outside the department. It will be useful to know the scope of all the research expertise.

It is also important to find out about the other departmental staff: the secretaries, the administrators, the post-doctoral researchers and, in some fields of study, the technical staff. Their friendship and support can be invaluable, but can all too easily be abused.

Use the following activity as a stimulus for finding out about staff and research groups in the department.

 ACTIVITY

What are the areas of research in the department and who heads them?

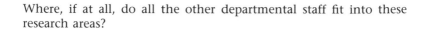

Where, if at all, do all the other departmental staff fit into these research areas?

If you are to be part of a research group in which one or more research students work on parts of a single large topic, what, in general terms, are the boundaries of the work of each of you?

Do any research groups have activities which it could be worth keeping informed about or being involved in?

What links are there between research groups?

What are the areas of responsibility of the secretarial, administrative and, where appropriate, library and technical staff in the department?

Do such staff ask that research students follow any particular procedures when requesting their services?

Familiarizing yourself with departmental and institutional procedures

Every department and institution has its own way of doing things. Some of this will be documented as formal procedures, although much will be implicit and undocumented. It is too easy to become drowned in paper, emails and web pages, so seek guidance about what documents are worth having and when. Use the activity below as a checklist.

 ACTIVITY

Find out whether there are documented departmental or institutional procedures on any of the following.

• Study contracts for students on research programmes

• Notes of guidance for students undertaking research

• Roles and responsibilities of supervisors and students

• Procedures for monitoring research students' progress and traversing hurdles such as the (common in the United Kingdom) transfer from MPhil to PhD

• Complaints and appeals

• Health and safety regulations, where appropriate for the field of study

What other useful or important and relevant documents exist, and at what stage is it worth studying them?

● DISCUSSION OF ACTIVITY

Some departments operate a form of study contract (also called 'learning contract') which documents the results of negotiations between student and supervisor and is amended, by mutual agreement, over time. Such contracts form a sound basis for understanding what is required of students and what they have a right to expect. Contracts are not, however, used everywhere, as some people feel that they are too trivial and patronizing for work between mature and independent adults at research degree level and that they could have unpleasant legal consequences. Most supervisors, though, would probably institute some form of informal contractual working if their students requested it.

Familiarizing yourself with departmental resource centres and institutional and other libraries

All institutions of higher education have a library or libraries, usually with librarians who specialize in particular disciplines. If such individuals exist in your library for your field of study, you would be well advised to cultivate their acquaintance. They can be of real help during your research programme.

Many departments have their own resource areas which house reading matter of particular interest to their staff and students – for example, past theses, conference literature and journal articles to which the department or individual staff members subscribe. These have the advantage of being directly relevant to students' broad areas of interest.

There may be nearby libraries which are open to members of your institution, and there may be specialist libraries elsewhere which you can arrange to use, possibly on a fee-paying basis. Public libraries can also be extremely helpful for researchers, and may be more readily accessible than the institutional library for students working at a distance. Most libraries have their own websites, which can be immensely useful throughout a research programme. Not only do they offer a quick and relatively easy way to find out about the library's stock and mode of operation, they almost certainly link to other useful websites. Web access to certain libraries does, however, depend on the subscription arrangements.

ACTIVITY

Does your department have a resource area of literature pertinent to the general discipline? If so:

• What types of material does it contain?

• What is the policy on borrowing?

It may be worth accessing the website of your institutional library now. (New users may find it easiest to go via links on the institution's home page.) See how many of the following questions can be answered without having to resort to asking someone or visiting the library.

• How many books are students on your programme of study allowed to borrow, and for how long?

• How can your library's on-site catalogue be accessed via the web to find out what is in stock or on loan?

• How can the site be used to link to similar information about other libraries?

• What, if anything, is the cost to you of using the library's inter-library loan services? Is there a limit on the number of such loans allowed without charge?

• How is the library arranged and is there an area for students to work undisturbed? For example, can private study areas be booked?

• If there is an institutional librarian specializing in your field of study, who is he or she?

- How can you access:

    - catalogues of works currently 'in print' worldwide (or capable of being acquired if they are media-based)

    - catalogues of all works that have been available in the recent past?

    - journals available on-line?

    - on-line citation indexes?

    - databases available on-line?

◉ DISCUSSION OF ACTIVITY

All institutional libraries (and good-sized public libraries) have their own catalogues on the web. Specialist catalogues should also be accessible from regularly updated CD-ROMs, although their use may require a personal visit. Of related interest are the websites of bookshops and publishers. The former are widely advertised and the latter can be readily located using a simple search. Of related interest is the service provided by some journal publishers by which one can request and receive the current contents of certain journals to see what articles seem worth the time to seek out. Advice should be readily on hand in your institution.

Fortunately there always seems to be a member of staff in any library who is more than happy to help on any query.

Locating other institutional facilities and services

Institutions normally have a wide range of facilities and services, such as: a students' union; computing services; print services; counselling services; financial services; services to help with language problems; centres for major religions; accommodation services; careers services; shops; eating places; etc. Some also have a research students' support group and a nursery for students' young children. You may like to check the web to peruse what is available, or you may prefer to check as needs arise.

If you are living away from home, you should find out fairly urgently about the institutional health centre and how, if necessary, to register with a local doctor. Next in urgency, if English is not your first language, is to find out what institutional support exists for you – perhaps a language centre to help with written and spoken English and/or a social club.

Identifying national and international sources of support

One of the best supports outside the department and institution may come from the learned or professional society for your field of study, particularly the postgraduate section if one exists. It can provide access to all sorts of useful information and support, such as email discussion groups, newsletters, journals and conferences. It may also provide certain facilities free or at reduced charge.

There are also national organizations which exist to support and/ or develop policies for research students, and they too provide access to information, such as email discussion groups, newsletters, journals and conferences. It would be useful, in due course, to familiarize yourself with their remits. Contact information for some of the main ones is in the *websites* section at the end of this book.

The National Postgraduate Committee (of the United Kingdom) is particularly worth noting, as it is run by students for students, and it represents the interests and aspirations of all postgraduates, whether on taught courses or undertaking research. Box 5.4 gives the idea. It lists some of the topics that have been aired recently by students through its email discussion group, and contributors are from outside as well as inside the United Kingdom. Box 11.3 in Chapter 11 is one example of the extremely valuable information that users provide for one another. Countries other than the United Kingdom have similar postgraduate groups, and information about them can be found via the website of the National Postgraduate Committee (see the *websites* section).

The British Council and the Council for International Education (still known as UKCOSA which stood for its old name, United Kingdom Council for Overseas Students' Affairs) should both prove useful for students from overseas.

Box 5.4 Examples, in no particular order, of the wide range of topics considered in the email discussion group of the National Postgraduate Committee

- Bank loans
- Employment vacancies
- Funding sources for postgraduate study
- Career development
- Insurance
- Intellectual property
- Printing costs
- Fees while writing up the thesis
- Institutional status of research students (students versus staff)
- Induction (departmental and institutional)
- Electronic databases
- Types of postgraduate qualification
- Modular postgraduate programmes
- Research Council funding
- Appeals and complaints procedures
- Library loans (allowances, loan periods, costs of inter-library loans)
- Procedures of oral/viva examinations
- Teaching undergraduates (training and rates of pay)
- The British Library
- Institutional postgraduate societies
- Binding theses (timing and costs)
- Pensions and pension contributions
- Commercial thesis editing (for style and grammar)

 ACTIVITY

Find out, possibly by enquiring of your supervisor, other departmental or library staff or by searching the web, whether there is a learned or professional society for your field of study and, if so, how to contact it.

Use the web or take advice from your supervisor on what the society has to offer in the way of help with your research.

■ DISCUSSION OF ACTIVITY

Research tends to be an individual activity and, as a programme of lengthy research progresses, a major complaint from research students is the feeling of isolation. Unless you are working on a group project or as part of a large and active research department, you would be well advised to put effort into warding off isolation. You need to be on the constant lookout for people who know enough about your field to be able to discuss it meaningfully and have the time to do so. You may find such people in your family, in your social group or in your department. Visiting staff on sabbatical leave are ideal, as are email discussion groups.

6 TOWARDS RECOGNIZING QUALITY IN RESEARCH

A PhD from a UK university is widely (if not universally) admired in terms of its quality.

(Clark 1995: 101–2)

The importance of recognizing quality in research

Many students start their research with research experience from elsewhere. This chapter is for those who do not have such advantages. Its aim is to provide a 'feel' for what contributes to good research through a guided tour of research articles and theses. If you think you would benefit from this, ask your supervisor or other students to recommend a few research articles that are respected in your area, together with some masters-level theses and a few PhD theses. Ask for the PhD theses even if your research is less ambitious, because only PhD theses will be able to illustrate certain points, and it will help you to be aware of these, even if only to know that they need not concern you. Most libraries do not allow theses or journals to be loaned out, but they can be studied on site, or the articles can be photocopied, or supervisors may be prepared to lend out personal copies.

Before starting the guided tour, a word of warning. Each field of study has its own norms, which have been built up over many years through dealing with the types of research with which the discipline is concerned (see Box 6.1). There is thus no way that this chapter can give specific guidance which would be acceptable across all fields of study. Nevertheless, the general guidance should be useful as a starting point for discussion with your supervisor and others in your discipline. That is its purpose.

Box 6.1 Postgraduate research is different in different disciplines

In science, research education is strongly shaped by the conditions required for maximising the productivity of specialised research groups. Students are recruited to a research group geared towards defining discrete sets of problems. Students will undoubtedly contribute to their solution. But sometimes the needs of the research are difficult to combine with those of the student. It might, for example, be in a highly competitive and rapidly changing field where speed is of the essence . . . Students' contribution to the work of their group may often be substantial. But their contribution to disciplinary knowledge is normally predefined by their supervisor and expectations of originality are limited.

. . . In the humanities the traditional emphasis has been on individual modes of inquiry and on the importance of the freedom of the student to select his or her research topic. Originality and independence are strongly held values . . . Claims of substantial contributions to knowledge on the part of PhD students are still made, but only from the most prestigious institutions.

. . . In the social sciences . . . the ideal remains that of the individual pursuing the problem of his or her choice and making a more or less original contribution. Concepts of originality are usually but not always fairly modest . . .

(Becher *et al.* 1995: 13–14)

Research areas, topics, themes, foci and problems

Research students normally start their work with a general area of interest. At some stage this may be expressed as a precise problem (or set of linked problems) known as a 'research problem'. The idea of a 'research problem' is extremely useful. It provides a sense of direction and hence of security because problems are there to be solved. So the whole thrust of students' research must be to use the tools and techniques of research to find solutions to their research problems. However, the term 'research problem' is not universally used, and it is worth taking a little time to understand where it is and where it isn't, and what terminology may be used instead.

The term 'research problem' tends to be most commonly used where the precise purpose of the research is known fairly clearly from the outset. Usually the whole research programme can be mapped out in some detail; the boundaries of the work are fairly neatly defined; and the term 'project' may be used to describe it.

On the other hand students may start their research with only a general area of interest, and the emphasis is on exploring that interest. Each new phase of the work takes up and further explores interesting or significant parts of what emerged from previous stages (which is known as 'progressive focusing'). Over time, the research tends to focus on specific and significant issues, which may not have been identifiable at the outset, and it is these that form the foci or themes of the thesis. The thesis itself has to be written, or at least edited, with hindsight to make a feature of the foci or themes that have emerged, and the title is finalized at quite a late stage so as to encapsulate these foci or themes. At the outset, the research is not neatly contained inside obvious boundaries, and it does not have a clear end point. Indeed part of the skill of the student is to create and impose boundaries so that the work can be terminated within the time and resources available and in such a way as to be presentable as a self-contained package (Chapters 17, 18 and 19 elaborate). Since neither the scope of work nor its eventual focus (or foci) or theme (or themes) are precisely known until the work is considerably under way, the terms 'project' and 'research problem' tend not to be used. It is as if the purpose of much of the research is to identify a problem which it can solve or has already solved. Then the processes of identifying the problem and solving it both feature in the thesis. The well-known saying about 'the solution looking for the problem' captures the idea.

The drawing in Figure 6.1 also captures the idea of identifying a research problem with hindsight, i.e. after the event. The way one normally thinks of going about hitting a target with an arrow is to start by noting where the target is, then to develop the skills to hit it and then actually to hit it. That is analogous to conducting research which is neatly defined and contained by a pre-specified research problem which one directs one's energies to solving. Yet the woman in Figure 6.1 merely shoots her arrow in the right general direction, notes where it lands and then paints a target around it. So it is with identifying the research problem (or theme or focus) once a viable solution has become apparent, and then putting one's time and energies into ring-fencing various possibly nebulous studies so that they can appear as a self-contained piece of research.

The concept of a research problem suggests roles in which research students have to operate, and this, too, provides a sense of direction and security. The first role is that of an explorer to

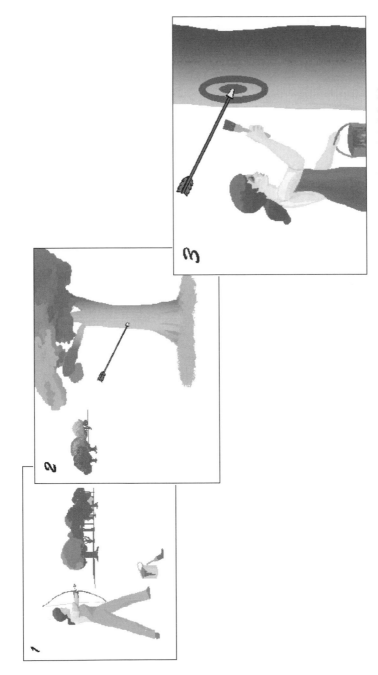

Figure 6.1 Identifying a research problem, focus or theme with hindsight: an analogy with archery. (Modified from an unattributed drawing supplied by the Graduate School of the Australian National University)

Box 6.2   Roles in which research students need to operate

The following roles are roughly in the order in which research students need to occupy them, although there will inevitably be a certain amount of cycling backwards and forwards between roles.

- Explorer – to discover a gap (or gaps) in knowledge around which to form a research problem.
- Detective and/or inventor – to find solution(s) to the research problem that defines the gap(s).
- Visionary – to develop an original twist or perspective on the work and a fall-back strategy in case the work doesn't go according to plan, and (where necessary) to find a way of ring-fencing nebulous or discrete investigations into a self-contained piece of research appropriate for the award being sought.
- Barrister – to make a case in the thesis for solution(s) to the research problem.

Other roles may be helpful for particular tasks but are less helpful for providing an overall sense of direction.

---

discover a gap in knowledge around which to form the research problem or set of linked problems. For those students who know their research problems from the outset, the time spent in this role can be very short, although not non-existent because the problem still needs some refinement. Other students can spend a considerable time in this role.

The second role is that of a detective and/or inventor to find solution(s) to the research problem(s): a detective where the problem is about something unknown and an inventor where the problem is to produce something. Box 6.2 shows these two roles, together with two further ones: a visionary and a barrister. Something of the requirement for the visionary role has already been mentioned in connection with finding a way to ring-fence nebulous investigations, and more will be said of this in Chapters 17, 18 and 19. The need for the barrister role is explained later in this chapter. Research students may, of course, occupy other roles at times, such as fire-fighter, manager, negotiator, etc., but these reflect the sorts of routine matter which everyone has to handle on occasions and do not stimulate any sense of overall direction in research.

The usual starting point to defining a research problem – and this is true irrespective of whether the term is used explicitly or implicitly and whether the research problem is identified early or late in the research programme – is to read round the subject to get to know the background and to identify unanswered questions or controversies. Small-scale investigations or pilot studies may also be conducted, to identify significant issues for further exploration. Where the research problem is identified early on, a common way forward is to break it down into a set of questions or hypotheses. Then care and attention are given to make these so detailed and specific that the research design falls naturally into place. The process of getting the research questions or hypotheses into a form which has the right amount of detail is known as 'operationalizing' them.

Because the concept of a research problem is so useful, it should help to keep it in mind, even if terminology such as theme or focus is more appropriate in your own field of study. The following activity invites you to get a feel for how research problems (or themes or foci) tend to be identified in your field of study. The purpose is to raise issues to discuss further with your supervisor and other research students. Make sure that you do so, and don't be surprised if they feel that both the terminology and the questions need considerable modification to be applicable for your field of study.

(■) ACTIVITY

Scan the theses in your sample (don't attempt to read them in full). Does it seem usual in your field to define the research problem explicitly, possibly in terms of a list of specific research questions or hypotheses? Or does it seem usual for the focus (or foci) or theme (or themes) of the research to emerge as the work progresses?

Does there seem to be any indication in the theses that the research problem, topic, theme or focus changed in direction or in emphasis during the research?

If a research problem was formulated early on in terms of fully operationalized research questions or hypotheses, how well do these seem to lead naturally and easily to decisions about how the research had to be designed?

Research methodologies

A rationale for the methods used to gather and process data, in what sequence and on what samples, together constitute a research methodology. This is not a grand term for 'list of methods', but an informed and properly argued case for designing a piece of research in a particular way. A research methodology needs to be appropriate for the research problem (or 'project', or 'piece of research', or whatever is the more usual terminology in the field of study concerned), and the justification that this is so should form part of a thesis. Box 6.3 gives some definitions of 'methodology' quite generally. The suffix '-ology' means 'the study of'; hence the terms sociology, psychology, etc.

Box 6.3   Some dictionary definitions of 'methodology'

The science of method.
                                    (*Shorter Oxford English Dictionary*)

A body of methods, procedures, working concepts, rules and postulates.
                                    (*Webster's International Unabridged Dictionary*)

It takes experience of research in the discipline concerned to comment on the appropriateness of a research methodology for a particular piece of research, but you should be able to see how well methodologies are argued for in the theses in your sample and how reasonable they seem in the articles. Good argument involves paying attention to counter-arguments. So – at PhD level at least – the theses should show a familiarity with alternative methodologies, and an argument in favour of one methodology for any piece of research should include arguments, however brief, against others for that piece of research.

ACTIVITY

How well do you think that each of the articles and theses makes its case for the methodologies that it uses?

Competence in research

Once the investigations have been carried out, data of some sort should have accumulated. Data* needs to be as relevant and accurate as possible for several reasons. One reason is to inspire confidence in the eventual solution to the research problem (or conclusions or findings, whatever is the appropriate terminology for the discipline). The extract in Box 6.4 is about the criticisms that careless researchers can lay themselves open to in this connection.

Box 6.4   The importance of data being relevant

Hans Eysenck has the following to say of the psychologist Cyril Burt:

Burt, while outstanding in his ability to use statistical methods in the analysis of data relating to intellectual or personality differences, was rather careless about the quality of the data he analysed. As I once told him: 'You use the most advanced methods of psychometrics in your analyses, but you use them on data that are quite dubious – tests done unsupervised by teachers, for instance . . .' This did not increase his liking for me . . .

(Eysenck 1994)

Another reason why data needs to be as relevant and accurate as possible is that sometimes something unexpected turns up which can lead to an entirely new and important line of investigation.

---

* In line with modern and idiomatic usage, this book takes 'data' as a collective singular noun.

Box 6.5   The importance of data being untainted

The British astronomy research student Joscelyn Bell noticed scuffs on photographic plates of the night sky which she was routinely surveying. Since she had confidence in how well she was keeping the plates, she knew that the scuffs could not just be dirt or stray light. So she investigated them further and as a result 'pulsars'* were discovered. On the basis of this, a Nobel prize was awarded to her supervisor Antony Hewish and his colleague, but not to her. She went on to become a professor of physics at The Open University.

* Pulsars are stars which send out pulses of radio waves.

Before pursuing this line, however, the researcher needs to be reasonably confident that the anomaly is not just 'noise in the system'. The anecdote in Box 6.5 is about a careful and competent researcher who was able to have just such confidence.

Yet another reason is that constraints of time, location or availability of source material often prevent a data collection exercise from being repeated as a check.

 ACTIVITY

Scan theses and articles. To what extent do they convince you that the investigations concerned were competently conducted?

Academic argument and academic discourse

One of the most important things to learn in connection with good research is that a thesis or research article should be much more than a presentation of the data collected or a report on the work carried out. It should be a well-documented and well-argued case for one or more specific solutions to a research problem (or whatever is the accepted alternative terminology). The idea of a thesis or report being a 'case' is helpful, because it suggests the barrister role in which students have to operate – i.e. the fourth bullet point in Box 6.2. Unfortunately many students write up their theses in the role of a journalist, which is totally unacceptable for postgraduate work.

In order to make a sound case, evidence has to be collected and presented so as to take argument forwards. The evidence can be data taken directly from literature (facts, findings, etc. processed and discussed by others, and acknowledged as such) or it can be the data collected in the research. These must be clearly distinguished from each other. Theses almost certainly contain a number of streams of argument, which may be intertwined: minimally for how the research problem or gap in knowledge was identified; how it was investigated; what the solutions or outcomes were and their importance and limitations. Arguments need to be convincing, and counter-arguments need to be explored and dealt with rigorously and fairly. The extract in Box 6.6 puts this well.

Box 6.6   Argument and academic discourse

One may give all the stylistic indications of setting out a case in a rigorous fashion, using devices such as 'it follows from what I have just said', when in fact nothing follows; 'I have argued that . . .', when in fact no argument has been offered; 'I refute the suggestion that . . .', when the suggestion is merely contradicted, not argued against; 'it has been shown that . . . , when nothing of the kind has been done and so on, without setting out a case.

(Fairbairn and Winch 1996: 169)

The language in which the case is argued has to be precise, and not blurred with irrelevancies. This is part of what is known as 'academic discourse'. Chapters 13 and 20 give advice for your own writing.

 ACTIVITY

Summarize the main case that is being made in each of the research articles in your sample.

Try to identify the cases that are being made in each thesis in your sample. The places to scan are the abstract, preface, introduction or overview (whatever is the norm in the subject area), contents list, the first and last paragraphs of each chapter and the final chapter. (At this level there will almost certainly be more than one case in each thesis, and the streams of argument are probably intertwined. Disentangling and identifying them could take some considerable time and is probably not worth attempting in any detail at this stage.)

To what extent do you feel that the theses in your sample have cogent, convincing arguments? Do you feel anywhere that the cases being made are blurred with 'padding'?

To what extent do you feel that the theses in your sample acknowledge and deal fairly with counter-arguments?

In terms of quality of argument and academic discourse, can you identify any significant differences between the masters-level and the PhD theses?

⬤ DISCUSSION OF ACTIVITY

All the theses in your sample should be logically and convincingly argued, but some will inevitably be better argued than others. You may feel that the PhD theses are more soundly argued than the masters ones. Certainly inability to argue is one reason, but only one, why students are not permitted to pass through certain probationary hurdles – notably, in the United Kingdom, the transfer from MPhil to PhD.

Outcomes of research

It is not at all uncommon for research to throw up some unexpected findings which are so important that the direction of the research is changed to pursue them further, irrespective of any previously defined research problems or topics. You need to be alert to this possibility in your own work. So it is worth thinking about what sorts of outcome (or solutions to a suitably phrased research problem) are usual and possible in your field of study. This should stimulate you, in due course, to be more creative in the formulation or later reformulation of your own (possibly implicit) research problem, and to recognize the significance of the unexpected when it arises in your own work. So use the following activity to see the sorts of outcome which seem to be usual in your field.

 ACTIVITY

On the basis of the articles and theses in your sample, is it possible to generalize about the sorts of research problems (or outcomes or foci or themes, etc.) which are common in your field of study?

Talk to research students who are near completion to see what sorts of research problem they are addressing or what outcomes they are anticipating.

Check your conclusions about possible and usual types of solution or outcome by discussing them with your supervisor and members of your department or group.

◉ DISCUSSION OF ACTIVITY

Outcomes of research can be wide-ranging. Look at the list in Box 6.7, which is used to stimulate thinking in workshops for research students. Some of the examples are abstract and others are tangible. In fact there is no significant difference in the processes known as 'research', 'research and development', and 'research and design'. How much development or design can be included in a thesis depends on the field of study and the institutional regulations.

Box 6.7 Research problems and the outcomes of research

Research problems can be in terms of 'to produce', 'to design', or 'to develop' something, and research outcomes can be in terms of having 'produced', 'designed' or 'developed' something. The following are examples from a wide range of possibilities:

- *A new or improved product.* There are many examples in all fields of study – for example, a book, a synthetic fabric, a synthetic food. There is a hazy borderline between a new product and an improvement on an existing one. For example, a design for a five-bedroom house could be regarded as new in itself or as a development of a design for a two-bedroom house. For the purpose of developing a research problem, the distinction is unimportant.
- *A new theory or a reinterpretation of an existing theory.* The best-known examples of what were once new theories happen to be in the natural sciences – for example, Darwin's theory of evolution and Einstein's theory of relativity. The research problems of research students normally involve reinterpretations of existing theories, rather than the development of new theories – for example, how far an existing theory is valid in a new context or how far it needs to be reappraised in the light of new evidence.
- *A new or improved research tool or technique.* An example could be a measuring device; a computer package to undertake certain tasks; a piece of equipment to identify disease; or a set of questionnaires to identify problem areas in certain sections of the community.
- *A new or improved model or perspective.* In all fields of study, knowledge can be interpreted or looked at in a fresh way. An example from science fiction would be the perspective of thinking about time as a fourth dimension, which can be travelled through, like the other dimensions of length, breadth and height.

- *An in-depth study.* In all fields of study there can be the opportunity to study something that has never been studied before, such as the moons of Jupiter, following the enormous amount of data collected by the Galileo probe, or the Van Gogh painting which was thought to be lost and has recently been rediscovered.
- *An exploration of a topic, area or field.* This is a particularly useful starting point where the main features of the work are not known at the outset.
- *A critical analysis.* Examples might be an analysis or re-analysis of a novel or of the effects of a government on the economy.
- *A portfolio of work based on research.* Professionals in many fields can produce these.
- *A fact or conclusion, or a collection of facts or conclusions.* This is a particularly common outcome of research in all fields. Examples might be the determination of a scientific constant or factors which favour or militate against crime on housing estates.

Documentation of literature

Properly written-up research should cite source material in a consistent manner according to the norms of the discipline. Three methods are in common use:

- References are indicated in the text by the author's surname and the year of publication; and the sources are collected together at the end of the thesis presented in alphabetical order of authors. (All good word processors can readily sort paragraphs, such as references, into alphabetical ordering by author's name.)
- References are numbered consecutively in the text and the sources are collected together at the end of the thesis in the order cited. (All good word processors can take care of the renumbering automatically when another reference is added mid-text.)
- References are given as footnotes on the page where they appear, denoted by a symbol or number. (Again, good word processors can take care of this automatically.)

Students should already be familiar with normal practice in their discipline for listing references. However, if you need to remind yourself of the details for the various types of publication, use the following activity as an *aide-mémoire*.

(■) ACTIVITY

Which reference method is used for referring to a publication within the text of the articles and theses in your sample?

What information is given, and in what order, about each of the following in the reference sections of the articles and theses in your sample?

• A book written by a single author

• A book written by several authors

• A book of contributions from several authors

• A print-based journal article

• An electronic journal

• A conference paper

• A thesis

• A website

• Information on a CD-ROM

• A document which does not give authors' names, such as a government publication or a law report

• Anything else that may need referencing in your field

If any abbreviations used in the references are new to you, list them.

Is there both a reference section and a bibliography section at the end of the theses? If so, what appears to be the difference between them?

(■) DISCUSSION OF ACTIVITY

Note, in particular, that full references of paper-based documents require page numbers. It is all too easy to forget to note them when examining a text; and it can be very time-consuming and irritating to have to find them again later. Also note that the information on websites may be out of date (as well, of course, as being in no way controlled for accuracy). Ideally all websites should contain a note of when they were last updated, but this is by no means standard practice. So referencing websites is a matter to be discussed with supervisors and library staff. The same is true of entries in databases. For your own work, it is important to keep full and detailed references. (Chapter 8 offers advice).

It is common practice in many fields of study for there to be a distinct difference between a reference section and a bibliography section. The first lists works referenced in the main text and the second lists works which were consulted during the work and which fed into the author's thinking. It is important to find out whether this distinction is normal in your subject area. Whether it is or not, there should be no literature alluded to in the main text which is not fully referenced later.

Use of literature

Properly written up research should always make a case of some sort (often more than one case), and it is helpful to think of literature as 'evidence' in that case. Literature should be used only to support argument or counter-argument and to move understanding forwards. Mere lists of references, as in a 'catalogue' of vaguely relevant items, are not acceptable. Direct quotations should be used only for purposes of illustration, never as a replacement for a soundly argued case.

In theses, literature should additionally be used to show a thorough knowledge of the field. So, where seminal works are not directly pertinent to the case in hand, skill and thought are required to bring them in meaningfully.

The absence (or apparent absence) of literature on certain topics can also serve as evidence, provided that this is set in a wider field of knowledge and is clearly not a ploy for an inadequate literature survey.

(■) ACTIVITY

Look at where literature is referenced in the articles or theses in your sample. To what extent does the literature seem to be used for the following purposes?

• Merely to demonstrate a knowledge of the field

• As evidence to make or support a case of some sort

• An effective mix of both purposes

There are wide-ranging possibilities for the types of case that literature can be used to support. Check on whether a case for any of the following is made in your sample:

• The existence of a gap in knowledge or the specification of the research problem.

• The suitability of a research design, including the technique for collecting data.

• The validity of, or limitations on the accuracy of data, findings or conclusions.

• Something else. What?

In terms of effective use of literature, would you judge the quality of some of the articles or theses in your sample to be better than others?

Do some chapters of the theses seem to include more referenced literature than others? Does it seem normal in your field of study for a thesis to have a chapter specifically devoted to literature?

⬛ DISCUSSION OF ACTIVITY

With some types of research it is normal to have a single chapter devoted to the literature survey. However, literature, where it exists, should be used to support all aspects of the research, and may therefore appear to some extent throughout a thesis. If any of the theses in your sample do contain a single chapter on literature, it is worth raising this for discussion with your supervisor.

Use of data

The data that researchers collect needs to be presented in the articles and theses, but that alone is not enough. The data has to be processed and then meaning has to be imposed on the findings or conclusions. (This is so, irrespective of whether the data is quantitative or qualitative.)

⬛ ACTIVITY

Scan the data that has been collected for the articles and theses in your sample.

• Has the data been processed in a way that seems appropriate?

• Have the authors argued their cases for their findings or conclusions meaning something?

• Is there any argument for the limitations or conditions for which that meaning is valid?

Originality in research

All institutions require theses to show some originality, but this is particularly important at doctoral level. The originality can be in terms of the research design, the research process or the outcomes of the research, and it can have a single major aspect or several minor ones. The theses and the research articles should make their claims to originality clear, even if only implicitly. Originality is considered at length in Chapter 17.

Significance of research

All institutions require theses to be significant contributions to the field, and the higher the level of the award, the more significance is expected. That some theses achieve this is beyond question. With others, however, it can be a matter of opinion and debate, guided by normal expectations in the field of study concerned.

Reliability in research

Where different researchers can repeat a piece of research and obtain precisely the same results, the research is said to be entirely 'reliable'. In practice, though, reliability can never be total, and it is important to understand why.

Consider first the type of research that is concerned in some way with people, animals, plants or other living organisms. Their individual vagaries all come into play. With people, variables, such as 'hungry', 'happy' or 'slept well' are highly influential on behaviour. They vary from one point in time to another; they cannot be measured numerically; and different observers may interpret the signs differently. Similar arguments could apply to studies on animals and even plants and the lower organisms. Consequently, such research cannot be entirely reproducible when conducted on different occasions by different researchers. It cannot therefore be totally reliable.

Reliability is less complex where the research is with inanimate objects and the data is numerical (i.e. measurable), as is usually the case in the natural sciences. To a first approximation, the research is reproducible – although there are still issues of competence, limitations of measuring instruments and minor perturbations. All measurements have an error associated with them, which limits reliability.

Validity in research

Where a piece of research does what it is intended to do, it is said to be 'valid'. The achievement of good validity at the same time as good reliability may be feasible, but it may not be. Figure 6.2 shows some of the possible combinations of reliability and validity in archery. An example in research could be the use of examinations as a research tool to judge or grade students. The most reliable form of assessment consists of tick-in-boxes types of question, marked by computer, because all suitably programmed computers would come to the same judgement about the same student, given the same script. However, if an important part of the assessment is to understand students' thought processes, as well as the outcomes of their thinking, then tick-in-boxes forms of assessment are not particularly valid. Other forms such as essay questions are more valid. Unfortunately, though, they are inevitably less reliable, since examiners' judgements are involved in the marking, and these are always somewhat subjective. There are means of increasing the reliability of essay questions (e.g. through double marking), but in the end it has to be accepted that the reliability cannot be total – although there are means of improving the overall reliability and validity of the whole assessment process (e.g. by using tick-in-boxes types of assessment alongside essays, orals, project work, etc.).

Where there has to be a trade-off between reliability and validity, validity must always be the more important. Achieving it starts with an understanding of the nature of 'truth' as it can be revealed by research. This, in turn, leads to the choice of an appropriate 'research paradigm' in which to set the research. Both are considered in the next section.

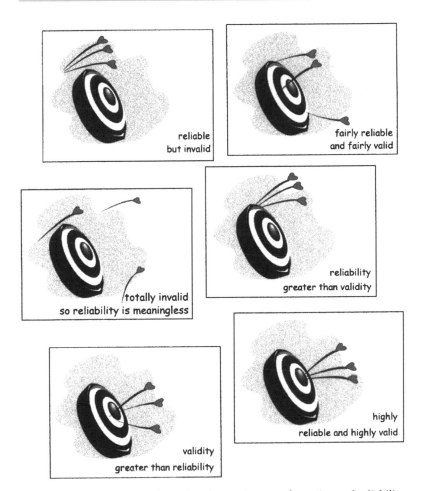

Figure 6.2   An archery analogy showing various configurations of reliability and validity

The nature of 'truth' in research: research paradigms and frameworks

Just as a paradigm, quite generally, is a viewpoint which shapes ideas and actions, a 'research paradigm' is a 'school of thought' or 'a framework for thinking' about how research ought to be conducted to ascertain truth. Different writers use different terminologies when discussing research paradigms, even when the paradigms are broadly similar, and consequently it is impossible to say how many there are. This book will simplify them into two, which it will call the 'traditional' research paradigm and the 'interpretivist' research paradigm.*

The traditional research paradigm relies on numerical (i.e. quantitative) data and mathematical or statistical treatment of that data. The 'truth' that is uncovered is thus grounded in mathematical logic. The traditional research paradigm lends itself to highly valid and highly reliable research, but only where the variables that affect the work can be identified, isolated and relatively precisely measured – and possibly, but not necessarily, also manipulated – which is how research in the natural sciences normally operates. Researchers who can work in this paradigm are fortunate because high reliability and validity are held in high esteem. The proponents of the paradigm tend to take it for granted, and theses grounded in it generally take the fact as self-evident.

The traditional research paradigm also lends itself to research touched by human and other animate behaviour if the data is numerical (i.e. quantitative and capable of being measured) and if the sample is sufficiently large for the effects of individual vagaries effectively to cancel one another out. An example could be the performance of school-leavers in national examinations across a country over a period of years. Another example could be an investigation into the yields of a hybrid crop using fields of control and experimental plants. Research set in the traditional research paradigm can answer questions about what is happening and the statistical chances of something happening in the future, but it cannot directly answer questions about *why* something is happening or may happen, nor about the existence of anything else that may be relevant. Answers to such questions may, however, be provided by an established theory within which the research fits.

The traditional research paradigm is generally inappropriate for research involving small samples of living beings. Then, the variables which stem from individual vagaries and subjectivity do not cancel one another out; neither can variables be readily identified or measured, let alone isolated and held constant while others are varied. Even with a large sample there are sometimes ethical or pragmatic reasons why variables cannot be held constant or manipulated experimentally. Then research has to be set in the interpretivist research paradigm. What this involves is more like in-depth investigations to establish a verdict in a court of law than experiments in a laboratory.

---

* The term 'interpretivist research paradigm' has been coined comparatively recently and is due to Denzin and Lincoln (1994: 536).

The evidence can be circumstantial and even where there are eye-witness accounts, doubt can always be cast on the veracity or reliability of the observers. A verdict must be reached on what is reasonable (i.e. the weight of evidence one way or the other) and on the power of the argument. Data gathered within the interpretivist research paradigm is primarily descriptive, although it may be quantitative, as for example in sizes of living areas, coded questionnaires or documentary analysis. The emphasis is on exploration and insight rather than experiment and the mathematical treatment of data.

Research set in the interpretivist research paradigm can answer questions about how and why something is happening. If it also addresses questions about what is happening in a wider context and what is likely to happen in the future, it can seldom do so with statistical confidence, because the 'truth' is not grounded in mathematical logic. The 'truth' has to be a conclusion in the mind of a reader (or listener), based on the researcher's power of argument, and different recipients of the research may come to understand different 'truths'. So it is important for those who use the interpretivist research paradigm to present their work as convincingly as possible. The extract in Box 6.8 offers some advice, and, if you are working in this paradigm, your supervisor will advise you further.

Research paradigms tend to be associated with particular disciplines, because of the sort of questions that research in those disciplines tends to address. Nevertheless, even within the same disciplines, there can be intense rivalries between individuals who have loyalties to a

---

Box 6.8   Towards making a thesis convincing

The following is part of an unpublished discussion document used in training supervisors of postgraduate research students at the University of Reading.

Choice of research paradigm
All research inevitably requires the selection of an appropriate philosophical and methodological framework. Since all such frameworks have limitations, this choice involves selecting the one which fits the questions and objectives of the research best while rejecting others even if they may have some salience. In order to demonstrate that this selection has been grounded in understanding, rather than being an arbitrary decision or one based on habit, it is important that the rationale for the selection includes both the argument for selecting a particular one and the reasons why others were deemed unsuitable for this research.

Selection of relevant literature
The literature section(s) of a thesis is/are intended to demonstrate that the student is conversant with the field and can use evidence from the literature to focus enquiries. This is most effectively achieved by:

- the selection from what might be a plethora of authors, those who are significant in the field;
- the provision of a critical review of the works, with particular respect to the focus of and relevance to the current research;
- the support, or illustration, of statements and contentions made by the student using apposite quotations from the literature.

To elaborate on the last point, since quotations out of context can be misleading, it is important that exact references, including page numbers, are provided so that readers can check both their accuracy and the intent in the original works. Similarly, it is good practice to provide some context to quotations, such as 'in a debate about such appropriateness, Bloggs (1999: 123) provided the following critique: . . .'

Demonstrating the salience of the data
The source, context and relevance of data used to justify interpretations is critical. It should be clear that evidence has been assiduously collected, compiled and reviewed, with alternative perspectives given credence and weight, and attributed suitably to origin. This is especially important when the data is derived from an interpretive framework with sources such as interviews and other narrative material. A data trail should be explicit, including for instance: a table of sources (participant, method, location in the temporal frame of the fieldwork); samples of transcripts showing the style and contextual structure; lists of categories derived from the data; lists of quotations used to determine particular categories, including a miscellaneous category to include material that does not fit into any other category. Much of this material is most appropriately contained in referenced appendices so that the reader can audit the instances cited for illustration in the text of the thesis, find other examples of the category and check on the validity of the interpretations drawn.

(Denicolo 1999)

particular research paradigm because of the nature of the truth that it uncovers.

Different parts of a complex investigation may need to be set in different research paradigms. For example, research into the effects of a new drug may involve the measurement and statistical treatment of, say, blood pressure, but the subjective views of patients have to be taken into account in the search for side-effects.

Alternative terms for research paradigms which are broadly similar to the traditional research paradigm are: quantitative, scientific, experimental, hard, reductionist, prescriptive, psychometric – and there are probably others. Alternative terms for research paradigms which are broadly similar to the interpretivist research paradigm are: qualitative, soft, non-traditional, holistic, descriptive, phenomenological, anthropological, naturalistic, illuminative – and again there are probably others. It must be emphasized that the similarities are in broad terms only. Many academics would argue fiercely about the significances of the differences.

(■) ACTIVITY

If the articles and theses in your sample are concerned in any way with the vagaries of human behaviour, check on the various ways in which they deal with these.

If the articles and theses in your sample are concerned with animals, plants or other living entities, how are individual differences addressed?

Do any of the articles fall into the trap of ignoring subjectivity and other individual vagaries by focusing on what can be measured and measuring it, even though the central aspects of the research ought in fact to be variables which cannot be isolated and measured?

■ DISCUSSION OF ACTIVITY

Because the traditional research paradigm is so highly esteemed, researchers often try to use it even where it is not appropriate – in other words, to sacrifice validity for reliability. This is reminiscent of a well-known analogy, which is reported in various forms, about someone looking for what he has lost under a lamppost, because that is where the light is, even though he knows that he lost it somewhere else. Working inappropriately within the traditional research paradigm is no less absurd, even though it is often done.

Where next?

This chapter has oversimplified a complex topic in order to present a grounding that is understandable to new researchers in all disciplines. The purpose is to raise awareness and to stimulate discussion. Make sure that this happens, and remember not to be surprised if modifications in terminology and perspective turn out to be necessary for your field of study.

You may feel that the chapter leaves you with a sense of frustration that it does not say more. However the 'more' that individuals seem to want always turns out to be intimately associated with the requirements of their own particular research projects or disciplines. This book is cross-disciplinary; so it does not consider aspects of research which could be seen as irrelevant in some disciplines, however important they may be in others. Fortunately there is no shortage of books on research design, research methods and research techniques appropriate for particular fields of study, and you should find out what they are and study a selection. The *further reading* section at the end of the book should serve to start you off. Then, under the guidance of others in your field of study (in particular, your supervisor) you should extend your journey into recognizing and conducting quality research. It is a journey that will never completely end.

7 INTERACTING WITH YOUR SUPERVISOR(S)

When a supervisor accepts a student, whatever the formal rules may be, both have entered into an implied moral contract which lasts until one of the three – supervisor, student, or research undertaking – expires.
(National Postgraduate Committee 1995: 2)

The importance of the student–supervisor relationship

The relationship between a research student and a supervisor can be a precious thing, particularly where supervisors and students work closely together over a number of years on something which fascinates them both. Mutual respect and trust can and should develop, together with a working relationship that can continue, as between equals, long after the research is completed. It is in your own interests to develop and nurture this relationship. Only highly unusual students successfully complete their research degrees if their relationship with their supervisors is poor. A research degree is about research training as well as contributing to knowledge, and although it is not impossible to find ways of training oneself, the whole process is designed to be guided by a supervisor. This chapter is about interacting with your supervisor, i.e. the single academic who has day-to-day responsibility for you. Where you have additional supervisory support, you will need to adapt what you read for your own circumstances. (See Chapter 2 for supervisory issues to consider prior to taking up a place at the institution.)

There are two aspects to developing and nurturing the relationship with a supervisor, and they are valid irrespective of the award for which you are registered and how many supervisors you may have. One is administrative and starts with finding out the respective roles of students and supervisors, as laid out formally by the institution. The other is interpersonal and involves treating a supervisor as a human being who has strengths and weaknesses, personal satisfactions and disappointments, good days and bad days, just like everyone else.

The roles and responsibilities of supervisors and students

Essentially, a supervisor's principal professional responsibility is to develop his or her research students so that they can think and behave as academic researchers in the field of study concerned. As Box 7.1 highlights, students are then in a position to achieve the award for which they are registered. The students, in turn, must take responsibility for doing their own work conscientiously. Some ramifications and implications are considered shortly.

The extracts in Boxes 7.2 and 7.3, which are in terms of the

Box 7.1   How to recognize an outstanding supervisor

The following conclusion was reached in an Australian research project which looked at postgraduate work in a range of academic departments. It has a face validity which suggests universal applicability.

One of the hallmarks of outstanding supervisors appeared . . . to be that their students felt driven very hard to impress them.

(Parry and Hayden 1994: 75)

Box 7.2   The (recommended) responsibilities of the supervisor

According to National Postgraduate Committee (1995: 5), the (recommended) responsibilities of a supervisor are:

1 *The supervisor should have knowledge of a student's subject area and/or theoretical approach to be applied.*
2 *If a student's work goes significantly outside the supervisor's field, the supervisor and the department should be responsible for putting the student in touch with specialists either inside or outside the institution who could help.*
3 *There should be regular supervisory sessions between students and supervisor, ideally at least once a fortnight. It is usually advisable to arrange for the time of the next meeting at the end of each session.*

4 Supervisory sessions will naturally vary in length but on average they should last for at least one hour. It is important that they should be largely uninterrupted by telephone calls, personal callers or departmental business.

5 If the student has an urgent problem, the supervisor should deal with the matter over the telephone or arrange a meeting at short notice.

6 The supervisor should read and critically comment on written work as it is produced.

7 The supervisor should assist new students to plan their time, draw up a programme of work and monitor their subsequent progress. The supervisor should be aware of the requirements of some funding bodies and/or institutions that renewal of funding can depend on successful upgrade from MPhil to PhD and should help students on such contracts to plan their work accordingly.

8 The supervisor should submit a report to the Postgraduate Study Committee every six months and keep the student's record file maintained.

9 The supervisor must ensure that the student is made aware if either progress or the standard of work is unsatisfactory, and arrange any necessary supportive action.

10 It is the responsibility of the supervisor to ensure that the data, results and information garnered by the student during their research is freely available to the student.

11 Research students should be eligible to attend free of charge any course of lectures run in the institution. Supervisors should advise on courses which may complement their field of research.

12 The supervisor should take an active part in introducing the student to meetings of learned societies, seminars and workshops and to other research workers in the field. The supervisor should give advice on publication and put the student in touch with publishers where appropriate. The supervisor should give advice on writing up the research work in the form of papers and the final thesis. The supervisor should ensure that the student receives due recognition for their contribution to any publication, according to the usual conventions in the field.

13 The supervisor must make clear the institution's regulations governing the nomination of the external and internal examiners for a student's viva (oral). Subject to the decision of the relevant bodies, the supervisor should arrange a mutually convenient date for the examiners and the student for the viva.

Box 7.3 The (recommended) responsibilities of the research student

According to the National Postgraduate Committee (1995: 6), the (recommended) responsibilities of a research student are:

1 *By the end of the first year (the first 18 months in the case of part-time students) (subject to specific, published departmental practices which may, because of the nature of the subject, vary from this model) the student should have defined the area of research, become acquainted with the background knowledge required, completed the literature review and have a framework for the future progress of the research with a timetable for the next 2 or 3 years (3 or 4 years in the case of part-time students). The student should have produced a 'substantial' amount of written work, even if only in draft form. 'Substantial' should be defined by the supervisor or department at the outset.*
2 *The responsibility is on students to have their own topics that they would like to discuss with the supervisor.*
3 *Students must submit written work regularly to their supervisors.*
4 *Students should take note of the guidance and feedback from their supervisors.*
5 *Students should generally produce all material in word-processed or typed form. Material containing complex equations may be exempted, but the presentation of such must be neat and legible.*
6 *Students must inform their supervisor of other people with whom their work is being discussed.*
7 *It is the student's responsibility to seek out the supervisor. Any serious problems a student has with the supervisor, including those of access, should be initially taken up by the student with the supervisor at the time.*

United Kingdom PhD and MPhil, lay out the responsibilities of supervisors and students respectively, as recommended by the National Postgraduate Committee. Most institutions have something similar. Such guidelines are useful to stimulate discussion and thought, but they may not be right for all supervisor–student partnerships, and you and your supervisor may already have something better in operation.

The developing nature of supervision

New students tend to expect supervisors to tell them what to do. Indeed, this may be justified for very short research projects or where the work is tied into a group project and bounded by the efficient use of expensive and heavily utilized equipment. Where this is not so, students may wait for their supervisors to tell them what to do because they think that demonstrating dependence in this way also demonstrates respect. Fortunately, good supervisors realize that they have to wean many students gradually into independence; so they may provide a well-defined task as something on which both supervisor and student can build – perhaps a pilot project of some sort. If this is what your supervisor does, it may give you a sense of security, but things are unlikely to carry on that way. Many people would argue that they ought not to carry on that way.

At the other extreme, some supervisors toss out a multitude of ideas at the first meeting, which can be overwhelming. If this happens to you, just realize that the ideas are merely possibilities for you to consider, not tasks that you necessarily have to do. Your best course of action is probably to make a note of them and take them away to think about, considering which ones comprise essential groundwork and which ones are merely alternative possibilities. There is no single best way to research into a topic, although there are numerous bad and non-viable ways. The point is that it is you and you alone who have to be intimately involved with your work over a considerable period, and, for all but the shortest of projects, it is essential that you design your work so that it appeals to you as well as being acceptable to your supervisor.

As your work progresses, supervisions should become two-way dialogues. Your supervisor will expect you to develop your own ideas – which may have to be bounded for various reasons – but will want to discuss them with you, to give advice and to warn in good time against possible dangers. It is not a sound interpretation of 'independent work' for students to continue along their own way, on the mistaken assumption that they do not need supervision.

Since research means going beyond published work and developing something new, your relationship with your supervisor must accommodate the natural and inevitable fact that you will eventually come to know more about your work than your supervisor. You will need to become comfortable with this and with engaging him or her in academic debate as between equals.

Arranging meetings with a supervisor

Some departments distinguish between formal supervisions and informal meetings; and they have specific policies about the timing and duration of the former, sometimes laying them out in advance for an entire programme of research and requiring specific documents to be completed and signed at each meeting. Other departments do not make the distinction, and may not specify arrangements for the mode of operation of meetings.

Where meeting schedules are not pre-defined, many supervisors are torn in two directions as far as scheduling supervisions is concerned, and it is helpful to understand why. On the one hand supervisors want to do what they can to be supportive, but on the other they do not want to interfere on the grounds that independent students ought to take the initiative when they need to discuss work which should, after all, be their own. This latter view is reinforced by the formal dictate of most institutions that it is the responsibility of the student to take the initiative in raising problems or difficulties, however elementary they may seem, and to agree a schedule of meetings with the supervisor.

The practical way forward is for you to take steps early on to find out how scheduling supervisions is likely to work best for the unique partnership between you and your supervisor. It is polite to wait a while, to see if there are departmental codes of practice and to give your supervisor time to make suggestions, but if this does not happen, raise the matter yourself. The following activity provides a checklist of the crucial issues.

(■) ACTIVITY

Find out how comfortable you and your supervisor are with the following ways of interacting:

• Dates and times of meetings are arranged a considerable time ahead according to departmental requirements. In this case, are there distinctions between formal and informal meetings?

• You take the initiative by emailing or phoning in a request for a meeting.

- Your supervisor timetables regular meetings irrespective of whether there is anything new or special to discuss.

- You provide something in writing about what you want to talk about so that it can be considered before you meet. Or your supervisor prefers to cut down the burden of non-essential reading and react to you on the spot when you meet.

- If either you or your supervisor think there is any reason to meet, one of you arranges it when you next happen to see each other.

- Much of the informal interaction is provided without meeting, via email. If so, how much?

- You simply turn up at your supervisor's office in the expectation of him or her having time for you.

- Some other arrangement. What?

How are you expected to go about setting up an additional meeting in an emergency?

⬛ DISCUSSION OF ACTIVITY

Each of the above possibilities will suit some partnerships of students and supervisors, but some will be intensely disagreeable to some supervisors. So you and your supervisor must develop a mode of working that suits you both.

Supervisors are busy people, and their workload is increasing all the time. So be sensitive about taking up your supervisor's time. Remember, though, that legally the responsibility for not raising matters with your supervisor is likely to be yours, and if you neglect to communicate ideas and findings to your supervisor you may overlook obvious interpretations, waste your time pursuing something that is not viable and wander into dead ends. Supervisors who feel that they are being worried unnecessarily should say so.

Frequency of meetings also has to be considered, where there are no departmental requirements. Some supervisors like to see full-time students three times a term and part-time students twice a term; some much more often. Some supervisors like to have two or more meetings booked ahead in diaries, on the proviso that they can be cancelled nearer the time if there is no need to meet. Other supervisors feel that meetings should be set up flexibly, according to the needs of the student, which are likely to be greatest when the direction of the work is being decided and during the final stages of the writing-up. As the relationship develops and confidence in each other grows, some supervisors may welcome forgoing the time outlay of a formal meeting in favour of interaction by email.

The location and timings of meetings is particularly important for part-time students. Most supervisors are sensitive to this.

Taking notes during meetings with a supervisor

Students need to have a sufficient record of what takes place during supervisions to be able to think the discussion over before taking action. Memory may not be enough. The record needs to include dates, times and locations, topics discussed, objectives set and attained, advice given and the decisions made, but it should go further. Degrees of conviction about decisions need to be captured. So do ideas presented on the off chance rather than in the certainty that they might prove useful.

Taking notes is a personal matter, and what suits one student may not suit another. Students may find that it gives them confidence to ask their supervisors if they may audiotape supervisions, even if, in the event, they never find it necessary to listen to a tape. Not only does the tape give a verbatim record of ideas and conclusions, and the strength of feeling behind them, it also records forms of expression and explanation which may be superior to anything used so far, and which may be ideal for putting into reports and the thesis.

Asking a supervisor for feedback and advice

Most students are entirely satisfied with how their supervisor responds to their requests for feedback and advice; and any initial problems tend to sort themselves out as the relationship develops. You can help by understanding some of the pressures that your supervisor may be under, and acting accordingly.

Supervisors are human beings who are exceptionally busy and who may also be shy or inexperienced. Any of these may be reasons for unhelpful, throwaway remarks rather than considered responses. There are other possible reasons. For example, a supervisor may not want to stunt the development of your independence by rejecting your ideas. Or he or she may feel embarrassed at rejecting your ideas, perhaps because you are a mature student with an impressive career record, or because you are a colleague in the department. If you think that any of these may be the case, a good technique is not to ask for a reaction to a single idea. Suggest several alternatives. Then there is something to discuss and an implicit ground-rule is that some ideas will have to be rejected.

Overwork could be affecting a supervisor. If you think that this may be so, be sensitive about how you raise issues for discussion. He or she may react most favourably to a written outline of your ideas, to study and respond to at leisure or convenience. On the other hand, an informal chat, to ease interaction with burgeoning paperwork, may be more acceptable. In your own interests, you should find out.

It is a well-researched and accepted fact that people tend to reject ideas if they feel forced into quick decisions. If you think that this may be a problem when you interact with a supervisor, give him or her plenty of thinking time by outlining the situation and then suggesting that he or she might like to mull it over in readiness for talking again in a few days.

If you think that a supervisor may be suffering from the shyness of inexperience, put him or her at ease by asking for answers to simple questions, to which you may even already know the answers. If, of course, the problem is also overwork, this tactic would make matters worse rather than better.

Responding to feedback and criticism from a supervisor

It is in your own interests that your supervisor gives full and comprehensive feedback on your work. This is difficult on both sides where the feedback is critical, and you need to help in every way you can.

Start by accepting that certain emotions are normal. You may be embarrassed at what you think your supervisor is seeing as your inadequacy, and you may be angry at how he or she appears to be misunderstanding you. Understandable as these emotions are, it is counter-productive to let them show, and the chances are that, when you calm down, you will realize that they were somewhat unjustified anyway.

So if it is necessary, mask negative emotions. Try to show gratitude that your supervisor is going to so much trouble to give the feedback, and to show interest in its content.

It is not necessary to agree with all the criticisms, either while they are being made or later. Only you know the ramifications for your own work and situation. So only when you have taken time to consider can you decide how much to accept, reject or adapt. Agreeing instantly with criticism indicates compliance and lack of independent thinking. Seek clarification if necessary and then say that you will go away and do some thinking, ready for talking again about any points that may need further discussion.

Only in exceptional circumstances is it sensible to launch into a justification of why the criticism is inappropriate. You may want to justify some points, but do this only when your supervisor has finished his or her say on that point. Then ask if he or she would like you to explain the reasons for what you did.

At the close of the meeting, reiterate your thanks. Say nothing more, other than general pleasantries.

Handling unprofessional behaviour from a supervisor

Unprofessional behaviour from supervisors is rare. Nevertheless, when it does happen it can cause a great deal of distress to the student who has to cope with it, particularly because of the implicit power relationship that accompanies it.

The behaviour may be due to some sort of prejudice – perhaps racism, sexism, ageism or some other '-ism'. Although institutions normally have – or state that they are working towards – equal opportunities policies, these are normally only of help when matters have already got out of hand. The best course of action for a student is to realize that prejudice in highly intelligent and educated people is often due to ignorance and/or a sense of inferiority. The way forward is to train them out of it by ignoring the insinuations and innuendoes, referring only to work and acting in words, dress and manner totally professionally. Supervisors are unlikely to persist with attitudes and behaviour where students keep supplying evidence that these are inappropriate. Sadly, this course of action will take time. Support and advice should be available from other students,

---

Box 7.4 A view, a comment and a counter-view on sexual harassment and relationships between academics and students

[There are] principled reasons for avoiding staff-student love affairs, because of the power advantage lecturers have as assessors, as well as pragmatic reasons. 'You have to take into account the views of the student's peer group. Even if you think you are being as even-handed as possible I can guarantee you that the peer group suspects there is favour.'

(Mary Davis, as reported in
Times Higher Education Supplement 1995: 4)

In the event of involvement in a relationship with a student, particularly when it is a romantic or sexual one, the member of staff is encouraged to declare it to an appropriate supervisor or colleague or to a third party designated by the university for the purpose after consultation with AUT.

(From the code of conduct governing
staff–student relationships, produced by the
Women's Committee of the Association of University
Teachers (AUT), as reported in Bristow 1995)

The [AUT] code has been adopted by a number of universities and while most students are unaware that it even exists, those students and lecturers on the receiving end are more than a little sceptical . . . This view that female students are all really vulnerable little girls in need of attention is simply patronising.

(Bristow 1995)

---

the member of staff (if he or she exists) who has departmental responsibility for research students, the head of department, formal institutional documents and the students' union. Box 7.4 considers another form of unprofessional behaviour, as does Box 11.2 in Chapter 11.

It is crucial to do whatever one can informally early on, rather than formally later, once things seem to have got out of hand. Appeals in connection with equal opportunities policies are difficult to substantiate and stressful; and rightly or wrongly, the wronged person may be regarded as a troublemaker.

Changing a supervisor

Although most student–supervisor partnerships work well, there are those which do not. Perhaps there is continuing unprofessional behaviour as discussed in the previous section; or a clash of personalities; or a lack of interest. Perhaps a supervisor does not seem to have adequate expertise in the subject area; perhaps he or she does not seem to respect arguments and judgement when the student, after genuine and lengthy consideration, feels that they are valid. If giving it time does not work, diplomacy is needed. Not only is it impolite to compromise a supervisor, it is probably pointless and is likely, however justified, to discredit the person doing it in the eyes of others.

If a change of supervisor does seem inevitable, find out as diplomatically as possible what the procedures are. Sources of advice are the member of staff (if he or she exists) who has departmental responsibility for research students, the head of department, formal institutional documents and the students' union. The final recourse would be to make enquiries at the registry.

Again, it is crucial to do whatever one can informally early on, rather than formally later, once things seem to have got out of hand. Some institutions do allow appeals on the grounds of inadequate supervision, but most do not. Whatever the validity of appeals, they are stressful, time-consuming and often public; and sadly in the eyes of the world, 'mud sticks', even to innocent parties. At best, students will recover no more than lost fees.

Getting a co-supervisor

Students whose research is collaborative or cross-disciplinary may have had more than one supervisor from the outset. Other students may identify a need for an additional supervisor only as the work develops and steps outside the expertise of their current supervisor. Being supervised by more than one supervisor may work well in some circumstances, but reports of it working badly are so widespread that co-supervision needs to be considered very carefully before being adopted.

The misgivings do not apply where the co-supervisor is merely overseeing the normal supervisor–student interactions because the day-to-day supervisor is inexperienced. Neither do they apply to backup supervisors – individuals who agree to help while the day-to-day supervisor is away or ill, so that work is not delayed. Neither do they apply to team, panel or committee supervision, where the roles of the individual members are negotiated and formally agreed at the outset, and where all the supervisors meet regularly to review progress together.

The predominant misgivings apply where one (or more than one) co-supervisor is brought in because the work is likely to develop or has developed outside the expertise of the first supervisor, but where the individual roles and responsibilities of each supervisor are not fully discussed, agreed and defined at the time. It is a fortunate student who is co-supervised by individuals who have a completely common understanding of what the research is to be about. Perhaps an academic supervisor may be primarily concerned with keeping the work to manageable proportions for the award concerned, whereas an outside supervisor may be primarily concerned with using the research to solve problems in a particular workplace, and these two concerns may not entirely overlap. Or perhaps neither co-supervisor may fully understand the expertise of the other which can put considerable burdens on the student who has to integrate the understanding of both and satisfy both. The student all too often ends up satisfying neither, and each co-supervisor can tacitly abdicate responsibility to the other. It is worth students' while to keep a wary eye open for signs that the implicit expectations of co-supervisors are conflicting. Explicit differences can then be openly discussed and dealt with early. Implicit ones, which are not so readily recognized, can cause considerable difficulty later.

A single supervisor, on the other hand, carries full professional and personal – although not necessarily legal – responsibility for the research student. With such support, the student is in a good position to complete the programme of work satisfactorily. So it is worth thinking carefully before agreeing to joint supervision in a situation where the roles of the co-supervisors are not formalized. One alternative, when your work seems to be moving outside the expertise of your supervisor, is that you both visit experts and learn together about the new area. Another alternative is that you constrain your research to stay within the expertise of your supervisor.

The formal position

The respective duties and responsibilities of supervisors, students and the institution are normally laid out formally in institutional documents, the contents of which, for most institutions, may come as a surprise to students. In particular, the formal and legal responsibilities are unlikely to lie where you may expect. So it can be very important to have sight of the documents and to read them thoroughly.

Use the following activity as a checklist. Without it you may find out too late that you have been labouring under the illusion of misassigned responsibilities.

⬛ ACTIVITY

Study your institution's documentation on the duties and responsibilities of supervisors, students and the institution. In particular, note the formal position regarding:

• Making complaints

• Who takes responsibility for the thesis being ready to be examined

• Rights of appeal against inadequate supervision

⬛ DISCUSSION OF ACTIVITY

In most institutions, it is the student's responsibility to decide when the thesis is ready to be examined, even though of course the supervisor will give an opinion. There is thus no recourse, other than the formal appeals procedures already mentioned, if the award is not given. So, if you see things going wrong, it is in your own interests to act in good time to do something about them yourself. You may feel that some form of informal agreement or contract would help, as mentioned in Chapter 5.

8 KEEPING RECORDS

Meet it is I set it down.

(Shakespeare, *Hamlet*, act I, scene v)

The importance of keeping records

It is crucially important for all students, irrespective of the nature and level of their research, to keep full and detailed records. How to do so is a matter of personal preference, guided by the norms of the field of study, the experience of other workers in similar fields and the requirements of the supervisor or department.

There is an inevitable compromise between the ease of putting information into whatever device you choose for keeping your records and the ease of retrieving it. For example, a particularly straightforward way of inputting information would be to keep handwritten notes on scraps of paper. Yet this would be the least straightforward for quick and easy retrieval, as it would require sorting through to find what is there, and interpreting handwriting. The choice is personal: to go for ease of inputting, ease of retrieval or a balance somewhere between the two; and you will not regret investing time and effort in looking for and setting up systems that seem right for you.

Purposes of keeping records

Your choice of a system for keeping records must depend on the purposes to which you may need to put those records. Here are some possibilities, but the list is intended to stimulate your thinking, not to be exhaustive.

- To document interactions with your supervisor (see Chapter 7).
- To preserve data that you collect, for later processing.

- To preserve information that you read, for later processing.
- To preserve information about what you do and how long you spend doing it, as an aid to reflection; to keep on track and to suggest ways of improving your time management.
- To provide material for progress reports and the thesis.
- To provide ideas for future directions of the work.
- To provide information for setting targets, possibly including provisional dates and planning schedules.
- To document demarcations between your work and the work of others in group projects. (You will need to be able to show this unambiguously in your thesis.)
- To deliver that information back to you, as and when you wish to retrieve it.
- To satisfy supervisors or departments, where they require such records.
- To show records or examples of achievement to potential employers (see Chapter 15).
- To submit, where applicable, with an application for chartered status with a professional body.
- To use in conjunction with formal complaints or appeals procedures.

(■) ACTIVITY

Which of the above purposes and what additional purposes might you have for keeping records?

Keeping records of supervisions

It is important to keep a well-documented record of supervisions. Most reasons are obvious, but others include a safeguard against the unlikely possibility of having to use the documentation in support of a formal appeal or complaint. What to put into records of supervisions was considered in Chapter 7. Ask the advice of your supervisor and others in the department about suitable formats.

Keeping records of ongoing work

Of the variety of possible ways of keeping records of ongoing work, the most obvious is logbooks or diaries. In some fields of study it is usual for these to be in a pre-bound form so that every mistake and doodle is recorded in sequence alongside the more formalized records. The idea is that such apparently extraneous material meant something when originally done, and even though its significance may not have been obvious at the time, it can turn out to be important later. In other fields of study it may be considered appropriate to keep a more formalized diary, either using the day-to-a-page sort available from stationers or loose-leaf pages, filed in sequence. Logbooks and diaries should record such things as:

- what you do, and where, how and why you do it, with dates, possibly with an indication of time spent;
- what you read (see later in this chapter);
- what data you collect, how you process it and what the outcomes are;
- particular achievements, dead ends and surprises;
- what you think or feel about what is happening;
- any thoughts that come into your mind that may be relevant for your research;
- what your supervisor's reactions are, possibly in note form or as appended audiocassette tapes;
- anything else that is influencing you.

One possibility for recording data is to use a computerized database. Although it may require time and effort to set up and slightly more discipline when inputting, retrieval is straightforward and rapid, irrespective of the amount of data. Where such records include data on individuals, they are subject to the Data Protection Act. Each institution should have someone who is responsible for ensuring that the provisions of that Act are observed and who may be consulted for advice in this connection.

If your records are on a computer, it is essential to keep backups on floppy disks or CD-ROMS. Most experienced researchers can tell horrific stories of how days or even months of work were lost when a computer crashed and they had not bothered to keep backups. Box 8.1 tells a typical such story.

Before deciding on the best way to keep a record of your ongoing work, talk to several people, including your supervisor and other research students, who keep their records in different ways. Use the bullet points in the following activity as a checklist.

Box 8.1 Keep backup copies! Sheila's story

From the start I was aware that I should keep a copy of my work on back-up disk in case of accidents. However, perhaps as with plague, famine, war and terminal illnesses, we like to imagine that they happen to other people but never to ourselves. It was only after I lost a whole week's work, which simply disappeared from a disk, that I now make not only one but three back-up disks of each chapter.

(Salmon 1992: 112)

 ACTIVITY

How do other workers in the field keep records of their work?

How well do they think that different methods help them to:

• retrieve data later?

• reflect on their time and resource management?

• get ideas for future work?

• set targets for future work?

What advantages and disadvantages do they see in how they keep their records, and what general advice do they give?

Keeping records of what you read

Research students need to preserve information that they read, particularly so that they can use it later to support the various streams of argument and counter-argument in the thesis. As always there is a balance to be struck between ease of input and ease of retrieval. Prime examples of easy inputting are photocopying parts of articles and books (which copyright law generally allows for individual use) and saving potentially interesting web pages and on-line journal articles. However, at some stage, all need to be read and processed.

Database computer packages can be useful for keeping records. Once set up for bibliographic entry and retrieval, they throw up a checklist of all the information that is needed for a full reference of any item, and they allow quick and easy retrieval by author, date, keywords, etc. There are also dedicated bibliographic computer packages. Some supervisors still recommend index cards, suitably cross-referenced. This is effectively the manual equivalent of a computerized database, but the space required for storage is likely to be a major problem, as can be the reordering into newly required categories, identified as work progresses.

A word processor can also be used, with information typed or scanned in. It can be in chronological or any other order, and retrieval is with the 'find' command on any words which may seem useful either at the time or at a later date.

Some of the most productive reading takes place on a casual basis, perhaps while relaxing with books or articles away from the workplace. Important points and ideas can then easily get forgotten or lost. A way of marking a page for processing later without seriously interrupting the flow of the activity is with a peel-off sticker of the 'post-it' type. It is worth keeping a pack readily to hand for the purpose, along with a pen or pencil. No damage is caused to the book or article.

Similarly productive reading can take place on a casual basis, while surfing the web, so it is helpful to be able to mark a site for later attention and carry on surfing. To do this, you may need technical help. One way is to add the site to your 'favorites'* or 'bookmark' it. (Both are essentially the same action, but the terminology depends on the web-accessing software, known as the 'browser'.) Another way is to set the site to be available off-line. Another is to download the site onto your own computer. It is crucially important to

---

* The American spelling is as used by Internet Explorer.

document the publication details of a site, just as with any printed publication. These details include the address of the site, known as its 'URL' (which stands for 'universal resource locator'), the date accessed and the date that the site was last updated. (If this is not stated, record it as missing rather than just omit it.) A simple and reliable recording device is to put such useful information into a separate text file which you create yourself and keep on your computer with the saved page. Don't fall into the trap of thinking that you can always revisit a site to document or examine it more fully, because websites often have transient lives. They may have disappeared next time you look or have been updated such that the precise information that seemed so appealing earlier is no longer there. It is of course entirely in order to use information from an out-of-date site provided that it is fully referenced.

There is no completely satisfactory way of keeping records of what you read because it is seldom possible to know at the time precisely how the item or quotation might best be used, if indeed it can be used at all. Hence, difficult decisions have to be made about how much to record and with what keywords. There is no formalized procedure which can entirely support the burden of this, and there is no substitute for a mind that can provide a partial retrieval system of its own. The sheer size of the literature makes it impossible to keep personal records of everything, so it may be best to start with an overview of what sort of thing can be found where.

Before deciding what is best for you, talk to your supervisor, other research students and possibly other academic staff, who keep their literature records in different ways. Use the following activity as a stimulus.

(■) ACTIVITY

How do other workers in the field keep records of their literature searches? (Consider literature in its widest sense – e.g. paper based, such as articles and books; CD-ROM based; and web based.)

What advantages and disadvantages do they find with their method?

How do other workers deal with the difficulty of the sheer size of the literature?

If you are not comfortable about setting up 'bookmarks' or 'favorites' on a web browser, saving web pages to your own computer and/or saving them to be available off-line, find someone with the technical expertise to advise you.

⬛ DISCUSSION OF ACTIVITY

However you eventually decide to keep records of what you read, the details of references should be complete so that items can be found again if necessary and can be properly cited in the thesis. As an emergency measure it may be possible to salvage some parts of some incomplete references from the stock lists of the British Library via the web, from the CD-ROM catalogues held by most public and institutional libraries or from the web generally. However, it is unsafe to rely on this practice.

Keeping records as draft thesis chapters

A common way of keeping records is to draft parts of the thesis as you go along, within a draft outline. Although it is not possible to envisage in advance the exact form of a thesis, it may be possible, where the objectives and plan of the research are unlikely to change, for a general outline to be prepared, once preliminary work has been completed. This can serve as a map to guide you. Although at the outset it will contain only a few major landmarks and will change considerably as the work progresses, it may still be recognizable in the final thesis. The thesis outline can provide a basic shape to your work; it facilitates thinking about what you are doing: why you are doing it, what you ought to do next and what the outcomes are likely to be. All are powerful motivators.

Keeping records of achievements

It is a good idea to keep a special box, drawer or file of things that demonstrate your ongoing achievements. You can then, whenever necessary, select items from it to show to various interest groups: perhaps a departmental meeting; a meeting of a professional body; or an interview for future employment. Here are some ideas for inclusion, but they are not exhaustive.

- Your current curriculum vitae.
- Any letters or documents that may serve as testimonials to your work. It is sometimes worth requesting these in writing whenever someone praises or thanks you in connection with work.
- Copies of progress reports.
- Copies of your publications (if any).
- Statements of courses or other training undertaken.
- Flyers or programmes for meetings, seminars or conferences attended.
- Notes of participation in professional-body activities.
- Notes of participation in team/community activities.
- Flyers or programmes for any teaching or laboratory demonstration undertaken.
- Any agreed study plan or contract with records of amendments made to it.
- Diaries or formal notes of meetings with supervisor(s).
- Departmental or subject-based codes of practice, where relevant, with which you comply.
- Any permits, licences or agreements which you have been awarded.
- Photographs showing what your research is about and/or situations in which you are using skills that might impress others.

(■) ACTIVITY

What have you got tucked away that could usefully demonstrate your achievements?

◉ DISCUSSION OF ACTIVITY

You may like to look ahead to Chapter 15, which develops the idea of demonstrating achievements to prospective employers.

9 PLANNING AHEAD

If your supervisor does not believe in planning, then plan to change your supervisor.
(James Irvine, Chair of the National Postgraduate Committee, 1993–5, personal communication, 1994)

The importance of planning

Irrespective of the field of your research or the level of award for which you are registered, you need to map out some sort of plan for the work ahead. A feature of research is that the major deadlines are relatively long term – or at least longer term than is usual for taught courses. A formal plan will help you to come to terms with this, but it will do more – for example, it will:

- ease anxiety by externalizing your planning so that it need not be constantly occupying your mind;
- provide a focus in discussion with supervisors and others;
- provide a sense of security that you are on track;
- prevent you from spending too long on only vaguely relevant activities just because you enjoy them;
- allow you to enjoy taking time off with a clear conscience;
- provide a basis for reflection so that you can plan more realistically in future.

Detailed plans inevitably need regular amendment (see Box 9.1). How much and how often tends to depend on the nature of the work. Plans can normally be made on longer timescales where objectives can be clearly laid out in advance, and where a team is working on a single large project. They can normally be made only on fairly short timescales where the direction of any one stage of the work is based on recognizing and grasping opportunities

> **Box 9.1** Planning does not mean blueprinting
>
> *Here, then, is perhaps the first lesson of research; it can, in a very general way, be planned, but not blueprinted. One simply does not know what one is going to discover. These discoveries may lead to a complete change of direction.*
>
> (Berry 1986: 5)

which present themselves as the work progresses and which cannot be foreseen; where understanding grows holistically; or where changes of direction are frequent, normal or imposed through circumstances.

This chapter is about planning your programme of work. It is not about developing a research methodology for it. That has to rely on knowing and understanding the use of the various research strategies, methods and techniques that are normal in your field – and possibly outside it – and matching them to the needs of your particular topic or research problem (see Chapter 6). For this, only your supervisor and others in your field can help.

Departmental planning schedules

The norms of research in some disciplines are such that some departments can and do provide their students with a common framework of essential or required landmarks, with projected dates, over the full period available. These landmarks may be primarily events, such as formal meetings with supervisors, progress reports and presentation of seminars. Or they may extend to lengthier activities, such as studying the literature, negotiating the research plan, collecting data, writing reports, etc., each with a projected timespan. Such a framework can form a useful basis for planning. However, research in many fields requires more flexibility because the type and direction of work at any stage depends on the outcome of a previous stage. Then the planning has to be on shorter timescales and more ongoing.

ACTIVITY

Does your department suggest a plan which is in common for the work of all its research students? If so:

• Over what timescale does the plan operate?

• How detailed is it?

• How much do supervisors expect students to veer away from it?

• What do you think about its usefulness?

The project management approach to planning

Project management is a formalized approach to planning which can be as simple or as sophisticated as users care to make it.

A basic technique, which would repay the time and effort of any student in any field of study, would be a bar chart of activities marked on a timescale, as shown in Figure 9.1. Different colours could be used to indicate:

• tasks expected to occupy all of the allocated time – in Figure 9.1, scanning the journals and writing the report;
• short tasks to be done at some stage during the allocated time – in Figure 9.1, meeting the visiting professor;
• tasks which must fit the allocated time-slot if they are to be done at all because they link in with arrangements which are firmly fixed – in Figure 9.1, attending the conference.

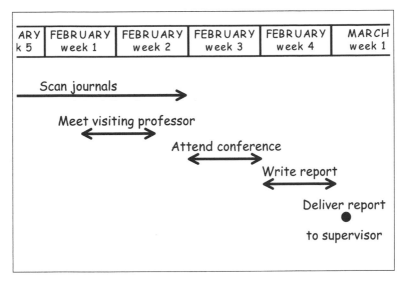

ARY k 5	FEBRUARY week 1	FEBRUARY week 2	FEBRUARY week 3	FEBRUARY week 4	MARCH week 1

Figure 9.1   A simple bar chart for a student's plan of work

Different symbols can be used to indicate when something has to be completed. The symbols are known as 'milestones' and the 'something' as a 'deliverable'. In Figure 9.1, the deliverable is the report and the milestone is the date it is to be handed in.

Bar charts are snapshots which capture how things are or are expected to be at a moment in time. They will rapidly become out of date and need revision, because the unanticipated is in the very nature of research.

All students, working alone, could sketch out a simple bar chart such as that in Figure 9.1. However, much more sophisticated project management packages can be run on computers. They can manage the interacting work of individuals in a team and the anticipated use of resources, and they have the advantage that they can be simply and easily updated. You will probably want to involve yourself seriously with computerized project management only if your supervisor already operates it and is concerned that everyone involved should be able to see the progress of everyone else at a glance, together with the usage of resources. If, however, you have ready access to such a computer package, such as Microsoft Project, you may like to check out what it can offer.

There is another technique which may be useful for the common problem of not knowing where to start among a sea of activities. It helps with the sequencing of activities, so that work is not held up while one aspect waits for another on which it relies. The technique is known as 'critical path analysis'. In its simplest form, it involves marking each task on a sheet of paper and then drawing arrows between them, linking them together in the order in which one relies on another. This may involve a certain amount of trial and error and possibly also, if one cares about aesthetic appearance, redrawing with tasks positioned differently on the page. Where there is considerable interrelationship between tasks, critical path diagrams look more like networks than linear paths, and it may be worth using computerized methods.

⬛ ACTIVITY

Draw a rough bar chart for the next stage of your work, basing it on the style of Figure 9.1. Include:

- key tasks, their start dates and periods over which they have to be done;
- milestones and deliverables – your own or any that may be imposed.

Annotate the bar chart with:

- the resources you want or need at each stage, together with their availability and costs;
- when and how your work links with and depends on input from other people.

How far ahead did you feel it reasonable to plan and how realistic or helpful did you find the planning?

If you feel uncertain about where to start any stage of your work, see if developing a critical path diagram might help.

If you have access to a computerized project management package, check out what it can offer. Is the extra sophistication helpful for you and your work?

● DISCUSSION OF ACTIVITY

It should be enlightening to reflect on the start date that you gave your plan. There is a tendency to make this sometime in the future rather than today or tomorrow. Students undertaking research as part of an otherwise taught course are particularly prone to taking time off between the taught modules and the research. Then the research may never get started or be so rushed that it is below standard.

Developing a style of plan for your own use

The ways in which most people develop and document their plans of work are highly personal, guided by the ideas and norms of others in similar fields and refined through personal experience. Planning is an ongoing activity and you may never feel that you have it quite right for your sort of work. This hardly matters because the act of progressively refining plans should markedly improve your work and your attitude towards it.

● ACTIVITY

Discuss planning techniques with other students and your supervisor(s) and develop a style that seems to suit you.

Practise and refine this through use.

Identifying what is to go into your plan

If you are working alone in an area where others are not closely involved, you may find it difficult to identify the activities that need to go into your plan. Any of the creative thinking techniques of Chapter 18 can help.

 ACTIVITY

Look at Chapter 18 and note the various techniques for creative thinking. Try some of them to develop ideas for the activities that ought to go into your plan. With the mind map technique, suitable spokes might be 'required outcomes', 'deadlines', 'resources' and 'other people', but there are many possibilities.

Planning extended work on location

Planning for extended work away from your institutional or work base requires special attention because, if not done properly, lack of finance and lack of opportunity may mean that there be no second chance to have another go.

The following activity lists some of the planning issues to consider. Use it as a checklist for what is relevant for your planning if you have to work away from base for an extended period.

 ACTIVITY

If your anticipated work is at some considerable distance from your normal base, particularly if it is in another country, what plans do you intend to make, or have you made, for the following?

- Financing your travel, accommodation and living expenses while away. How far in advance ought you to start organizing this?

- Arranging meetings with individuals or access to buildings or resources at the new location. How far in advance ought you to start organizing this? Who needs to be contacted?

- Identifying someone to talk things over with while you are away. When should you contact them to get their agreement?

- Using a computer and printer, and accessing the Internet (for web work and email).

- Keeping in touch with your supervisor.

- Backup data collection (where relevant) if the intended source of data becomes unavailable.

- Resources to take with you, such as money, stationery and equipment.

- Anything else.

Have you checked that the time you wish to spend away from the institution is allowed within institutional regulations?

(■) DISCUSSION OF ACTIVITY

Supervisors will advise on the general planning for work away from base over an extended period. However, if any of the above points give cause for concern, do mention them specifically to your supervisor. In particular, note the possible need to make alternative or back-up plans before you leave. It may be too late to do so afterwards.

It will be helpful to identify someone local who can act as a mentor while you are away. Some knowledge of the subject is desirable, but it is not as important as sound, logical and creative thinking ability; a commitment to being supportive; and time to be so. Provided that you can find such a person, your own creative thinking and academic training should help you cope with the unexpected, at least until you can get in touch with your supervisor.

Email is the obvious cheap, fast and reliable way of keeping in touch with your supervisor and others. Someone local may allow you to use their email address while you are away or arrange for you to have your own temporary account there. Or you could access your existing home account by phone, or set up a 'Hotmail' account which is accessible anywhere via the Internet. Access to a fax machine is also likely to be useful. Try to set up communication mechanisms before departure.

A laptop, notebook or palmtop computer will be extremely useful. If you don't own one yourself, it may be worth trying to borrow one to use while you are away.

Institutional regulations invariably state the proportion of time that has to be spent 'on campus' for various awards. Application for study leave must normally be formally supported by the supervisor and made to the registry, and approval must be given before departure.

There will, of course, be other administrative issues relating to your particular subject area and to the location of the work, and there will certainly be methodological issues. These need to be considered in advance by you and your supervisor together.

Coping with things not going according to plan

Quite generally all research students seem to report that they had unusually bad luck somewhere along the way that played havoc with their plans. In fact it was probably not bad luck, or at least not in the way that bad luck is usually understood. Instead it was and is a normal feature of research: perhaps equipment is not delivered on time or breaks down; perhaps people are not available when wanted; perhaps crucial information centres are closed for refurbishment; perhaps an essential book takes weeks to filter through the inter-library loan system. Then there is always illness. The list could be endless.

The way of coping with unpredictable delays is in two parts. First, build in 40 per cent more time than you expect for everything, without getting lulled into the sense of security that this allows a more laid-back approach. Second, have a list to hand of all the other related tasks that you always meant get round to, but never had time for or that you mean to do at some stage in the future. Examples might be:

- getting to grips with the more sophisticated features of word processing;
- tidying up your store of references from the literature;
- checking on websites that have come to your attention or have proved helpful in the past;
- surfing the web;
- acquiring any important keyboard skills which you don't already have, such as learning to touch-type using all fingers;
- getting to grips with computer-aided projection for making presentations (such as PowerPoint);
- producing neat diagrams or tables for reports or the thesis;
- visiting a library some distance away that specializes in something that might be relevant;
- writing a draft of a chapter of the thesis;
- going to see someone;
- a treat of some sort in the way of leisure activities or a short holiday.

The next activity invites you to make your own list. Then, when an unforeseen delay presents some unexpected free time, use it for one of the items on the list.

⬛ ACTIVITY

Make your own list of things that are non-urgent and somewhat peripheral to your main work, but which nevertheless would support it.

Beside each one, jot down a reasonable estimate of the time-slot that it would require.

10 MANAGING YOURSELF AND YOUR TIME

Dost thou love life?, then do not squander time, for that's the stuff life is made of.
(Benjamin Franklin, quoted in Tripp 1976: 640, item 19)

The importance of managing yourself and your time

It has been said that research is 1 per cent inspiration and 99 per cent perspiration. The 1 per cent inspiration relies on creativity and is discussed in Chapter 18. The 99 per cent perspiration is the routine work – for example, attending meetings, reading around the subject, gathering data, keeping records, writing drafts and then rewriting in the light of feedback. Although opinions differ about the relative magnitudes of the inspiration and the perspiration, the adage does stress that both are important and that the routine work is always likely to be much the greater in terms of outlay of time. This chapter considers some ideas which may be new to you for making routine work more efficient.

Finding out where your time goes

It is a common experience that time seems to disappear and one wonders where it has gone and what has been achieved. Whereas this probably does no harm when it happens occasionally, something must be done if it becomes a regular occurrence. The first step lies with finding out where the time goes, to provide a basis for re-evaluating activities. Some people like to do this by keeping a diary over a period of time, logging the various activities in each day. The task can be an amusing and even essential activity, but it does itself take considerable time which the benefit may not repay. Nevertheless, you may like to try it for a short period or for certain days.

(■) ACTIVITY

If you feel that time is disappearing without any noticeable achievements, try keeping some form of log of what you do. This can be as accurate or as rough as you please or think you need.

Does the log show up any surprisingly large usages of time?

Do you think you need to make any major changes in your use of time?

(■) DISCUSSION OF ACTIVITY

There are no hard and fast rules on how to spend time while undertaking research. What matters is that you should be content with your own use of time. Do realize that time spent on leisure activities or talking to people is not necessarily time wasted. You need them to maintain your physical and mental health (see later in this chapter), and they can, as Chapters 12 and 18 explain, also help your work.

Using time efficiently when supervisions and seminars are cancelled

Supervisions and seminars do sometimes have to be cancelled at short notice, and it is worth taking all possible steps to ensure that you are informed in good time, so that you use the time to your best advantage.

 ACTIVITY

Whose responsibility is it to let you know if a supervision or seminar has to be cancelled at short notice?

Make sure that this person has your current contact telephone number.

 DISCUSSION OF ACTIVITY

When free time-slots arrive unexpectedly it is worth making full use of them. Chapter 9 makes some suggestions.

Matching the task to the time-slot

Sometimes the urgency of certain tasks must dictate the order in which they have to be done. Although this may occasionally be unavoidable, it is seldom ideal. First, it may mean that an important task has to be rushed; and second, it may be an inefficient use of a time-slot. Try the following activity to get a feel for the benefits of taking the trouble to match tasks to available time-slots.

 ACTIVITY

Imagine that you have the following tasks ahead of you. If you like, replace them with tasks which fit better into your own type of research.

- Sticking stamps on 100 envelopes
- Making two five-minute personal telephone calls
- Writing-up notes of an interview you have conducted and analysing its meaning
- Arranging a meeting to help another student

Arrange these tasks into your personal timetable for the next week or month, ensuring that the use of time is as efficient as possible. Have you merely filled the next blank slot? If not, what principles were you using, explicitly or implicitly?

■ DISCUSSION OF ACTIVITY

Arranging tasks such as these efficiently is a personal matter, but here are some principles to consider. They may appear self-evident, but you may be surprised to see the extent to which you have or have not applied them.

Tasks which require considerable concentration need periods of uninterrupted time and they are also best done at a time of day which suits the individual's metabolism. This is one's prime time, and it may be early in the morning or late at night, depending on the person. Tasks which rely significantly on what is in short-term memory need to be completed as soon as possible, and this is true irrespective of the detail of any notes taken at the time, because notes can never record everything and are often difficult to transcribe. Tasks which do not rely on concentration can be done at the same time as, for example, talking to people or watching television.

In the activity, you may have felt that the most important aspect of writing-up the interview was that the concentration it required demanded no interruptions. If so, it would be sensible to schedule it into a lengthy period of uninterrupted time – perhaps at home when other people in the family have gone to bed or during a weekend when they are out, or perhaps when a room in the department is quiet. Alternatively or additionally, you may have felt that the concentration demanded your prime time. Or you may have felt that the most important aspect of writing-up the interview was that it had to be dealt with immediately while it was still fresh in your mind. If so, you would have scheduled it for immediately and moved other tasks accordingly.

Least concentration would be needed for sticking on the stamps. So it would be efficient to do this at a time when interruption is likely, or when you are likely to be tired or watching television. Try not to waste precious prime time on such things.

Did you think of suggesting the meeting for a time which would least disrupt you? Perhaps in the middle of the day if you wanted to use it as a break; or at the beginning or end of the day if you wanted it to interfere as little as possible with a task requiring extended time. Timetabling to suit yourself is not selfish or self-centred, provided that the other person's preferences are also allowed for, and it is one of the most important aspects of time management.

Handling interruptions

Some people can work with interruptions, but most people, particularly as they get older, prefer to work without them. The following activity provides a stimulus for developing your own ways of dealing with interruptions.

 ACTIVITY

Is there a place to work where you won't be interrupted, such as at home when everyone is out, or in a library?

Is it reasonable to put a notice on a door somewhere giving a time when you will be available and requesting not to be disturbed until then?

Can you work in a room in the department or at work, out of hours so that no one else is there?

Can you let the phone ring when you are really busy or use an answerphone and call back at your convenience?

Managing time at home with partners and family

Particular difficulties arise when working at home and having to deal with interruptions from members of the family. It is natural for them to feel that the home is a place for being together; it is not that they are unsympathetic or insensitive. Some people find the following tactics useful:

- At the outset of the research, negotiate an informal contract with partners, older children and other relatives about time commitments; their implications; and how long a period of time you expect the contract to have to last. (If you didn't do this at the time, it's probably not too late to do it now.)
- Every weekend, or at some other convenient time, go through your diary with your family, to agree what periods you can spend with them and when you ought to be alone working. Work periods are likely to increase considerably while writing up or finalizing the thesis, and sensitivity is needed on how and when to let the family know this.
- When you start a period of work at home, consider role-playing the 'joke' of saying a formal 'Goodbye, I'm going off to the office now' and a formal 'Hello, I've come back' when you are ready again for disturbances.

 ACTIVITY

Can you adapt any of the above suggestions to fit your own circumstances?

Managing time on the Internet and at the computer

It is a waste of time and effort to do tasks 'manually' which the right IT tools can do very much faster and more efficiently. In the long run, for example, it certainly saves time to learn how to consult a library catalogue on the web rather than having to visit the library for it. Furthermore, web skills and other IT skills are important in their own right and are expected of today's professionals (see Chapter 15). So it is crucially important to take time to find out about the right tools for a job and to learn how to use them. Unfortunately, though, computers and the Internet can run away with time.

Although some of the information on the web is the most up to date and pertinent available, which is reason enough for accessing it, much of what also seems, on the face of it, to be fascinating and useful often turns out to be trivial, peripheral and frustrating. The web can all too easily consume time to little or no value, and this is made worse if access is via a slow modem. So it is important to be firm with yourself, and decide in advance what precisely you are going to use the web for, and stick to it; or to allow yourself a specific small amount of surfing as a treat or a break from work.

Chatting via email can similarly run away with time. So you again need to be firm with yourself. Essential aspects of email apart, you need to establish a balance between wasting time chatting electronically and invigorating yourself through interaction with others. You also need to learn to recognize junk mail quickly and not spend time on it.

Playing games on the computer can obviously run away with time, but perhaps the worst time-waster is 'playing' which masquerades as work, because it carries a spurious acceptability. Creating a PowerPoint presentation that you don't need, ostensibly to 'learn how to use the most sophisticated aspects of the package', is just one of many possible examples. You can almost certainly think of others to which you may be particularly prone.

When you find yourself spending more time at a computer than you originally anticipated, think of it as 'spending' time which ought to be 'buying' something worthwhile. Try a cost-benefit analysis to see whether you ought to move on to another task or take a break to do something else.

Keeping 'office hours' versus using the 'psychological moment'

As the adage about research being 99 per cent perspiration suggests, research certainly does involve long periods of routine work. Some students recommend keeping to 'office hours' during these periods, to ensure a balance between work and social and leisure activities.

Often, however, the routine work needs to be sparked off by an idea. Indeed, many students say that they can go for days without producing seemingly productive work; then an idea occurs to them, together with immense enthusiasm for pursuing it. If they can work on it then, they produce a great deal of high-quality work very quickly. If, on the other hand, other commitments force them to delay for any reason, the moment seems to have gone, and the work, when it is eventually started, is slow and hard going. It is worth trying to recognize these 'psychological moments', and, if at all possible, to let them take over, even at the expense of other commitments and office hours.

Keeping going for hours at a time

During some parts of the research, particularly while writing reports or finalizing the thesis, it is not unusual for students to keep working at their books or their computer for 13 or more hours at a time. This can be due to the pressures of work or due to pure delight and fascination. Do realize the dangers of sitting in front of a computer screen for long periods: eye strain, excessive tiredness, unknown effects on pregnant women, repetitive strain injury (see Box 10.1), etc. Humans need to take regular breaks. Cups of coffee and biscuits or chocolate bars often seem the obvious ways of justifying and filling them, but what generally works better is some form of physical activity for five to ten minutes. It can be exercise or it can simply be one of the essential chores, like washing up. It can be a good idea to delay doing these, then use them to fill breaks, rather than rushing to get them all done before starting work.

Not infrequently, students work far into the night. Only you can decide the extent to which it is advisable for you to go without

---

Box 10.1 Repetitive strain injury

Repetitive strain injury (RSI) is an acute inflammation of the muscles, ligaments and tendons and it's caused by performing the same physical task over and over again . . . Poor posture, sitting in a fixed position for too long, even stress and a tense body, can all combine to form RSI . . . The warning signs of RSI are aches or tingling in the fingers, wrists, elbows or shoulders. At the first sign of discomfort you should act. If you continue typing without improving your work habits, just hoping that the ache will go away, it may well develop into the shooting, burning pain that real sufferers know so well. In severe cases, they are hardly able to use their hands at all and a few end up disabled for life. Why some people and not others fall victim is all a bit of a mystery. But if RSI really gets you in its agonising grip, your doctor's first order will be to stop typing and possibly stop using your hands altogether for a time. Physiotherapy, ultrasound and even osteopathy can all help the sufferer. But it may take as long as six months before any activity is pain free . . . Prevention, as always, is easier than cure. For more advice contact The RSI Association, 152 High Street, Yiewsley, West Drayton, Middlesex, UB7 7BE.

(Prima Magazine 1994: 57)

sleep. It is not advisable as normal procedure, although it may be appropriate in certain circumstances.

Matching your approach to your preferred learning style

Managing yourself can be made much more efficient if you get to know your own personal preferred learning style and then try to match your approach to it.

You may have already identified your preferred learning style. However, many new students have never realized that there are alternative ways of setting about work. Consequently, they have never consciously analysed how they prefer to do it. Try the following activity.

 ACTIVITY

When faced with a deadline for a task, do you tend to finish it with time to spare, to fill the time available with it, or not to get properly started until the deadline is upon you?

When faced with a large task, do you find yourself breaking it down into small parts and then starting just with one small, well-defined part, and only after completing it going on to another part? Or do you find yourself spending time trying to understand the full context of the large task before attempting any part of it? (If you are unsure, try to think of a concrete example, which need not be to do with work, like designing a dinner party or a touring holiday.)

Do you find yourself starting with the easiest parts of a large task to get them out of the way, before concentrating on the harder ones, or do you prefer starting with the harder parts to 'break the back' of the large task?

When faced with new information, do you consciously consider whether your aim is simply to reproduce parts of it; to understand certain parts of it; or to understand as many implications and ramifications as possible?

(■) DISCUSSION OF ACTIVITY

There is no right or wrong learning style. It should be a matter for personal preference, dictated by the purpose behind the task. However, everyone's work could be made much more efficient by using a repertoire of learning styles which could be called on according to the situation.

In particular, starting a task only when the deadline approaches may be ideal where crucial aspects are changing by the moment, but for postgraduate research a better approach is likely to be to allow oneself time to mull things over and develop and improve on one's thinking. Some students, though, do take this to extremes. For them it may be sensible to aim to do several good jobs rather than one excellent one. Be guided on this by your supervisor, once he or she has had the opportunity to get to know you.

Letting a context emerge gradually by completing one aspect at a time is described as 'serialist' thinking. Needing to see the whole context before studying any part of it is described as 'holistic' thinking. The adage about 'not seeing the wood for the trees' is relevant here. It is normally used disparagingly to imply that someone cannot see clearly what they ought to be doing and where they ought to be going, and there is a lesson in this for research students for whom it is important to be able to see the wood *as well as* the trees. Doing so requires holistic thinking, which will probably have to be cultivated, because early education tends to train children into serialist thinking at the expense of holistic thinking, because high priority subjects such as languages and mathematics require a step-by-step approach. Subjects which foster holistic thinking tend to have a lower priority in the school system. Art appreciation is an example because it can require the complete picture to be taken in at a glance before the detail is considered. A technique to foster holistic thinking is the use of mind maps, which are considered in Chapter 18.

The intention to reproduce material without understanding it involves what is called a 'surface approach' to learning, and the intention to develop understanding involves what is called a 'deep approach'. It is not true that students should always use the deep approach, although of course no academic work could progress with an entirely surface approach. Both approaches have their places, and what is important is to decide which approach to use in which circumstances and why.

Using music to manage yourself

Some people work best with complete quiet. Others find that music can increase their efficiency. Most people know their musical preferences by the time they become students. What they may not appreciate is that different types of music can be better for different types of work. Use the following activity as a basis for discussion with others, to see if they can make any suggestions about the use of music.

(■) ACTIVITY

If you like to work with background music, what pieces or styles are your preferences for the following?

• Reading

• Writing

• Creative thought

• Routine administrative work

(■) DISCUSSION OF ACTIVITY

Some people find that certain routine administrative work, such as the sticking of stamps on envelopes mentioned earlier, can wind them up because it is occupying only part of their mind. Music can occupy the other part, and hence make the work more relaxing – but the music has to be the right sort.

Playing taped music or CDs serves another purpose in that the end of a tape forces people to realize how long they have been working and that it is time for a break, even if that break is simply changing the tape.

Directing your research to suit your personal needs and preferences

There is usually some flexibility in designing a research programme, particularly where the precise formulation of the research problem grows out of choices made at the various stages of the research. So it makes sense to build in personal preferences, because doing what one likes aids efficiency. Use the following activity to set yourself thinking.

(■) ACTIVITY

Give an approximate rating for how much the following modes of working appeal to you personally. Then see how far people who know you well agree.

• Working alone

• Work involving being with or talking to people generally

• Work involving being with or talking to specific types of people

• Work involving long hours of private study

• Work involving using the Internet

• Work involving making or using equipment

- Work which is primarily out of doors

- Work which is primarily of use to others

- Work which is primarily of personal fascination

- Work which involves travelling

⬛ DISCUSSION OF ACTIVITY

Some or all of the above modes of working, and other modes as well, are required to some extent in all research degrees, but students usually have more freedom than they realize in terms of designing their work around the modes of working that are most enjoyable or fascinating to them personally. The freedom is greatest where the research students are working individually in a mode in which decisions about the direction of the work at any stage grow out of the findings of previous stages. The freedom is least where the research involves a closely pre-defined research problem or working as part of a team, particularly in laboratory-based subjects.

As an example of flexibility, if you happen to prefer working away from other people, it should be perfectly possible to define or redefine the direction of your research to involve reinterpreting data which is entirely secondary (that is, already collected by other researchers and probably already published). Then contact with others will be kept to a minimum. If you happen to prefer working with people, out of doors or in any other particular situation, you should be able to define or redefine the direction of your research to maximize this.

Fitting in teaching work

Students working for higher degrees are often offered teaching or laboratory demonstration work within their departments. It may indeed be a prerequisite of accepting a bursary of some sort. Teaching and demonstrating have the advantage of providing money and experience, but care needs to be taken that they do not seriously

---

Box 10.2   Recommendations on preparing postgraduates for teaching

The following responsibilities are summarized from a report produced by a working party on the subject.

- *Postgraduates with teaching responsibilities should be appropriately prepared for teaching.*
- *Every department should appoint a mentor to offer guidance and support.*
- *A member of staff should also be involved with the outcome if GTAs [graduate teaching assistants] are engaged in any form of assessment that contributes to the award of a degree.*
- *Appropriate bodies – for example the UK Council in association with ILTHE [Institute for Learning and Teaching in Higher Education, now the Institute for Learning and Teaching – ILT] should develop a Code of Practice for GTA contracts of employment.*
- *Preparation for teaching should be integrated into the study programmes of research students.*

(UK Council for Graduate Education 1999: 2)

---

detract from the business of the research. Some people find that a 'teaching session' overshadows the complete day because they work themselves up for it and then need time to unwind afterwards. Before you agree to take on teaching work, make sure that it suits your disposition, that you receive suitable training and are paid at a fair rate. The National Postgraduate Committee has produced guidelines for the employment of postgraduate students as teachers (see the *further reading* section) and the Careers Service Unit (CSU) Prospects site also has helpful advice (see the *websites* section). Box 10.2 summarizes recommendations from the UK Council for Graduate Education.

Teaching and laboratory demonstration work should be at your choice and never imposed, unless of course it is part of a bursary agreement.

Maintaining a healthy lifestyle

Part of managing oneself must be to maintain a healthy lifestyle, giving attention to adequate and appropriate exercise and to healthy eating. This is particularly important for students who feel that things are getting on top of them. Dealing with this includes maintaining a balanced outlook by keeping physically fit.

According to a television documentary (*The Lady Killers*, ITV, 16 August 1995, 10.40 p.m.), long term, serious depression is readily avoidable and treatable on three levels, according to its severity: physical exercise, which releases natural therapeutic chemicals into the body; talking things over; and then – if these fail – taking drugs prescribed by a doctor. The dangers of taking drugs which are not prescribed by a doctor are well known.

Being realistic with yourself

It is all too easy to be unrealistic about what it is reasonable or possible for you or anyone else to do in a given time. If you aim at too much, you will get fraught and disappointed when you fail to achieve. If you aim at too little, you will never complete the re-search programme. You have to get to know yourself, and then be firm with yourself while at the same time treating yourself with gen-erosity and understanding. Box 10.3 encapsulates what is realistic.

Box 10.3   A maxim for realism

A doctoral thesis is a piece of work which a capable, well-qualified [full-time] student, who is properly supported and supervised, can produce in three years.

(British Academy 1992, para. 12)

---

11 TAKING RESPONSIBILITY FOR YOUR OWN PROGRESS

The people who get on in this world are the people who get up and look for the circumstances they want, and if they can't find them, make them.

(George Bernard Shaw, *Mrs Warren's Profession*, act II)

The importance of taking responsibility upon yourself

There is a core of basic knowledge and basic research skills that all students need for their research programmes, and you may be fortunate enough to belong to a department that is sufficiently large to provide this training on a formal basis. However, all students' work is unique and everyone's needs in terms of research skills and knowledge is similarly unique, at least in some respects. It is not reasonable to expect your unique needs to be satisfied without taking some of the initiative yourself. This chapter considers ways of going about it.

Taking up formal training

If you belong to a department that runs a formal programme of training for its research students, you may wish to do no more than scan this chapter. If you don't belong to such a department or if you are part-time in a department which does not extend such training to its part-timers, you may like to use the activity below as a checklist to identify where you may need to top up.

⬛ ACTIVITY

The following is a list of topics which could be in an inter-disciplinary core research training programme. (It is not meant to be ideal or comprehensive.) Does it spark off ideas about any topic that you feel you ought to know more about? When doing this activity, do bear in mind that each discipline has its own vocabulary and its own way of looking at research, so some topics may require different names, and some topics may naturally fit within others.

- Designing a research project
- Conducting a literature search
- Ways of gathering data
- Ways of analysing data
- Developing academic discourse and constructing arguments and counter-arguments
- Writing the thesis
- Giving a seminar on one's work
- Giving a conference paper
- Writing a journal article
- The nature of 'truth' and research paradigms
- Ethical issues
- Intellectual copyright
- Keyboard skills
- Use the worldwide web
- Use of email
- Use of computer packages, such as word processing, spreadsheets, databases and presentation applications (such as Microsoft PowerPoint)
- General key skills (see Chapter 15)
- Career planning (also see Chapter 15)

⬤ DISCUSSION OF ACTIVITY

It is difficult to identify the boundary between basic training for research and learning about research on the job. The latter is an ongoing activity with ever more to learn. However, time is of the essence for students; so they have to find a balance between, on the one hand, ensuring that their basic training is adequate and, on the other hand, not wasting time learning things they may never use. If the activity has stimulated the feeling that you really do need a particular aspect of basic research training, do speak to your supervisor about it and possibly ask him or her to recommend courses, books or someone to talk to.

There is also the issue that the meaning and scope of research training are interpreted differently from one field of study to another. In the arts, humanities and social sciences it is widely assumed that once students are trained in how to go about research they can find out about various methods or techniques for themselves, should this become necessary. In the natural sciences, each research method tends to require a unique competence with specialized equipment; and students often feel justified in demanding a wide range of experience of different methods, irrespective of their applicability to any research problems in hand. Then they can quote this experience in job applications.

Keeping up with your subject

All students undertaking research are expected to get to know what is regarded as 'all the basic and important literature in the field'. So you need to try to keep abreast with developments by reading core and closely related literature. The difficult balancing act is drawing a line between the core and the related. You don't have the time to read everything.

Students also need to keep abreast with new developments by sitting in on various courses and seminars. However, this too is a matter of balancing the potential usefulness of the information with the time spent acquiring it. In an academic community it would be quite possible to spend all one's time following only marginally related interests, and, fascinating as they may be, they cannot write a thesis for you.

Networking and serendipity

As your work develops, you will probably find the need for research tools and techniques that you did not learn about in any formalized training. These may be things that everyone knows the existence of, even if they do not know how to use them, such as the statistical treatment of data. Or they may be something that no one can reasonably be expected to have heard of. To find out about these, you have to go out and meet other researchers, to talk to them and let them know what you are doing – i.e. to use networking and serendipity. Box 11.1 gives an example of their many uses.

Box 11.1   The value of serendipity in research

Lewis Elton tells the story – which he admits dates him! – of how he first learnt about computers at a time when they were very new. He was giving a conference presentation in which he regretted that he could not follow up a particular approach because the calculations would be impossibly onerous. One of the participants came up to him afterwards and suggested that the mathematics would not be at all onerous if he used a computer with a suitable program. Between them they did indeed use a suitably programmed computer, and the work was completed successfully.

If you are part-time in the institution or working at a distance from it you will have to find your own means of networking, guided by the time and resources at your disposal. Colleagues in the work-place may help. So will support groups, particularly electronic ones (see Chapter 5 and the *websites* section at the end of the book).

Using research seminars

Most departments run regular research seminars. The discussion that takes place afterwards is often as important as the content of the presentation. Although your first thought may be to doubt the value of attending a seminar where the topic is far removed from your own, your further thoughts should be very different unless you are very near the end of your research programme. There are several reasons for this.

- Research seminars may be your only access to academic staff other than your supervisor. Not that these individuals will be objectively in any way superior to a supervisor, but they will have different ranges of experience to call on and different ways of expressing themselves. You should learn a lot about what does and does not constitute good research by listening to their contributions to the discussion and then testing out the quality of your own work against their reactions.
- Research seminars provide easy access to what is going on in different and related areas, in case you may need or wish to link it to your own work (see Chapter 17).
- Research seminars provide excellent opportunities for developing an appreciation of the research culture of your discipline.
- Research seminars provide excellent opportunities to learn about how to give a seminar yourself.
- Research seminars are good occasions for using serendipity.

A valid reason for not attending research seminars is that they are so badly attended by others that it is not possible to gain the benefits outlined above. It may be possible, though, if you choose the right time and place so as not to cause offence, to have a word with the seminar organizer to suggest ways of boosting attendance – for example, by moving the seminars to a different time of day.

Protecting the ownership of your work

It is a normal part of academic life for people to help one another (see Chapter 12). However, it is regarded as misconduct for people to take the work of others and present it as their own (see Box 11.2). Everyone has what is known as 'intellectual copyright' or 'intellectual property rights' on their own work. If you think that there could be some aspect of your work that others may want to claim as their own, perhaps for financial or commercial reasons, or even just to be able to produce a journal article or thesis, you should take it upon yourself to raise the matter with your supervisor.

The best way to show that work is yours is to publish it in a journal article, but this is a slow process. The work has to be packaged in a 'complete' form, and then more than a year can elapse before a submitted article gets to press. Peer-reviewed electronic journals may be a little quicker, but not much. One way forward is to put down an ownership marker by presenting your ongoing work at a conference (see Chapter 14). Another is to publish something about it yourself on the web. Neither are particularly valued

Box 11.2 The nature of misconduct in research

Misconduct in research includes:

(a) *The fabrication of data: claiming results where none has been obtained.*
(b) *The falsification of data including changing records.*
(c) *Plagiarism, including the direct copying of textural material, the use of other people's data without acknowledgement and the use of ideas from other people without adequate attribution.*
(d) *Misleading ascription of authorship including the listing of authors without their permission, attributing work to others who have not in fact contributed in the research, and the lack of appropriate acknowledgement of work primarily produced by a research student/trainee or associate.*
(e) *Other practices that seriously deviate from those commonly accepted within the research community for proposing, conducting or reporting research.*
(f) *Intentional infringement of the institution's published code of conduct for the responsible conduct of research.*

Misconduct does not include honest errors or honest differences in interpretation on judgements of data.
  This list is not meant to be all inclusive.
(Australian Vice-Chancellors' Committee 1990: 5)

academically. The first lacks rigorous peer review and the second lacks any quality control. Nevertheless, both do provide public markers of ownership, although they are also, sadly, ways of getting work stolen.

Supervisors themselves are generally entirely open and honest if they wish to use their students' work in some way, and they see to it that the student gets full credit and a fair share of any financial remuneration. If, however, you suspect that you are not being treated fairly in this respect the best way forward is probably to speak to the individual who takes special responsibility for research students in your department or an officer of the students' union.

The websites in Box 11.3 may provide some helpful information on intellectual property rights, but the law is complicated and does keep changing.

Box 11.3 Sources of advice on intellectual property rights

The following sites were offered via the email discussion group of the National Postgraduate Committee. With the approval of the author, they were edited for availability just prior to the publication of this book, but inevitably they won't all be available by the time you come to read them. Neither will they be current nor comprehensive. So take the purpose of this Box as (i) to indicate the informality, generosity and usefulness of the help that is commonplace with postgraduate email discussion groups, and (ii) to indicate the sort of support that is available on the web.

Hi,

Thank you to everyone who helped with this. It is the result of my searches, and might be of use to some of you, some day.

Andree

A good, readable text is:

Pearson, H. and Miller, C. (1990), Commercial exploitation of intellectual property, Blackstone Press Limited, London.

The following web links should work, but are by no means comprehensive:

(a) http://www.fplc.edu/#web. This site is from the USA based Franklin Pierce Law Centre. This is USA based but has a potpourri of different sites and information. Of particular interest might be the sections on patents, trademarks, copyright on the net, visual arts, patents and the market value of inventions.

(b) The Association of University Technology Managers presents a site at http://www.autm.net. It provides links to the various useful sites including: Patent, Copyright and Trademark Resources.

(c) Bristol University – http://www.bris.ac.uk/Depts/IPMU

(d) University of Newcastle – http://www.ncl.ac.uk/rsu/tto/index.htm

(e) European Commission's IPR helpdesk – http://www.cordis.lu/ipr-helpdesk/home.html

(f) Links to Patent Offices – http://www.aber.ac.uk/~dgw/patent.htm

(g) Basic information on patents, from the Patent Agency – http://www.cipa.org.uk/cipa/

(h) UK Patent Office – http://www.patent.gov.uk/index.html
(Andree Woodcock 1999,
NPC mail-base discussion group, 20 April)

12 COOPERATING WITH OTHERS FOR MUTUAL HELP AND SUPPORT

No man is an island.

(John Donne, 'Meditation XVII',
Devotions upon Emergent Occasions (1624))

The importance of mutual help and support

Although doing research can mean a great deal of working in isolation, students who are successful invariably rely heavily on the support of others – to suggest leads, to give informed judgements, to provide constructive criticism and to boost motivation. This chapter is about giving and receiving help and support from others: other students; other academics; partners, family and friends; and other professionals in the department, institution, workplace or elsewhere.

Receiving advice, feedback and criticism

Receiving advice, feedback and criticism from others is very similar to receiving it from a supervisor (see Chapter 7). They will want you to take the trouble to understand what they are saying; will hope that you are pleased about it; and will want you to take time to consider it. So the best thing to do is simply to thank the persons concerned, to seek clarification if necessary and then to say that you will go away and do some thinking. It is seldom worth launching into a justification of why what they say may be inappropriate. If you do, you may irritate them and probably prevent them from giving further help in future. It is quite in order not to accept the advice, feedback or criticism exactly as it stands, and it is important to realize this.

Occasionally people give feedback which seems designed only to make themselves feel superior by denigrating others. This can be because the individuals concerned have been caught at a bad moment, in which case they usually apologize later. People who give destructive feedback as a norm invariably lose the respect of those around them. If you find that you are receiving destructive criticism on a regular basis, stay polite and take whatever steps are necessary to put an end to it.

It is important to learn to recognize other forms of advice which can be very depressing and damaging to progress. Their tell-tale signs are that accepting them would involve any of the following:

- undertaking major changes of direction which are unnecessary for the purposes of the award;
- not fitting comfortably within the boundaries of a consolidated piece of research;
- not being of a suitable academic standard;
- unreasonably extending the period of the research;
- not fitting within your area of interest;
- an unappealing change in ideology or methodology, particularly when the existing one is valid;
- undue expense.

Such advice is usually well-meant, but it tends to come from someone who does not know the ins and outs of a student's work, is making invalid assumptions about it, has a vested interest in a different slant on the research or has different ideological or methodological predilections. There is no one way of undertaking research into a general area or of teasing out a research problem or theme or focus, and if advice makes you feel uncomfortable, even when you have given it due consideration, it is almost certainly best to reject it. Your supervisor's help should guide your decision.

Normally, though, it is only when you have taken time to consider advice, feedback and criticism that you can decide how much to accept, reject or adapt. If the advice is substantial and you do accept it, formal acknowledgement is warranted.

The ethics of using help from other people

In an academic community there is no shortage of ideas, and there is nothing inherently wrong in finding out about them and using them. If you turn a lead into a significant part of your research work, it is you and you alone who deserve the credit for recognizing its significance and developing it into something forceful and academically convincing. This is neither cheating nor plagiarism nor any other form of misconduct, provided that you acknowledge sources. Published sources should be fully referenced, so that other people can, if they wish, go back to check the originals, which is why references need page numbers. When you come to write up your work, you should include an acknowledgements section in which you thank individuals for informal as well as formal help and advice.

The ethics of giving help to other people

Just as it is unethical to take other people's work and present it as your own, it is equally unethical for other people to take your work and present it as their own. Chapter 11 considers ways of guarding against serious abuse. However there can be a fine dividing line between general helping and giving something that could be of financial, commercial or academic use to others. You may need to think sensitively on this.

It is entirely reasonable for you to bat around ideas freely in informal discussion (see the next section), although you may expect some formal acknowledgement if others develop an idea of yours into something significant.

Supporting and getting support from other students

Students in the same department or research group may be able to give advice and support relating specifically to the subject of your research. This should work both ways, in that you should be willing to give advice and support in return. Students from other departments and other institutions can give advice and support of a more general nature. If you can build up a mutual support group with one or more students, all of you will benefit. Such groups can be large or small; formal or informal; ongoing or transient. In any form, they can serve their members well.

Some of the most useful support groups are email discussion groups. The information in Box 11.3 of Chapter 11, from such a discussion group, is a collation of suggestions given to the group member by some of the members in response to his earlier email query. It will almost certainly be worth your while asking around and keeping your eyes and ears open for email discussion groups that are pertinent to your own work.

Getting support from academic staff

Other academics can be used in the same way as other students: to suggest useful references or information on what is going on and leads to explore. However, academics are busy people and will not welcome being expected to spend time solving your problems. Also they have a professional duty towards their colleagues. So do not put them in the position of having to listen to what could be construed as criticism of how a supervisor supervises you. Also, if you want a formal consultation, do clear it with your supervisor first.

Soliciting help from academics in other institutions

Most academics have stories to tell of receiving letters and emails from students they have never met, asking for information. Academics seldom look favourably on such requests. First, they smack of the students apparently trying to get someone else to do their work for them; and second, they show a lack of understanding of what students' research work ought to be about. General leads can, after all, be gathered from institutional libraries, and research for a degree ought to be about students processing ideas themselves and then following through the themes that develop.

Unfavourable reactions do not extend to requests for specific unpublished pieces of information in an academic's own published research area, where these are phrased in such a way as to show that students have already done sufficient groundwork themselves to recognize the significance of their requests. Then academics usually do what they can to help and their advice can be very valuable (see Box 12.1). It is only reasonable to thank them for it.

Box 12.1 A definition of an expert

[An expert* is] someone who knows some of the worst mistakes that can be made in his subject, and how to avoid them.
(Heisenberg 1971: 210)

* Or someone who answers questions you didn't know were important to ask.

(■) ACTIVITY

On the basis of your reading, name a few national and international experts in your field.

Develop a few questions that you would ask each of them if you were to meet them. These should be questions that would further your work while not causing them irritation.

If this activity stimulates questions that really seem worth following up, mull them over for a few days, to see if they 'answer themselves' or if you can answer them from your own resources. If you and your supervisor both agree that it is reasonable to contact the expert, then think about doing so.

Getting support from family and friends

If you are a mature student living with your partner or family, you will realize that they will have much to put up with while you are working on your research. You may work late into the night, or over weekends, or at other times that might be considered as 'belonging' to them. You may be short of money and they may have to go without. You may be preoccupied for much of the time. Tell them what to expect from the outset, negotiate ways of meeting their needs as well as yours, and get their support.

If family members have also studied for a qualification involving research, you may be able to enlist their help in the same way as with academics and fellow students. They do not need to have a background in your subject. If you talk about your work, they can come to know it almost as well as you do. They can react by pointing out logical inconsistencies and they can also suggest ideas and new directions.

Getting support from colleagues in the workplace

Colleagues in a workplace can provide valuable support in various ways. However, if your research topic is intended to be of value to your place of employment, you need to watch out for colleagues there who are not familiar with what you are doing, have misunderstood its point and have vested interests in a somewhat different, and possibly non-existent, piece of research. Their advice can be depressing and destructive and should be politely 'forgotten'.

Giving advice, feedback and criticism

Helping others involves giving them advice, feedback and criticism on their work. Before going ahead with this, do make sure that they actually want your help, and don't proceed otherwise. Try to understand their insecurity and put them at ease by starting with a comment about something you like. You will always be able to find something if you set your mind to it. Before moving to anything critical, suggest extenuating circumstances if this seems appropriate, and ask how they would do it differently another time. Propose realistic ways forward. Make your suggestions for consideration, not as unequivocal statements of what must be done. Take the attitude that you can comment constructively because you are not so close to the work, not because you are in any way superior. Close with good wishes and offers of future help if they so wish.

If you don't have time to prepare feedback properly, it is usually safest not to give it at all. It is unfair to give weak, ill-considered platitudes which are of no help, or to upset people by giving feedback destructively. Being able to give constructive, acceptable feedback takes time, but is worth working at. It is a hallmark of academic ability and will serve you well along any career path which involves working with people.

13 PRODUCING REPORTS

> *Woolly writing is frequently a reflection of woolly thinking, and a student who has trained himself to write clearly will soon discover that a problem of expression often arises from a lack of understanding, whereas a student who writes poor English can write rubbish without even realising it.*
>
> (Science and Engineering Research Council 1992: 16)

The value of reports in a research programme

Reports may have to be produced for various reasons during a research programme. At one extreme are the informal and private reports that students may choose to write for their own records, to help them develop their work. At the other extreme are formal reports which may be required by the department or funding agency at specified stages of a research programme. Between these extremes are less formal reports required by supervisors as part of general supervisory practice.

Report writing may benefit you in any of the following ways, although the relative importance of each will change as your programme of work progresses:

- to see whether you are on target with your work, so that any problems can be spotted in time to be attended to;
- to provide an opportunity for you to reflect on progress, consolidate arguments and identify any gaps in knowledge, data or methodology;
- to help you to develop an appreciation of standards and hence to learn to monitor your own progress;
- to provide practice in academic report writing and academic discourse, so that any additional training which may be necessary in this respect can be supplied at an early stage;
- to form a basis, in due course, for your thesis and possibly a journal article.

This chapter aims to help with the sorts of interim report that have to be written during a research programme. If your interest is in a final report for a research contract, you should also read Chapter 20 which is concerned with the thesis, although a contract report seldom needs to be as scholarly as a thesis. The suggestions in both chapters are general and are not necessarily appropriate for every field of study. They should nevertheless stimulate your own thinking and indicate topics for discussion with your supervisor.

Developing the content of a report

The content of a report must depend on its purpose. For most fields of study, the content of early informal reports probably ought to be such as to review progress to date and to identify a plan of action for the next phase of the work. Reviewing progress is not merely a matter of cataloguing what tasks you have done, although this will come into it. Rather, you should make a case that what you have done has been thoughtful, directed and competent.

You should probably include the following in the report, presented where possible as a substantiated argument rather than as a straight description:

- How you have defined or developed the research problem, question(s), topic(s) or theme(s) with which the report is concerned – possibly with reference to the original proposal.
- How you are developing your research methodology, stressing how it is appropriate.
- How you expect to ensure that you will collect appropriate data which is convincing for its purpose.
- How you are using the literature.
- How you are dealing with any constraints.
- How you are dealing, where necessary, with subjectivity.
- How far you have got.
- Problems or potential problems which you would like to flag up.
- General reflections – these should be relevant, not just padding, and the nature of what is required is likely to vary considerably from one discipline to another.
- A plan for the next phase of the work.

Interim reports should build on previous ones and, where appropriate, refer to them. Thus there should be no need for repetition of previously reported material that remains unchanged.

With a formal report, for which certain headings or sections are obligatory, it is probably a good idea to start by drafting brief notes along the lines indicated by the above bullet points, and then, in negotiation with your supervisor, to edit these together to fit within the required specifications. A supervisor's help can be essential where headings appear bureaucratic or irrelevant. They may be there to provide the institution or funding agency with data for quality assurance purposes, and you may need help with how to handle them.

The mind map technique of Chapter 18 can be helpful for developing the content of a report, see, in particular, page 209.

Structuring the report

A report should be structured to make a case for something, such as the validity of a conclusion to a piece of work or the design for the next stage of the work. If this means writing little or nothing about something which occupied a great deal of time and writing a lot about something which occupied little time, so be it.

To achieve a clear structure when developing a report, it is worth making the title and headings sufficiently detailed that a list of them summarizes the case that the report is making – i.e. making the list of contents show the 'storyline'. This can be an extremely powerful technique because shortcomings in structure are immediately obvious from the contents list and can be attended to immediately, before time is wasted on writing which might otherwise have to be rejected. If, of course, your discipline is one where standard practice is to write discursively in continuous prose, the storyline technique is not for you.

⬛ ACTIVITY

Look at some reports or journal articles in your own field. If there are headings, turn them into contents lists.

The chances are that the storylines could be clearer, either by differently worded headings or by having more or fewer headings. Make some suggestions.

DISCUSSION OF ACTIVITY

A good way to make contents lists communicate storylines can be to prefix headings with '-ing' words, such words as 'identifying', 'preparing', 'using', 'analysing'.

Using word processing features to aid structuring

Modern word processing features can display and update a 'contents list' – and hence the storyline – while a document is being prepared. They can only do so, though, if the writer specifies what headings are to be at what level by assigning them a 'style' via a pull-down menu (see Figure 13.1a). Merely emboldening or enlarging headings is not enough. Once a style is assigned to every heading the current contents list appears on the left of the screen when the 'document map' button is selected (see Figure 13.1b).

It is, of course, entirely possible for students to complete their research programmes and write all their reports and the thesis without making full use of the word processing features. However, you will make life much easier for yourself if you can get to grips with such features – and sooner rather than later. If you are not already comfortable with them or if formal training is not scheduled for the near future, it will be worth taking a couple of hours out of your normal schedule to work on them, if necessary with help from a more experienced user.

 ACTIVITY

If you are not familiar with your word processor's use of styles and the outline and document map views, see what you can learn about them using the built-in 'help' facility.

If necessary, ask around for someone to advise you informally, or request some formal training.

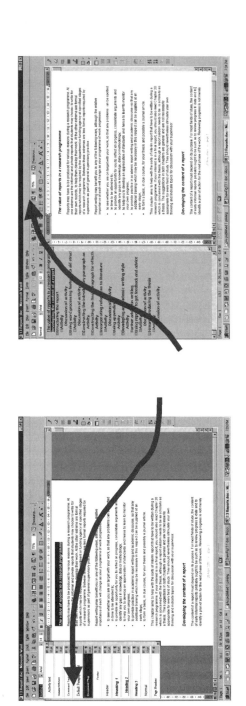

Figure 13.1 A typical screen display showing (a) the 'styles' menu, and (b) how the 'document map' button displays the 'contents list' on the left-hand-side of the screen

Try to get into the habit of dropping into 'outline' mode at intervals as you prepare documents, to check their structure.

⬤ DISCUSSION OF ACTIVITY

Another advantage of using styles is that any document you create using them can quickly and easily be reformatted at a later date to other specifications, for example, to satisfy journal requirements or requirements for thesis presentation. So it is well worth getting to grips with styles earlier rather than later.

Constructing the introductory paragraph as an orientation to the report

Readers of reports need to be orientated to what the report is about, and how it is structured. There is a presentational technique for achieving this. The first step is to write a few keywords or some notes under each of the following headings:

- Setting the scene for the report, i.e. the general area(s) that the report considers.
- The gap in knowledge or understanding which the report addresses.
- How the report fills the gap.
- A brief overview of what is in the report.

Then the notes are edited together to form the introductory paragraph.

⬤ ACTIVITY

Assume that you are about to write the introduction to a report on a piece of the work you have been doing recently. Write a few keywords or some notes under each of the headings indicated by the above bullet points, and then edit them together into an introductory paragraph.

Constructing the final paragraph for effective closure of the report

The concluding paragraph of a report should serve as an effective closure. The technique for doing this starts with writing a few keywords or some notes under each of the following headings:

- What the report has done.
- What new questions the reported work has identified.
- How, in broad terms, you will deal with these new questions or how you hope that others might do so.

Then the notes are edited together to form the concluding paragraph.

 ACTIVITY

Imagine that you are about to write the concluding paragraph to the report of the previous activity. Write a few keywords or some notes under each of the headings indicated by the above bullet points, and then edit them together into a concluding paragraph.

Incorporating references to literature

Literature should be used to substantiate and carry forward an argument. It should never be a catalogue of everything you could find that might seem remotely relevant. However, where seminal works in the general area are not directly relevant, you would be unwise to omit them. Try instead to find a way of bringing them in, possibly in terms of what they do not do, thus making a case for work that you will be doing or have done or that still needs to be done by someone at some future time.

The following activity illustrates the use of literature to carry an argument forward.

 ACTIVITY

Imagine that the following are two alternative versions of a paragraph from a journal article. Comment on the good, bad and interesting aspects of each.

1 Brown (1991) reports on a study based on questionnaires to explore the feelings of teachers in Poppleton School about using self-study materials to teach schoolchildren, but she does not tease out mathematics from the other subjects taught in the school. Smith (1992) uses interview techniques to elicit how a sample of mathematics lecturers in several universities feel about using self-study materials. No studies appear to be reported in the literature about the reactions from schoolteachers to using self-instructional materials for teaching mathematics to schoolchildren, although Jones (1989) argues strongly for the need for such studies if the teaching of mathematics in schools is to be made more efficient. This article reports on work which addresses this omission.

2 Questionnaires have been used to explore the reactions of teachers to using self-study materials to teach schoolchildren (Brown 1991). Interviews have been used with mathematics lecturers in several universities (Smith 1992). There is a need for studies with mathematics schoolteachers if the teaching of mathematics in

schools is to be made more efficient (Jones 1989). This article reports on work which addresses this need.

(■) DISCUSSION OF ACTIVITY

The following are some of the issues that you may have considered.

Words such as 'reported' and 'argued', as used in the first version, inspire confidence that the writer has read and understood the literature. In contrast, the second version leaves the reader in ignorance of the nature of the quoted work or its conclusions, and so gives the impression that the writer could be quoting secondary literature without having ever read or understood the primary literature.

The first version reinforces the feeling of conviction that its writer is intimately familiar with the referenced work because the sex of the workers is shown to be known.

The first version also gives what is absent from the literature as an argument for the reported work. This adds to the conviction that the writer has a good grasp of relevant literature and is using it to substantiate argument.

You may have found areas where you felt that the second version was better than the first – for example, in its brevity. You will probably also have identified further interesting differences between the alternative paragraphs.

Using appendices

Different disciplines have different norms about the use of appendices. A view at one extreme is that the main text of a report should be for making a substantiated case for something, and anything that interrupts the flow of the argument, such as tables of data or copies of instrumental documents, should be placed in an appendix and merely referred to in the text. A view at the other extreme is that if material is worthy of a place in a report, it should be in the main text.

ACTIVITY

Ask around in the department or look at some reports, journal articles and theses to find out normal practices for the use of appendices.

Developing an academic writing style

By the time students come to write a report, they may be thoroughly familiar with the accepted style of academic writing and academic argument in the discipline. However, they may not. If you feel ill-prepared for academic writing, you must work on your writing with your supervisor and other research students.

If English is not your first language, there can be particular difficulties with writing. Your reports should alert your supervisor to such difficulties sufficiently early for something to be done about them in time for the serious business of writing the thesis. It is not necessarily your supervisor's job to tutor you directly in writing, but he or she should be able to direct you to where help is available, possibly to the institutional language centre where one exists, or to independent specialists who advise on or correct writing for a fee. Alternatively you may like to enlist the help of a more linguistically able friend. At the level of a research degree, editorial help – if that is all it is – is not generally regarded as cheating. After all, authors who write for publication, even in their own language, always have someone nominated by the publisher to work through the manuscript in an editorial mode, and no one argues that the work is consequently not theirs. It should be pointed out, however, that a reasonable grasp of English is expected from graduates of English-speaking universities who may be expected to interact and teach in English afterwards. (In the unusual event of a supervisor claiming that a student's command of English is beyond help, the institution should never have accepted that student in the first place.)

Quite generally, academic writing relies on coherence, argument and precise meanings of terms. Other issues are whether it is normal in a discipline to:

- write discursively or use section headings and bullet points to break up the text and orientate the reader;
- use the active or the passive voice for reporting your own involvement (e.g. 'I did something' or 'something was done') (Box 13.1 illustrates some pros and cons);
- use the past tense or the timeless present (the first version of the paragraph in the last but one activity is written in the 'timeless' present to imply that the work is as valid now as when it was done);
- use complex sentence structure.

Box 13.1 Use of active and passive voices in academic writing

In some subject areas, the use of the active voice in academic writing is regarded as unacceptable because it would indicate subjectivity and lack of modesty. Yet consider the following:

'The liquid was evaporated.'

Which of the following might it mean?

- I heated the liquid as part of my work.
- Someone else did this part of the work for me.
- The liquid evaporated naturally over time without anyone doing anything to make it happen.

How far do you think it reasonable that academic writing which is supposed to be unambiguous should not permit clarification through use of the active voice?

 ACTIVITY

Select some theses or research articles in your subject area and examine the writing style.

If you are at all uncertain on any aspects of the style, discuss them with your supervisor, other research students or the institutional language centre, well in advance of doing any of your own writing.

Check out the complexity of your own writing. Either use the fog factor of Box 13.2 or the computer equivalent which is available on all modern word processors.

Box 13.2 The fog factor – a guide to clear writing

We are often told to use short words and write clearly. A helpful device here is the 'fog factor'.

For this, we count the words of three or more syllables and the number of sentences on about half a page of writing. (I count the long words in my head and the sentences on my fingers.) We then divide the number of long words by the number of sentences.

A piece with a fog factor of 2 or 3 remains easy to read. If the count goes up to 4 or 5, it becomes heavy going. Yet academic and technical writing often averages 6 to 8 long words per sentence and sometimes more than 10. Long words strain our short-term memory. They make it difficult to remember how a sentence started by the time we reach the end.

Good novelists cope with basics like life and death on a fog factor of less than 1. But in technical writing, we are handicapped. We need long jargon words like statistics, regression or correlation coefficient – they can be a useful shorthand if used often enough to be worth learning . . .

The definition of the fog factor is not watertight. Are there two syllables in 'ratio' or three? What about names, numbers and abbreviations? . . . Splitting a sentence in two will halve its fog factor . . . Not all sentences should however be short. That would make for too abrupt a style. But long sentences should be there for a reason, such as giving a qualification or illustration before the reader is allowed to stop and think.

(Ehrenberg 1982)

Further advice on writing

Writing a report, or indeed a journal article or thesis, can seldom be done in a single attempt. It is generally a matter of progressively refining parts in the light of others. This cannot be done quickly. People who are new to academic writing usually underestimate the time required.

The early emphasis should be on producing a reasonably coherent whole. It is a waste of time and effort spending hours refining style if what is written is likely to have to be discarded later – although of course there is a balance to be struck. No one can develop coherence in meaning if the style is too rough. It can be helpful to write at a time and in a place where you feel relatively relaxed. How and where are personal choices – perhaps by using a portable computer so that you can put your feet up or by working at a desk when no one else is around. Then write. Keep on writing until you feel intuitively that you have run out of what you have to say for the moment. Write as if you are writing for yourself alone. Don't worry too much about style or typing/spelling errors at this stage. The word processor should take care of them later anyway, and no one else is going to see what you are writing. With this approach, you will invariably find that you create a piece of writing which serves well as a framework for refining later.

All writing is improved by the 'drawer treatment', i.e. putting it away in a drawer (or on the computer) and coming back to it after an intervening time in which you have been concentrating on something else, preferably after at least a few days. Then, arriving fresh to what you have written, you can act on your second thoughts, and go into an editorial mode to tidy up the arguments and the writing. Several cycles of putting aside, editing and re-editing will probably be required.

Throughout the writing, be meticulous about keeping backups! It is false economy to save money on floppy disks or CD-ROMS. Have a plentiful supply of them, and keep backups by date of several previous versions as well as the latest version. There are two reasons for this. First, you may want to refer to what you wrote some time ago; and second, it is all too easy to overwrite a file on hard disk and then copy it on to a backup disk before realizing that you have lost your backup as well as the current file. Then having a backup of a previous version is a life-saver.

Using reports to get feedback and advice

If you are to get maximum benefit from your reports, it is important to get feedback on them. This may be done informally during the process of refining them with your supervisor, or more formally on the basis of a completed report. Either way, it needs to be done. Use the activity below as a checklist.

 ACTIVITY

Make sure that you receive feedback on your report which covers the following issues:

- Am I on target as far as expected progress is concerned, or are there any problems that ought to be addressed now?

- Am I reading adequately and demonstrating acceptable standards in my work?

- Am I reflecting sufficiently thoughtfully on my work?

- Is my writing style acceptable?

 DISCUSSION OF ACTIVITY

You should discuss with your supervisor how 'reflecting sufficiently thoughtfully' could be interpreted in your field of study, and what your particular needs are in this respect. For example, you may need to spot more effectively where, how and why others might argue differently from you, to acknowledge and explore this and then modify your own case accordingly; you may need to identify how and why it would be better to do things differently if certain constraints were not operating or how it might have been possible to have done things better anyway with the benefit of hindsight; you may need to consider the implications of your work more deeply; you may need to give your writing more of a 'drawer treatment' so that others (including your supervisor!) do not have to spend unnecessary time and effort trying to understand it. Maybe some other form of thoughtful reflection is what you need.

Towards producing the thesis

It is usual for reports or parts of reports to be edited together at some stage to contribute substantially to the thesis. So you should aim to become increasingly more proficient at producing them. It is therefore important to point out now that there are word processing features that can be extremely helpful for working with longer documents. They include: automatic dating of documents; automatic numbering; automatic cross-referencing; coloured highlights for emphasis; bookmarks for marking places to return to later; embedded messages or 'comments' for on-screen readers; templates; tools for producing tables, charts and pictures; production of contents lists, etc.

You should also find out when to start writing your thesis. Use the following activity as a stimulus for discussion with your supervisor.

(■) ACTIVITY

Ask around in the department about when other students start writing up their theses.

What word processing features do they find useful? (Talk to experienced as well as new computer users!)

(■) DISCUSSION OF ACTIVITY

You will probably find that there is no simple answer to the frequently asked question of when to start on the thesis, because even the earliest of reports is likely to feature in it, albeit in considerably edited form. The best advice is to start on the shape of your thesis as early as possible, but to appreciate that it will change considerably as the research progresses. Now may not be too early to consult Chapter 20, which is about producing the thesis.

14 GIVING PRESENTATIONS ON YOUR WORK

The communication of the results of research is an integral part of the research process, which is incomplete and ineffective if findings are not made available to others.
(Engineering and Physical Sciences Research Council 1995, Section 9:1)

The value of giving presentations on your work

It is important to be able to give confident and effective presentations on your work. Some departments require it as part of formal progress monitoring; some offer it as part of their training for career development; and some request it to support their interaction with outsiders such as funding bodies and prospective students. Having to give a presentation on your work has benefits for you. It forces you to structure and evaluate your work, so enabling you to spot, and hence remedy, flaws in arguments and to identify new ways forward; it then enables you to get feedback from others on what you have done so far and to benefit from their advice about what you might do in future.

Giving presentations is a large subject, and this chapter can only touch on those aspects that seem to be of particular concern to students working on research. If you would like further information, there is no shortage of advice (see the *further reading* section). If you are already a fairly experienced presenter, you may choose only to scan this chapter for revision purposes.

Good preparation for a presentation should never be a matter of working through certain steps in sequence, even though this chapter has to present its advice sequentially. Good preparation must be more of a cyclic activity, because decisions on one aspect of a presentation affect decisions on another. So it is best to start by planning each aspect in outline only and then progressively developing them all as the whole presentation takes shape.

Identifying the purposes of a presentation

A presentation may have a variety of purposes, and before you do any serious preparation, you should identify your purposes and prioritize them. Some possibilities include:

- to show what you or your group or department has achieved so far;
- to get advice and feedback from the audience;
- to provide a forum where everyone can learn and mutually support one another;
- to contribute to assessment or monitoring procedures;
- to make a case for something, such as the need for a continuation in funding;
- to impress, for example, a funding agency, prospective future students or a prospective employer.

For formal monitoring purposes or for an information-giving presentation near to or after completion of the research, the priorities should be to show what has been achieved and to provide a forum where everyone can learn from the speaker and from each other. Even at this stage, though, where you might be forgiven for regarding the work as entirely complete, it would be inappropriate not to solicit advice and feedback from the audience. After all, further work can always still be done, even if not by you or for this particular piece of research, and you would be well advised to show that you appreciate this.

For a departmental seminar that is not part of a formal monitoring process, your emphasis ought probably to be on getting advice and feedback, but you need to discuss the matter with your supervisor or the seminar organizer.

 ACTIVITY

Imagine that you are some way into your research and that you are going to give a 1–1$\frac{1}{2}$ hours seminar on it to the other students and academics in the department.

Rate your relative importance of each of the following purposes:

- To show what you have achieved so far
- To get help, advice and feedback
- To provide a forum for mutual help and support
- To contribute to assessment or monitoring processes

List several areas where you would like help, advice or feedback.

 DISCUSSION OF ACTIVITY

You will not impress if the areas where you want help are such that you could help yourself given a few hours in the library or a few minutes with your supervisor. You may even alienate people if you seem to be putting your supervisor down because he or she could or should have helped if only you had asked, without having to call on the rest of the department. The areas where you want help should link in some way to research methodology, research procedure, scholarship, argument or originality. There should not be too many of them, and you should clear them in advance with your supervisor.

Developing the content of a presentation

For all but the most experienced presenters, one's own presentation usually passes more quickly or slowly than expected. The difficulty is compounded because enough time may have to be left for audience participation afterwards. For some types of presentation, this time ought to be as long as the actual presentation. So, when you come to prepare a presentation, you have to overcome the natural tendency to prepare too much material.

You should think carefully about how much of your work needs to be described and explained for your particular purposes. Sound advice is to present no more than a minimum of background material and not to give details that your audience has a right to expect that you can be trusted to have handled competently on your own. This will inevitably vary from one type of audience to another.

The following are helpful starting points for thinking about what to put into a presentation:

- the purposes of the presentation;
- the purpose of the work on which the presentation will report;
- what has been achieved so far – for which the pointers for reports in Chapter 13 may be useful;
- options for ways forward, and their apparent advantages and disadvantages as you perceive them at the moment;
- what is likely to interest the audience.

It is probably sensible to start developing content in terms of topics. The mind map technique of Chapter 18 may help – but it may not, depending on your personal inclinations. It is a good idea to mark some topics as less important than others, so that you are ready to leave them out if you find yourself short of time on the day. Similarly it is worth making sure that you have some 'filler' material in reserve, to use if you find time on your hands.

(■) ACTIVITY

Think of some topics to put into the seminar of the last activity, using, if you like, the above bullet points to stimulate your thinking.

Mark some of the topics as suitable for leaving out, if time should catch up with you during the seminar.

Add a few additional topics that you could present if you should find yourself with spare time.

Structuring the presentation

Once you have developed the topics on which to present, they have to be put into a meaningful order. It will save you a lot of heartache if you accept that there is no single 'right' way of doing this. The most immediately obvious way is likely to be the order in which you did things, but this may not be as interesting or illuminating as, say, a problem-solving approach or an opportunistic approach. You will need to play around with a few possibilities to see what you feel comfortable with.

Box 14.1 gives a maxim on structuring presentations. Although it is somewhat flippant, it does make the point that presenters need to 'top-and-tail' their presentations to orientate the audience for what is to follow and to summarize the message afterwards.

Box 14.1   How to structure a presentation

Here is a maxim to help presenters get their message across.

Say what you are going to say, say it, then say what you've said.
                                                                  (Anon.)

 ACTIVITY

Arrange the topics into a logical sequence with which you feel comfortable.

How would you describe the logic of this sequence?

Developing the presentation and producing visual aids

Developing the presentation and producing visual aids are often most easily done in parallel with one another, because each affects the other. The process tends to be a matter of starting out with a rough idea of content and sequence, giving a rough test-presentation to yourself with rough or imaginary visual aids, noting where modifications are necessary, making the modifications and going through the whole process again. A computer-aided presentation package, such as PowerPoint, can simplify the process considerably, but it may not be available to you, or you may prefer to use more traditional methods. However, many people would argue that the effective use of computer-aided presentation is a skill which will be valuable in the careers of all professionals of the future. So try if you can to take the opportunity to become comfortable with it as a student. However, be prepared for the possibility, however slight, that the system may fail on the day. So print out a few transparencies or handouts as a back-stop.

PowerPoint takes care of most of the design issues in creating the 'slides' (which can become transparencies if printed onto acetates), and the slides can be modified as easily as with a word processor. Furthermore, it is easy to practise a presentation with PowerPoint, just using one's own computer to move from one slide to another, and many presenters like to do this, even if they know that the PowerPoint equipment will not to be available at the actual presentation. Once the practice is complete and the amendments are made, they print the slides out as transparencies (or onto paper to be photocopied onto acetates). Many experienced presenters choose the transparency approach rather than the fully computerized PowerPoint one, to maintain more flexibility to vary the sequence at the time. PowerPoint can produce handouts automatically from the 'slides' – and audiences do seem to like to have sheets of paper to take away from a presentation.

If you will not be using PowerPoint for developing your presentation, you will probably want to develop and practise using draft, and possibly handwritten, visual aids. Once you are happy with these, you can turn them into quality transparencies for use with an overhead projector and/or into handouts for the audience. A way to produce transparencies is to design them with a word processor, then either print them directly onto acetate, or print them onto paper and then photocopy them onto acetate. Less professional looking, but nevertheless effective transparencies can be made by writing with appropriate pens directly onto acetate sheets. The size of the lettering should be such that it can be read easily if the paper or the acetate sheet is propped up about a metre and a half from the eye, and this has implications for the amount of material that can be fitted in. If you want to include a diagram or a table that does not satisfy this test, make it into a handout as well as a transparency. Then the audience can read it from their own printed sheet while you point to the relevant parts of the transparency.

There is a balance to be struck between too many and too few visual aids and handouts: too many can be perceived as patronizing to a mature and intelligent audience, whereas too few will make the presentation difficult to follow. A commonly quoted guideline is one visual aid for every few minutes of talk, but it is ignored successfully by many good presenters.

The preparation and use of visual aids is a large topic. For further information, see the *further reading* section.

Rehearsing the presentation

Rehearse the presentation in private to check that the timing is about right. Some people find it helpful to keep a clock or watch on the table in front of them while rehearsing, although PowerPoint does have its own timing facility.

The actual presentation is likely to go more slowly or more quickly than during rehearsal, for all sorts of reasons. If you should find that you are overrunning, never speed up to cram everything in and do not shorten discussion time. Instead, simply be prepared to say what, if time had permitted, you would have spoken about. If you should find that you are seriously underrunning, use the extra material that you planned for just such a contingency. If you are only marginally underrunning, simply finish early. No one will mind extra discussion time or an early end.

Practise sounding enthusiastic. If you are not interested in your work, no one else is likely to be. You may find it helpful to practise the seminar in front of someone who can provide constructive help, such as a member of your family or another student. Do be open to their advice. If they spot a lack of consistency or an error, the chances are that they will be right and that the reason why you did not spot it yourself was not that it was unimportant, but that you are too familiar with your own work.

Other things to consider when you rehearse include whether you can be heard properly; whether to stand or sit; what clothes will look right and also stop you getting too hot; and body language to suggest the right degree of confidence. It seldom gives a good impression to read directly from a script, so you should experiment with the form of notes that enables you to feel most comfortable. Some people find that the prompts of the slides or transparencies are enough; others like to make notes on cards or annotations on a copy of the handouts.

If you feel nervous, it can help to learn the opening couple of sentences by rote, as it seems to be easier to ad lib from there on. It may also be helpful to plan answers to likely questions. Also think about how to respond to questions that you will not be able to answer or questions that seem designed primarily to show the expertise of questioners. For the former, it is probably best to admit that you don't know and ask if anyone in the audience can help. For the latter, one response could be to invite questioners to share their expertise with the audience.

It may be useful to set up someone to take notes for you on the comments and advice from the audience, as it will be difficult for you to concentrate fully on these while also attending to the process of the presentation.

In your own interests, find out at what stage your supervisor wishes to be involved in the preparation of your presentation. Never present it without giving him or her the opportunity to comment or advise first.

Finally, if you get the chance, visit the room where the presentation is to take place to get a feel for what it will be like being at the front and addressing people. In addition to an overhead projector or computer-aided projection, there may be the options of a microphone, a slide projector, video playback equipment, and lighting and blind controls. If you decide to use any of these, you need to find out, in advance, how to manage them yourself, or how to signal directions to a technician. Audiences are likely to be irritated if you waste time finding out how to use such facilities during the presentation.

Drumming up attendance for a seminar presentation

If a major purpose of giving a departmental seminar is to get advice and feedback, it is important that the audience should contain people who have the background and experience to give informed reactions. This usually means other academic staff. They are inevitably busy people, so it may be worth making a point of personally and individually asking them to attend. Even if they do not make particularly helpful comments at the time, they will get to know your work, and may therefore be able to pass on any useful tips which come their way later.

Giving a conference presentation

Your supervisor will suggest that you give a presentation at a conference only when you are far enough into your work to have some meaningful results, and he or she should certainly tutor you to make sure that you are a credit to the department. So only a few words are in order here. A conference presentation is not the same as an internal seminar presentation. The purpose is different. Also, time will be a much greater constraint.

The purpose of a conference presentation varies from one field of study to another, so check with your supervisor. It may be to put down a marker in the national or international academic community that it is you who are doing a specific piece of work, and to show that you are making good progress with it. A journal is the place for presenting completed work. Ideally, the conference presentation will result in publishers or other workers in related fields speaking or writing to you later to follow up on your work. So all you need to present is what you are doing, why it is so important or interesting, how far you have got, what your results are so far, what they mean to you, and where you intend to go next. Describe your research methods briefly, but do not delve into the difficulties unless they are likely to be of particular interest to others. It is important that visual aids and handouts be very professional-looking because you will want to convince your audience that you are someone to be taken seriously. Many a conference participant has been put off by slides that could not be read from the back of the room and by the presentation of too much material.

Since work is often publicized at conferences before it is formally published, conferences are good places to get information to keep ahead of the field and to find out who is heading what work in your general area. You may even meet your future examiners.

Giving other types of presentation

Students may find themselves giving presentations other than seminars or conference papers. Most likely are presentations to prospective employers or funding agents and to prospective students on departmental open days. The advice in this chapter can readily be adapted for such alternative presentations.

15 USING THE RESEARCH PROGRAMME AS PREPARATION FOR EMPLOYMENT

Postgraduate education was believed to be either essential or likely to promote their career development by those who planned to do further courses.

(Purcell and Pitcher 1997: Executive summary)

The importance of paying attention to skills

These days most people take on a variety of different jobs during their working lives, as existing jobs become obsolete following new technological developments and the changing requirements of society. Even professionals have to change their career directions, and this trend is expected to continue and grow. So students at all levels, on all educational programmes, whether they are already in a career or not, need to prepare themselves by thinking not so much about what they 'know' but more about what they will be able to 'do' for a possible employer. Terms which reflect this way of thinking have become common currency. They include: 'key skills', 'personal skills', 'core skills', 'transferable skills', 'skill sets', 'competencies' and 'lifelong learning'. Although there is little common agreement on their precise definitions, they all serve to illustrate the trend.

Broadly speaking, a skill is the ability to do something well with minimal time and effort. A skilled typist, for example, can type a report quickly and accurately, probably without even looking at the keyboard, whereas an unskilled person would have to keep looking for keys and would probably press the wrong ones by mistake. The typing would be awkward, would require excessive concentration and would take an excessive time. It might still get done, but the final product would almost certainly have an amateur look about it.

Typing is an example of a skill which is largely manual, but skills can also be interpersonal and intellectual. For example, a skilled speaker can comparatively effortlessly hold an audience spellbound; an unskilled speaker might have a go, but the task would consume a great deal of preparation time and emotional energy and would probably not be received well by the audience. The straight division of 'skilled' and 'unskilled' is of course an oversimplification, as there are varying degrees of skills proficiency.

The skills which are fundamental for success in so many walks of life are often called 'personal' and 'transferable' skills because, arguably, they can be used in a range of situations – i.e. they can be learnt in one situation and 'transferred' to another. Such skills are also called 'key' or 'core' skills. There is no definitive list of them, and lists vary according to emphases and degrees of breakdown. One published by the *Times Higher Education Supplement* (see Box 15.1) gives the general idea.

Box 15.1 Common definitions of key skills

- *personal skills such as ability to improve own learning and action planning*
- *interpersonal skills such as working with others*
- *communication*
- *literacy*
- *information technology skills*
- *problem-solving including critical and lateral thinking, reflection and objective reasoning*
- *positive attitudes to change including understanding the worlds of work, politics and society*

(Times Higher Education Supplement 1998: 6)

Employers obviously value skills because they want their employees to be able to produce professional results without undue expenditure of time and effort. You may be fortunate enough to be in a department or institution that recognizes its responsibilities to students in this connection and accordingly runs skills development activities. If so, you may want to do no more than scan this chapter. It is primarily for students on full research programmes who do not have such an advantage. Fortunately, as the chapter will show, much can be achieved with minimal outlay of time and effort, provided that you start sufficiently early.

Ways of thinking about skills

A useful way of thinking about skills is in the four categories which have been identified by the Association of Graduate Recruiters (AGR) (1995): specialist skills, generalist skills, self-reliant skills and group/ team skills. The 'complete graduate' is regarded as having competence in all the categories. Figure 15.1 is an adaptation for postgraduates. The skill-set of the 'complete postgraduate' is skewed towards specialist skills, because graduates of higher degrees ought to be able to claim superb skills in their specialisms.

'Specialist' skills are the skills of 'being an expert at something'. For students on research programmes, these are the skills associated with doing research, finding out knowledge, and being able to use understanding and scholarship in their subjects. For other postgraduates the same is true to varying extents which could be debated at length.

The AGR (1995) defines 'generalist' skills as 'general business skills and knowledge, e.g. finance/basic accounting, written communication, problem solving and use of information technology'. There may, in some circumstances, be an overlap between generalist skills

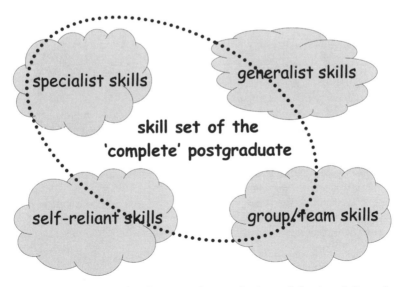

Figure 15.1 Clusters of skills, using the terminology of the Association of Graduate Recruiters (1995)

and specialist skills, as for example with the skills of foreign language proficiency, using certain computer packages or having expertise with the Internet, but the point at issue is not to be able to classify skills but to have a terminology for thinking about them. A skill which could be regarded as generalist and which many postgraduates develop to a high level is that of teaching – as in tutoring individuals and groups, demonstrating in the laboratory and even lecturing.

The skills that have been the focus of developments at undergraduate level are largely group/team skills and self-reliant skills. The AGR defines the former as those skills associated with 'team players, e.g. management skills, meetings skills, networking skills, and presentation skills'. It defines the latter in terms of being 'able to manage [one's] own career and personal development'. In summary: self-awareness, 'self promotion, exploring and creating opportunities, action planning, networking, decision making, negotiation, political awareness, coping with uncertainty, having a developmental focus, being able to transfer flexibly from one situation to another, and self-confidence'. There are clear links between the fashionable notion of 'emotional intelligence' (see Box 15.2) and the AGR's group/team skills and self-reliant skills.

Box 15.2 Emotional intelligence

When Goleman's book, Emotional Intelligence *came out, it was an instant hit . . . The main message [is that] IQ* is less important to how you do in life than what he calls 'emotional intelligence', a set of skills unrelated to academic ability . . . Goleman identifies five 'domains' of emotional intelligence. The first is 'self-awareness', the ability to recognise your own emotions, to know your strengths and weaknesses and to generate a sense of self-worth. The second is 'self-regulation', the ability to control your emotions rather than allowing them to control you. The third is 'motivation', the strength of will needed to achieve your goals and to pick yourself up after a fall. While these first three concern your own emotions, the last two, 'empathy' and 'social skills', relate to other people's emotions, the ability to recognise them and to nurture relationships or inspire others.*
(Ochert 1999: 20)

---

* Intelligence quotient, arguably regarded as a measure of intellectual ability.

Appreciating the skills that you already have

Everyone develops skills merely from everyday living, and similarly all students develop skills as a natural part of progressing through their studies. However, few students generally appreciate this fact if they are not regularly encouraged to make a link between performing a task and developing a related skill. For example, students on lengthy research programmes may implicitly accept that they have worked in isolation over many months, yet it does not generally occur to them that they have, in so doing, acquired the skill of 'working independently'. Even when students are invited to make links between tasks and skills, they are generally reluctant to claim that they are 'skilled' because that would imply a sophisticated proficiency which seems to them to be arrogant and inappropriate. Perhaps more surprisingly, there seems to be the same reluctance for claiming the specialist skills of research and scholarship as for the so-called key skills.

Box 15.3 suggests a framework for the sorts of skills that are most likely to be developed in a lengthy research degree such as the United Kingdom's MPhil and PhD. The Box provides no more than a framework because all the skills could be described differently, summarized, elaborated or subdivided. In fact, it is important to make adaptations yourself in order to make the terminology more relevant to you and your field of study. All the skills are more advanced and have a wider scope than those skills which first-degree graduates can normally claim, and they are developed quite naturally by able and well-supervised research students.

Box 15.3   A digest of a framework for a transferable skill set for MPhil/PhD students

All MPhil/PhD graduates who are adequately able and were properly supervised should be able to claim skills in the specialist research-related aspects of their MPhil/PhD topic. The extent to which these skills are 'transferable' to employment will depend on the individual concerned, the nature of the MPhil/PhD work and the requirements of the employment.

In addition, there are numerous skills which are highly 'transferable', which employers would understand and value, and which it is reasonable to expect from PhD and possibly MPhil graduates, over and above those transferable skills which have received so much attention at undergraduate level:

1 All MPhil/PhD students will, by the time they complete, have spent two, three or more years on a research programme, taking it from first inception through its many and various highs and lows. This is no mean feat and should develop the transferable skill of being able to see any prolonged task or project through to completion. It should include to varying extents which depend on the discipline and the research topic the abilities: to plan, to allocate resources of time and money, to trouble-shoot, to keep up with one's subject, to be flexible and able to change direction where necessary, and to be able to think laterally and creatively to develop alternative approaches. The skill of being able to accommodate to change is highly valued by employers who need people who can anticipate and lead change in a changing world, yet resist it where it is only for its own sake.

2 All MPhil/PhD students should have learned to set their work in a wider field of knowledge. The process requires extensive study of literature and should develop the transferable skills of being able to sift through large quantities of information, to take on board the points of view of others, challenge premises, question procedures and interpret meaning.

3 All MPhil/PhD students have to be able to present their work to the academic community, minimally through seminars, progress reports and the thesis. Seminars should develop the oral communication skills of being effective and confident in making formal presentations, in intervening in meetings, participating in group discussions, dealing with criticism and presenting cases. Report and thesis-writing should develop the transferable written communication skills needed for composing effective reports, manuals and press releases and for summarising bulky documents. These communication skills should go far beyond the level acquired during a first degree.

4 The road to completion of an MPhil/PhD can be a lonely one, particularly in the humanities and social sciences. Yet the skills of coping with isolation are 'transferable' and can be highly valued by employers. They include: self-direction; self-discipline; self-motivation; resilience; tenacity and the abilities to prioritise and juggle a number of tasks at once.

5 MPhil/PhD students working on group projects, which is most common in the sciences, should be able to claim advanced team-working skills.

Further examples of transferable skills are many and various and depend on the interests of the student and the nature of the research programme. Possibilities include advanced computer

> *literacy, facility with the Internet, the skills of being able to teach effectively, to negotiate access and resources, to network with others, to use project management techniques, and to find one's way around specialist libraries or archives.*
> (Extracted with minor modifications from Cryer 1997: i)

 ACTIVITY

Modify the framework of Box 15.3 and fill it out to make it applicable to your own field of study. You may like to scan the headings in this book as a prompt, as many can be readily reworded in terms of skills.

Collecting and using evidence to demonstrate skills proficiency

At undergraduate level, the generally accepted way of demonstrating the acquisition of skills is through a personalized collection of documentary evidence for showing to interested parties. Students build up their collections over a considerable period, often using a custom-designed box, called a 'portfolio', which may display the institution's logo. However, many of the standard examples of evidence (see Chapter 8) can seem rather trivial at research degree level, although it is always worth collecting them anyway, just in case.

A better way of making a convincing claim for proficiency in certain skills can be indirectly, through the fluency with which you can talk about your experiences and successes. To do so, though, you have to be ready and able to steer the discussion in your direction, and for this a limited portfolio can be helpful. Particularly useful are, for example, photographs or newspaper cuttings showing your involvement in certain activities; products or outcomes generated during the research (or plans, photographs or sketches representing them); and any special awards or commendations. Photographs are particularly useful because they can so easily be carried around in a pocket or bag.

An alternative and excellent way of taking the portfolio idea a stage further is by publishing your personal home page on the web, with photos and newsclips, etc. embedded in the text of your cv. (Web space is free via most of the free Internet service providers, and if you do not have the skills to set up the site yourself, you may be able to find a friend or relative who will enjoy doing it for you.) You can then cite your web address (URL) with your other personal details on your letterhead, in your email signature and anywhere else that seems appropriate. A personal home page has the added advantage that it sends a clear message that the person concerned is computer-aware and reasonably computer literate.

(■) ACTIVITY

Think about your life outside the institution, your research programme as it has developed so far and as you expect it to develop in future. What special skills do you think you have acquired or will have acquired, and what evidence could you provide to:

• Justify your claim to having acquired the skill?

• Stimulate discussion in which you could illustrate your proficiency in the skill?

Keeping your skill set up to date

Although much can be done by becoming aware of the skills that you are developing as a matter of course during your research programme, it goes without saying that you should do all that is reasonable to update old skills and develop new ones. Provided that this does not detract unacceptably from the progress of your research, it is worth chatting to other students who may be using a new technique or piece of equipment, so that you are at least familiar with its existence; it is worth attending departmental seminars to find out relatively easily about new developments; and it is extremely important to become comfortable with using IT where it is appropriate for every-day professional tasks.

The importance of elapsed time and good feedback in skills development cannot be overestimated. The development of a skill requires cyclic repetition of 'receiving feedback on performance', 'reflecting on that feedback' and 'practising the skill again'. The more times the cycle is repeated, the greater the eventual proficiency. This is why skills proficiency cannot be hurried, and it is important to start early. However, without informed and constructive feedback, the repetition merely reinforces bad habits.

Departmental and institutional skills-related activities

Some departments offer their students skills-related training, usually closely integrated with research programmes so as not to detract time or energy from essential work. The main difference between this and what other departments provide is often only in name and emphasis. For example, when students give presentations on their work there may be the opportunity for them to receive informal feedback on presentational aspects as well as content.

More formalized skills development activities for postgraduates may be offered centrally by an institution, but only a relatively small proportion of students tend to take them up. There may be army-style training over several days off-campus at special campsites to develop skills of leadership, teamwork and ingenuity. There may be workshop-style activities on-campus to develop advanced presentation skills, perhaps with the opportunity of video for in-depth analysis. Students may be guided to produce action plans and to keep journals logging their skills development.

Assessment of skills development activities is invariably either students' own or a mix of their own and that of other students, and it is specifically not graded. This is partly because there can be no definitive measure of skills proficiency, but it is also to help develop the very important skills of self-assessment and self-responsibility.

A particularly helpful aspect of some skills development and/or careers related activities is the help that they can give for understanding oneself and one's usefulness to others – what one likes and dislikes and what one can particularly contribute to a team. If you think that this should be obvious to any mature and sensible individual, you would be wrong. The standard forms of the tests rely not on common sense but on psychological research (such as the Myers Briggs test for personality type and the Belbin test for role function). Most people who experience the tests find them surprisingly enlightening and are profoundly grateful for having had them. Some suitable books are recommended in the *further reading* section, and the *websites* section links to some know-yourself style questionnaires which are offered and analysed free of charge over the Internet. However, there is really no substitute for being analysed by an experienced and accredited professional. Some experts would argue that it is harmful to play around by oneself without professional guidance. In fact the Myers Briggs test must be offered only by qualified practitioners.

⬛ ACTIVITY

Are you aware of the skills-related activities offered by your institution?

Can you identify any aspects of formalized skills development activities that you could profitably adopt informally, either for yourself alone or with a group of other students?

⬛ DISCUSSION OF ACTIVITY

Whether you decide to participate in institutional skills-related activities will probably depend on your other commitments. However, informal self-help or group-help approaches can be fitted in at your convenience, and the associated interaction may also support your research.

Professional careers services

Most educational institutions have careers offices and resource centres staffed by qualified professionals (see Box 15.4). These staff will almost certainly be prepared to give advice on careers guidance, job vacancies, preparation of curriculum vitae for job applications and the handling of job interviews; and they may run self-awareness sessions like those of Myers Briggs and Belbin.

Box 15.4 Responsibilities for career planning

Institutions are responsible for:

 i *providing access to careers library facilities and career planning resources;*
 ii *providing support in decision making about career directions, occupational opportunities and vocational education and training;*
 iii *providing information on vacancies;*
 iv *undertaking sample surveys and follow-up destinations of those leaving programmes [of study].*

Learners [students] are responsible for:

 i *making full use of careers and vacancy information, library and resource facilities;*
 ii *exploring career and occupational opportunities available through research, work shadowing, placements, applications, interviews;*
 iii *providing follow-up information on their employment/learning destination.*

(Higher Education Quality Council 1996: 66)

 ACTIVITY

Check on what your institution's careers office or unit is offering. This is probably on the web, and can be accessed from the institution's home page.

Is it worth asking your department to invite a professional – perhaps from the institution's careers office – to run a self-awareness activity along the lines of Belbin and/or Myers Briggs?

(■) DISCUSSION OF ACTIVITY

Institutional careers offices can be a valuable resource to students, and it is likely that you are not taking full advantage of what yours can offer. It is in your own interests to raise the matter with appropriate staff in your department or make contact yourself.

National skills and careers development programmes

The research councils of the United Kingdom run residential courses on skills and careers development for research students, and these are free to PhD students funded by the research councils. Other research students can apply for a fee-paying place. For details, see the *websites* section.

Finding a job

If you are looking for a job, the way forward is best regarded as a twofold attack. One is to grasp every opportunity to raise the subject with people who may be able to help, such as supervisors, other students, friends of the family, etc. The other is structured, using the facilities of the careers office and searching job advertisements. A number of university careers offices make a point of advertising job vacancies on the web, and there is no reason why you should not do a search on all of them, rather than limiting yourself to the provision of your own institution.

For the best possible sound-bites of advice on further career development, look ahead to Box 22.2 in Chapter 22.

16 PROGRESS CHECKS AND HURDLES – AND THE TRANSFER FROM MPHIL TO PHD

Landmarks and feedback provide emotional security and remove ambiguity and doubt.

(Mathias and Gale 1991: 9)

The rationale for progress checks

Most departments have a framework of formal and ongoing procedures to monitor and assess the progress of their students. Such procedures are to the students' ultimate benefit because they:

- enable departments to see whether the students are on target, so that if any problems exist, they can be spotted in time and attended to;
- provide a formalized opportunity for students to reflect on their progress, consolidate their arguments and identify any gaps in knowledge, data or methodology; and
- help students to develop an appreciation of standards, to enable them better to monitor their own progress.

This chapter provides some general principles for handling progress checks, which may differ considerably in form from one institution to another and one department to another.

In the United Kingdom it is widespread practice for research students who wish to take a PhD to register first for an MPhil degree, and then, in time, if the work is deemed worthy, to transfer or upgrade their registration to a PhD, backdated to the start of the MPhil. The transfer can be regarded as a very specific and high-profile progress check, and the chapter considers it specifically in its own right. The chapter is also relevant for students outside the United Kingdom who are subject to the probationary procedures of their own countries.

Handling progress checks

The straightforward path through progress checks depends on knowing the administrative requirements; being competent in one's work; and being able to produce credible documentation to justify oneself.

 ACTIVITY

In each of the following categories, what are the formal departmental procedures for monitoring the progress of students undertaking research? Where aspects are absent or ambiguous, how are they normally assumed or interpreted and how flexible are they?

• When and how often do the progress-monitoring events take place?

• What is required of students? For example:

    – Writing a report or proposal of some sort. What precisely?

    – Presenting a seminar

    – Attending departmental training/meetings/seminars

    – Submitting a paper to a refereed journal

• What is required of supervisors or other academics? For example:

    – Formally grading written work of some sort

– Writing a testimonial of some sort

• To whom should written material be submitted?

• To whom does it go for approval?

(■) DISCUSSION OF ACTIVITY

Departmental student-monitoring procedures normally require students to write some sort of report. Chapter 13 gives some general advice on writing reports, and parts of Chapter 20 (on writing theses) may also be helpful. Monitoring procedures may also include giving a presentation, on which Chapter 14 offers advice.

Some departments expect that, as a landmark of progress, students should submit an article or paper on their research to a refereed journal. This focuses the students' minds, as well as adding to the very important publications record of the department. However, whether students are pressurized to publish should depend on the progress of the research, their time commitments and the time commitments of their supervisors. If you publish, your supervisor will almost certainly advise and may be a joint author.

The special case of the transfer from MPhil to PhD

As previously mentioned, it is widespread practice in the United Kingdom for students to register for an MPhil degree, and then, in time, if they wish and if the work is deemed to be worthy, to transfer or upgrade that registration for a PhD. What this worthiness entails is well-known in general terms (see Box 16.1), although interpretations may differ considerably from one discipline to another and from one institution to another. Ongoing discussion with supervisors and other academics is essential for arriving at an understanding of the range of possible interpretations in your own field.

Institutions may impose rigorous and detailed transfer procedures on departments. Or departments may have autonomy to work with their own procedures, which may or may not be particularly rigorous. However, each student's transfer normally has to go through the formality of being ratified centrally by the institution.

Box 16.1   The distinction between an MPhil and a PhD

Subject to the institution's regulations, an MPhil thesis should be either a record of original work or an ordered and critical exposition of existing knowledge in any field. A PhD* thesis must form a distinct contribution to the knowledge of the subject and afford evidence of originality, shown by the discovery of new facts or by the exercise of independent critical power.

(National Postgraduate Committee 1995: 3)

* Additionally creeping into institutional regulations is that a PhD thesis must show work which, if rewritten in a suitable form, would be publishable.

Students wishing to transfer should find out what the procedures and requirements are, as laid out in official departmental or institutional documentation, and as normally interpreted in practice. Use the activity below as a checklist.

 ACTIVITY

In terms of each of the following, what are the formal procedures in your department or institution for transferring registration from MPhil to PhD? Where they are absent or ambiguous, how are they normally interpreted, and how flexible are they?

• When is the earliest (i.e. how soon after you have registered for the MPhil) and the latest (i.e. how near to the anticipated completion date of the PhD) that you can apply for transfer? When does your supervisor suggest that you start collecting your documentation together?

• What documentation is required? e.g.:

  – A supporting paper from you

  – A letter of support from your supervisor

  – Submission of logbooks or diaries

- Copies of previous progress reports

- Confirmation of attendance at formal training

- Confirmation of having given a seminar presentation

- A draft or published journal publication

- A testimonial from someone

- Something else. What?

• What, if any, are the formal requirements for the supporting paper from you? e.g.:

  - Length

  - Section headings

  - Appendices

• Which documents should be submitted to whom?

• To whom does the documentation go for consideration?

• What are the procedures by which the institution ratifies the decision to transfer registration?

Preparing your case for transfer from MPhil to PhD

The chances are that you will have to produce a paper to support your transfer. It should be your responsibility, although your supervisor will almost certainly advise on it and help you to improve it. It will probably be expected to do three things:

1 Review progress to date in the light of the original research proposal.
2 Identify one or more aspects in the work to date which are suitable for developing further to a PhD standard.
3 Produce a plan of action to complete the work.

With regard to (1), reviewing progress to date is not primarily a matter of how you have spent your time. The emphasis should be on showing that what you have done has been thoughtful and competent. The following should probably be included, presented as far as possible as a substantiated argument rather than as a straight description, with literature referenced fully and in the manner which is the norm for the discipline.

• How you defined the research topic or problem, taking your original proposal as the starting point.
• How you have developed your research methodology so far.
• How you have ensured that you have collected data which is appropriate and convincing for its purpose.
• How you have used literature.
• How you have dealt with any problems and constraints.
• How far you have got.

Most of this should come out of previous reports and records. If much of it is new, you probably ought to have been writing more as you went along.

The scope and depth of (2) and (3) must depend on the stage in the programme at which the transfer is to take place, which can differ markedly from one institution to another. Normally the next stage of the work has to be a significant contribution to knowledge and be sufficiently challenging to enable you to be able to demonstrate independent, critical and original scholarly work to a PhD standard. Also it must be such that it can be realistically achieved in the remaining time. All these invariably require narrowing the scope and focusing down. (The adage in Box 16.2, although intentionally flippant, does carry more than an element of truth.) With some work, the identification of a suitable next stage is obvious. Yet this is by no means always so, and Chapters 17 and 18 offer advice.

Box 16.2 At last! A definition of a PhD

Here is a flippant adage which carries more than an element of truth.

A PhD is about finding out more and more about less and less until one eventually knows everything about nothing.

(Anon.)

The plan of action for completing the work (i.e. (3) on previous page) should normally be in the form of a fully justified research design with attached timescales.

 ACTIVITY

Check out the advice of this section with your supervisor and develop an action plan for your own MPhil/PhD transfer.

17 COMING TO TERMS WITH ORIGINALITY IN RESEARCH

All good things which exist are the fruits of originality.
(John Stuart Mill, *On Liberty* (1859), Ch. 1)

The need for originality in research

'Originality' is a high-profile requirement for research at PhD level, although it should also exist to some extent in research at all levels. Unless you are fortunate enough to have it already built into your work in some way (as explained later in the chapter), developing it for yourself is a threefold process:

- appreciating the fullness and richness of what 'originality' is and can be;
- learning and using creative skills to recognize and/or develop originality;
- allowing a considerable incubation period for the creative skills to function effectively.

This chapter is concerned with the first of these, and Chapter 18 addresses the second and third.

A useful way to appreciate the scope and potential of originality is through an analogy, where the research programme is a major expedition of discovery, such as a trek into a wilderness or a voyage to new land at a time when the world was still largely unexplored and when leaders of such expeditions still had considerable personal autonomy. The leader, who is analogous to a student, may have certain visions in mind concerning what he or she hopes the expedition will achieve, but he or she is aware that these visions may not materialize and is open to alternatives. For ease of reading in the sections that follow the leader and the student are both taken to be male.

Originality in tools, techniques and procedures

In planning the expedition, the leader uses what information he can to firm up on why he wants to explore the area and how he might do so, within the resources at his command and within any constraints that may exist. He uses this information to work out and organize what background knowledge, procedures, tools, equipment and personnel he will need, tailored to the resources and constraints. Some procedures may have to be specially designed, some tools and equipment may have to be specially made and some personnel may have to be specially trained or brought in.

Similarly, the student studies the literature, talks to experts and attends relevant seminars or courses to get background knowledge and to develop an appropriate research methodology. This must include decisions about the procedures, tools and techniques, and possibly also the people to be involved. If these are fairly standard in the field of study, but the student uses them in new untested ways, this would justify a claim of originality. Or if the student develops new procedures, tools and techniques for a specific purpose, this, too would justify a claim of originality. If neither is the case, the claim for originality must lie in later stages of the work, as suggested in the next few sections.

Originality in exploring the unknown

The expedition begins along the preplanned route. If this is previously unexplored, the mere exploration is original work. Similarly, if the student is conducting a major investigation of something which has never been investigated before, such as a recently discovered insect, star or poem, the work will necessarily be original. This was what was meant above by originality being 'built into' the research.

Although 'originality' in some types of research is built in, in many fields of study it can be elusive. The extract in Box 17.1 puts this well. So students undertaking research have to learn to live with a certain amount of uncertainty, which Box 17.2 also puts well. Living with uncertainty may be difficult, but it is a fact of life, and can be ameliorated to some extent by welcoming the uncertainty as a precursor of creativity; thinking of the uncertainty as fascination with the unknown; and realizing that committed students do normally manage to complete their programmes of research and earn the award for which they are registered.

Box 17.1   Originality is unpredictable

A view from a Nobel laureate:

In real life . . . the truth is not in nature waiting to declare itself and we cannot know a priori which observations are relevant and which are not; every discovery, every enlargement of the understanding begins as an imaginative preconception of what the truth might be. This imaginative preconception – a hypothesis – arises by a process as easy or as difficult to understand as any other creative act of mind; it is a brainwave, an inspired guess, the product of a blaze of light. It comes, anyway, from within and cannot be arrived at by the exercise of any known calculus of discovery.

(Medawar 1981: 84)

Box 17.2   Uncertainty is a fact of life in research

A view from the President of Ireland:

Research is like putting your foot out at the edge of a precipice and hoping that there's territory underneath.

(MacAleese 1998)

Originality in exploring the unanticipated

The planned route may already have been broadly explored. However, the leader will, from time to time, come across unexpected and unexplored sidetracks. He may not notice them; or he may continue on the planned route anyway, in which case nothing original is involved.

If the leader does notice the sidetracks, he has to make decisions about whether to explore any of them, and if so, which ones. These decisions may be difficult because he cannot know whether anything of interest lies along the sidetracks without at least partially exploring them, and doing so will use resources of time and equipment which may delay the expedition on its main route. Yet, one or more of these sidetracks could contain something of such great interest and importance that it would be worth abandoning the expedition

---

Box 17.3   From the commonplace to the significant and original

*In 1980, Jack Sepkoski compiled a detailed database showing the dates when all the biological families lived on Earth. On the face of it, the database appeared to be rather uninteresting, but when David Raup carefully analysed the information, he found that the major extinctions of life on Earth occurred in cycles of roughly 26 million years.**

(Mathews and Taylor 1998: 17)

* This led to new theories on reasons for mass extinctions.

---

as first planned and putting all the resources into exploring the sidetrack. Similarly, in fairly mundane research, one phase of the work can open up alternative ways forward which have never previously been researched, and it is often these that can provide 'originality', as well as the fascination with the unknown that ought to accompany research. They can, on the other hand, equally turn out to be dead ends which consume time and effort fruitlessly.

The example in Box 17.3 illustrates how apparently mundane data can turn out to be significant. The claimant for the originality is the person who imposes meaning on the data, not the person who gathered that data.

Originality in use of data

The leader of the expedition may make and note observations along the way which cannot be processed properly on the expedition. Similarly, the student may find himself collecting much unprocessed data which he hopes may provide something usefully 'original' later, once processed or analysed. This is a perfectly possible way of incorporating originality into work, but it is not at all safe. To do it successfully students need either good hunches about how the data might be used to advantage or considerable creative abilities.

Originality in outcomes

The leader of the expedition may collect all manner of goodies along the way, ranging from what he hoped for when the expedition was planned to the entirely unanticipated. These goodies may have an obvious uniqueness, beauty or value, like gold or precious stones. Similarly the value of the outcomes of research may be self-evident. More likely, though, the goodies were commonplace where they were found, but unknown back home, like the potato which Sir Walter Raleigh brought to England from America. Similarly, original outcomes of research need not be new in absolute terms; they can merely be new to the situation or the discipline.

Originality in byproducts

Things may go so badly wrong on the expedition that it has to be abandoned with seemingly nothing achieved. Yet, the illnesses of the team could be used to testify to the diseases that are rampant in the area. Or the torrential storms that washed away the collections of specimens could be monitored for interpretation in terms of what is already known about storms in that type of terrain. Neither of these would have been the purpose of the expedition, but they would be none the less valuable and count as original work.

Similarly, the student may be able to capitalize on things that seem to go wrong. Important equipment may not work; crucial resources may not be available; people may not agree to being interviewed; funding may be withdrawn; or there may be other serious and unforeseen obstacles. Just as in the analogy, a little creative thinking can rescue the situation, which is the most important reason for the third bullet point in Box 6.2 of Chapter 6 about the visionary role in which students need to operate. There are almost always byproducts during any research – perhaps the development of a certain piece of equipment or some interesting secondary findings in the literature. These can be moved into the mainstream of the research, and focused on or developed further. When the thesis is written, the research problem, theme or focus merely needs to be reformulated to reflect the new nature of the work.

Originality in the experience

Whatever happens on the expedition, the leader should, provided that he did not give up and return home early, have some interesting stories to tell. Similarly, students who stay the course with their research should be able to tease out something worthwhile from an academic or scholarly standpoint. The creative thinking techniques of Chapter 18 should help.

Originality as 'potentially publishable'

Departing from the analogy, another useful way to stimulate thinking about originality is through the concept of 'potentially publishable' in a peer-reviewed journal. This is increasingly being equated to 'originality' for students' research. The work does not necessarily have to be published, only to be worthy of publication, in principle, if suitably written up at a later stage. 'Potentially publishable' is a useful notion, because most research, particularly at PhD level, ought to be able to generate at least one, and probably several, journal articles. The focus of any such article would provide an acceptable claim for originality.

The variety of interpretations and configurations of originality

It is not, in practice, difficult to develop new and original twists to research, although it may seem so and Box 19.1 in Chapter 19 gives some examples of how real students have done it. Use the following activity to see what you can do yourself.

 ACTIVITY

The following list was given in Box 6.7 of Chapter 6 as a checklist of possible solutions to research problems or other outcomes of research. Now, for your own general field, think of something 'original' for each item. It could be something that was original when it was first developed or something that would be original if it were developed in the future. It could even be something that you could develop yourself out of your own work. The emphasis is not on 'right answers' but on realizing that there really is a host of possibilities for originality in research, in all discipline areas, including your own.

• A new or improved product

• A new theory or a reinterpretation of an existing theory

• A new or improved research tool or technique

• A new or improved model or perspective

• An in-depth study

• An exploration of a topic, area or field

• A critical analysis

• A portfolio of work based on research

• A fact or conclusion, or a collection of facts or conclusions

• Something else

The balance between originality and conformity

Since the research components of all higher degrees are expected to show a certain amount of originality, the question is 'how much?' On the face of it, the more stunning and original a new development is – i.e. the more it is a significant contribution to knowledge, a seminal work in the field or a beneficial technological achievement – then the more highly it ought to be acclaimed. Unfortunately things do not always work like this, because it is a tendency of human nature for people to be slow to appreciate what is outside their understanding. Box 17.4 gives some examples.

Really original research is all too often slow to be accepted. To understand why, imagine overworked examiners faced with a thesis that is so original and significant that, if borne out, it would shake the very foundations of the subject. The first reaction of the examiners

---

Box 17.4   The highly original may be the unappreciated

These are examples of three different kinds of innovative work which are now highly acclaimed and respected but were not accepted or appreciated at the time, almost certainly because others could not grasp what was outside their present understanding.

Example 1: Charlotte Brontë, who in the nineteenth century wrote the novel *Jane Eyre*, submitted some of her work to Robert Southey. At the time she was the unknown daughter of a Yorkshire parson and he was the poet laureate. He counselled her that her vivid imagination could give her brain fever and 'a distempered state of mind' and that 'literature cannot be the business of a woman's life'; he described her work to his friends as 'flighty'. Yet her work was soon to become much more famous and widely read than his. *The Guardian* (15 July 1995: 8) described the episode as 'one of the most notorious put-downs in the history of English literature'.

Example 2: Nowadays few people would deny the significance of the cheap production of the hormone progesterone, a constituent of the contraceptive pill. Yet when Russell Marker of Pennsylvania State College tried to interest drug companies in a cheap way to produce it in quantity, they were not interested. He could have given up, but instead he rented a small laboratory in Mexico City and began producing by himself. Several years later he arrived at a drug company with two jars, about 2kg, of progesterone, equal to most of the world's supply at the time. When the company had recovered from the shock, they invited him to join them.

Example 3: The painter Van Gogh is reputed to have been so frustrated at his work that he cut off his own ear in a fit of frenzy! Although there are various versions of this story, the fact remains that his works were not recognized in his lifetime and only remain today because his brother collected them. Now they hang in prestigious galleries all over the world.

would be to wonder whether such a thesis really is valid – and to be fair, the chances are high that it would not be. However, it just might be. If so, the examiners might argue with themselves, then it would surely have come out of one of the major research centres, not from a mere research student. The examiners would realize that they would have to work through this thesis very carefully indeed, weighing every step of the argument and considering the reasonableness or otherwise of every piece of data, in order not to miss something that might invalidate the whole work. Even then, the examiners would fear that they still might overlook that crucial something. They know that if they ratify the thesis, its contents will spread like wildfire through the academic community; then someone else might find that something that actually invalidates everything. Then they, the examiners, would be seriously discredited.

So examiners' own reputations are at stake when they ratify a thesis. Consequently, before spending very much time on the details of a highly original and significant thesis, there would be the temptation to check first on more mundane matters and put the problem off. This might result in their returning the thesis for clarification on a few issues or for rewriting of certain parts more in the language of academic discourse. Where examiners are faced with a highly original and significant thesis that relies on bringing different academic disciplines together, one of which is not their own, and which they do not really understand, their immediate reactions would be the same. Box 17.5 gives an illustration. The extract in Box 17.6 documents similar experiences with regard to original and significant journal articles.

Although not all examiners would behave in this way, it has to be said that students with highly original PhD theses do seem to have them referred (returned for alteration) much more often than students with more commonplace ones. Many such students never bother to complete after a referral and become totally disillusioned with academia.

The lesson is that students whose work seems to be showing extreme originality must be guided by their supervisors. The supervisor may warn against pursuing a highly original theme, not because it is bad, but because it is unsafe. The supervisor may feel with some justification that the research student ought to be more established in the field before risking taking a novel idea further. On the other hand, the supervisor may see the original work as lying entirely within his or her own competence and expertise. If such a supervisor belongs to an internationally renowned research group and publicly endorses the work, then it is well worth pursuing. The supervisor's backing should enable the thesis to be safe.

Box 17.5 Risks of highly original research in terms of examiners' reactions

I once knew a student whose research was in a field on the border between two fields and so he had two examiners, one in each field. Each said that he would pass the candidate, if the other passed him, and so the student failed. He is now a professor and eminent researcher in his field.

(Elton 1999)

Box 17.6 Highly original articles and reactions of journal referees

There is much evidence that the best papers are more likely to be rejected [when submitted for publication in journals]. 'Current Contents' ran some articles by the authors of the most cited papers in the physical and biological sciences – those that were cited more than 1000 times in ten years. The authors complained: 'I had more difficulty in getting this published than anything else I have written.' Some of the more prolific authors in economics and statistics have found the same: it is easy to place a routine paper but it is difficult to place an original, important or controversial paper. I know a case where one journal rejected a paper as rubbish, but another, of higher status, accepted it as being 'the most important paper ever published in this journal'.

(Bowrick 1995: 11)

One of the safest and most common outcomes of a research degree is a set of findings or conclusions which are well substantiated through investigation and argument and which are generalizable from one situation to another. An example might be 'Factors which facilitate crime on housing estates'. These might not set the academic world afire, but they could certainly claim to be original if the work had never been done before. Properly substantiated, the PhD would be safe because examiners would have no difficulty in recognizing the value of the work.

The ownership of original work

Original work may have implications for the career advancement of the students and supervisors concerned. Or it may have commercial implications. So ownership needs protecting. This is considered in Chapter 11, particularly in Box 11.3.

Claiming ownership of work that is not one's own can have very serious consequences, both in terms of the award, which can be withdrawn if plagiarism comes to light, and possibly also in terms of litigation.

Putting originality into perspective

Originality is a crucial requirement for research at postgraduate level. However it must be put into perspective. Also crucial are adherence to the academic and scholarly norms and practices which ensure that a piece of research has the rigour to be convincing.

18 DEVELOPING SKILLS FOR CREATIVE THINKING

I envisage a dialogue between two voices, the one imaginative and the other critical.

(Medawar 1981: 85)

The importance of creative thinking

The identification of originality in research may depend on creative, rather than reasoned thinking (see Box 18.1). That is why a 'visionary' is one of the roles in which research students have to operate (see Box 6.2 in Chapter 6). Creativity can be encouraged through the use of certain techniques. This chapter presents some which have proved particularly useful to researchers.

Box 18.1 Logical analysis and creativity

If we look carefully at how creative, eminent scientists describe their own work, we find [a world] which uses logical analysis as a critical tool in the refinement of ideas, but which often begins in a very different place, where imagery, metaphor and analogy, intuitive hunches, kinesthetic feeling states, and even dreams or dream-like states are prepotent.

(Bargar and Duncan 1982: 3)

Recognizing how intellectual creativity works

Creative thinking works differently for different people, so, if you need it, you first have to recognize how it works for you. Try the following activity.

(■) ACTIVITY

Think back to a number of difficult problems that you had to solve – ones that needed creative (i.e. novel or unusual) solutions, not just the application of some standard procedure or formula. The examples need not be to do with research or even with your field of study. In fact, for this purpose, it is probably better if they are personal, family or financial. In each case write down some characteristics of the process by which you eventually arrived at the solutions. (What the solutions were is irrelevant.)

Now see if there is anything in common in the ways in which you developed solutions to these problems.

(■) DISCUSSION OF ACTIVITY

Most people find that some or all of the following are usually involved in arriving at a creative solution:

- There is a considerable mulling-over time before arriving at a solution, and there is no way of predicting how long this might be.
- The idea for a solution just pops into one's mind, usually when not consciously thinking about it and when not thinking particularly hard about anything else either.
- Once the creative part of the problem-solving is over, hard groundwork still needs to be done to make a solution viable.

Most lists also include the use of one or more creative thinking techniques, although these may go by different names, such as 'talking things over with other people'.

Techniques to facilitate creative thinking

Some techniques which facilitate creative thinking are well-known and well practised because they are common sense, second nature or fundamental to good research. Others are not widely known, which is a pity because students who do know about them usually find them very useful. The next few sections present a selection of techniques which are likely to be particularly useful in research. The first three are included for comprehensiveness and will already be familiar to most researchers. The same is unlikely to be true for the others. More techniques can be found in specialist books, as suggested in the *further reading* section.

You will probably feel that some of the following techniques will suit you but that some will not. However, it is best not to dismiss any of them immediately. Practise them from time to time, and see which ones prove their worth. You only need one really good idea to set your research off in a viable, original direction.

Talking things over

Talking things over with other people does not only provide the benefit of their views and ideas, the very act of talking seems to stimulate one's own thinking. Whether or not the other person needs to be an expert in the field must depend on the nature of the problem. Although one would, for example, go to an expert for expert information, that is not at all the same as going to someone in order to facilitate one's own creativity. This merely requires someone of sound judgement who can supply time and commitment. You might choose other students or members of your family, particularly if they have the time and inclination to help.

Keeping an open mind

Keeping an open mind should be fundamental to all research. So you may not appreciate that it can be a technique for creative thinking. It involves identifying all the unlikely or seemingly implausible interpretations and then considering them carefully to see if they might have any validity. Keeping an open mind is particularly important when talking to others; without it, one is liable to 'hear' (i.e. 'take in') only what one already knows.

Brainstorming

Brainstorming is a well-known problem-solving technique, particularly in groups. It is mentioned here for comprehensiveness, although it seems to be the least useful technique for the sorts of problems and issues that students have to address in research. It consists of listing as many ways forward as possible, however improbable, without pausing to evaluate them. Only when the list is complete may the value and feasibility of the possibilities be considered.

Negative brainstorming

Negative brainstorming is a technique that can be of considerable use for the sorts of problems and issues that students have to address in research, and it is suitable for individual as well as group use. It consists of listing as many ways as one can think of about how not to achieve a purpose, and then, when the list is complete, considering whether reversing any of them might be productive.

The idea of negative brainstorming may seem rather trite, and most of the reversed ideas usually turn out to be meaningless. Nevertheless, negative brainstorming really does have a proven worth, in that it can produce ideas that would never have been thought of via more direct methods – and only one needs to be worthwhile.

Viewing the problem from imaginative perspectives

Viewing the problem from imaginative perspectives is a technique that frees the mind from constraints which may have handicapped its creativity and which may in practice not be as binding as convention and normal expectations have led one to expect. The technique consists of giving the imagination free rein on the problem or issue in ways that may seem preposterous, to see if they generate any ideas that could be turned into something worthwhile. One asks oneself how one would feel about the problem or issue if one was, say, in outer space, or 200 years into the future, or living the sort of lifestyle that one has always dreamed of.

This technique is particularly valuable for generating originality in research and development (see, for example, Box 18.2).

Box 18.2   Creativity and imaginative perspectives

Einstein is reputed to have begun working on his theory of relativity by giving his imagination free rein and wondering what it would be like to ride on a light ray.

Concentrating on anomalies

Many researchers tend to concentrate on what they believe to be the main theme or central issue of their research, and when they come across some aspect that does not fit, they ignore it. The technique of concentrating on anomalies involves focusing on these anomalies and making a feature of them to see if they offer anything worth exploring or investigating. The anecdote in Box 18.3 is an example.

Box 18.3   Creativity and focusing on anomalies

The anecdote in Box 6.5 in Chapter 6 provides an example of the value of focusing on anomalies. When Joscelyn Bell, then an astronomy research student at Cambridge, noticed unexpected scuffs on her photographic plates while she was routinely surveying the night sky, she could have ignored them or assumed they were dirt. However, she chose to investigate the scuffs, which resulted in the major discovery of 'pulsars'.

Focusing on byproducts

Research students can be so committed to the main theme of their research that they do not recognize the significance of something that may have happened or that they may have developed along the way. Box 18.4 gives an example of how focusing on byproducts can be really helpful in research and development.

Interrogating imaginary experts

The technique of interrogating imaginary experts consists of imagining that one is able to interview and interrogate a real or imaginary

---

Box 18.4 Creativity and byproducts

It is said that the antibiotic penicillin would never have been discovered if Sir Alexander Fleming had not been interested enough to bother to investigate a stray contamination of mould.

---

expert in one's field. The interview doesn't have to take place. One just prepares some suitable questions. These often turn out to be surprisingly perceptive, and they may open up some unexpectedly original and valuable ways forward for the research.

Viewing the problem from the perspective of another discipline

Pushing back the frontiers of knowledge in a single discipline can be a rather formidable way of achieving original and significant work. Often a simpler alternative is to see what can be done by bringing different disciplines together. A technique is to talk the problem or issue over with people from other disciplines to see how they would approach it. If you happen to have a sound grounding in another discipline yourself, perhaps from your undergraduate work, or if you would feel stimulated to learn more about that discipline, you could try viewing the problem yourself from the perspective of that discipline. You may not need to have any great expertise in it. The anecdotes in Box 18.5 give examples.

Box 18.5 Creativity and linking with other disciplines

Example 1: Sir Alexander Graham Bell had a deaf wife and therefore was interested in developing a device that would amplify sound. He was a biologist by training, and he applied what he knew about the form of the human ear to develop the telephone. It is said that if he had just been a physicist, the idea of developing a telephone would have appeared too daunting ever to attempt.

Example 2: Crick and Watson were not molecular biologists. If they had been, it is said that they might not have dared to propose their model for the structure of DNA.

Using 'the solution looking for the problem': serendipity

A good creative technique is to keep one's eyes and ears constantly open, to question anything and everything to see if it might be used to provide a creative leap forward. The anecdotes in Box 18.6 are examples.

Box 18.6 Creativity and serendipity

Example 1: It is unlikely that anyone looking for a way of speeding customers through supermarket checkouts would have thought of developing the laser as a means of solving the problem. The fact was that the laser was there, already developed, and someone was bright enough to spot a new use for it. Other bright people have of course spotted other practical uses for it in a wide variety of different areas – replacing torn eye retinas, for example.

Example 2: George de Mestral had no intention of inventing the Velcro fastener when he looked to see why burs stuck tightly to his clothing.

Using mind maps

A mind map is a technique for freeing the mind from the constrained and ordered viewpoint from which it has been seeing a problem or issue. It provides an overview, which shows at a glance all the components of the problem or issue and the links between them. This tends to stimulate new and creative ideas. Much has been written on mind maps (see the *further reading* section). The technique is best explained by working through the next activity.

 ACTIVITY

To illustrate the procedure for making a mind map, think of a problem or issue which is currently concerning you. In order to illustrate the method, it may be best to make this fairly trivial, like what to have for supper or where to go next weekend, although if you prefer a research problem, feel free to choose one.

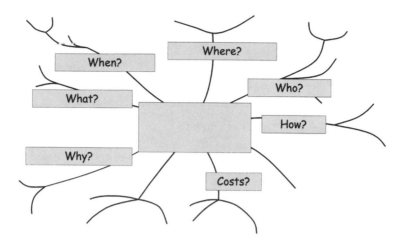

Figure 18.1 An example of a mind map

On the diagram in Figure 18.1:

- Write down what the problem or issue is inside the blank box.
- Note the seven spokes coming out of the box, labelled 'Why?', 'What?', 'When?', 'Where?', 'Who?', 'How?' and 'Costs?'
- Label the remaining two spokes coming out of the box with other questions that seem appropriate to the problem or issue, and draw more spokes and label them if you think there are further appropriate questions. Use a separate sheet of paper if you run out of space.
- Let your mind wander over the questions on each spoke and label keywords for your thoughts (any thoughts) on the further spokes.
- Draw more spokes, as the labelled ideas suggest further ideas, and label these new spokes, which may link up with existing ones.

Continue until you run out of ideas. Then mark any similar labels which are common to more than one spoke.

You may feel that a viable solution has already occurred to you. If not, put the paper aside and see if a solution pops into your head later.

 DISCUSSION OF ACTIVITY

Mind maps have widespread applicability in a variety of tasks that require creative thinking. They can, for example, with suitably labelled spokes, also be used to generate the content of reports, thesis chapters and presentations. Possible spoke labels might be 'purpose of report, chapter or presentation', 'links with previous knowledge', 'work to be reported' (from which there would be several sub-spokes), 'constraints on work' and 'outcomes'. Once the mind map has produced the ideas for content, these still have to be structured into a meaningful order, but that is a separate activity.

Creativity and free time

Solutions only pop into one's mind if it is not occupied – i.e. if it is thinking about nothing in particular. The anecdotes in Box 18.7 are examples. So, although it is important for students to study hard, doing it all the time is counter-productive. Take a few minutes over the following activity, to think about how to help your creative abilities operate.

Box 18.7 Creativity and letting the mind wander freely

Example 1: The mathematician Poincaré claimed to have thought of his most profound idea quite suddenly while boarding a bus.

Example 2: In the middle of the nineteenth century the constituent atoms of a molecule of benzene were known, but no stable molecular structure could be visualized. The problem was solved by Kekulé, who, while musing in a semi-dozing state, visualized snakes coiling round eating their own tails This gave him the idea, which has since come to be accepted, that the benzene molecule could be in the form of a ring.

 ACTIVITY

List activities which you enjoy and are practical for you to indulge in, and which free your mind from purposeful thinking.

◉ DISCUSSION OF ACTIVITY

You have probably identified some form of sport, or something like gardening, listening to music, or yoga. Perhaps you should force yourself to spend more time on these mind-freeing activities. Television and reading may seem relaxing but they seldom free the mind for creativity.

Many people find that creative ideas just pop into their mind when they wake up in the night, still half asleep. They recommend keeping a pen and paper beside the bed for jotting the ideas down, for full consideration later.

Testing out the techniques

Try the following activity to see which techniques seem helpful for your own work.

◉ ACTIVITY

Assume that you want to develop your research in a new direction. Try each of the following creative techniques:

- Negative brainstorming
- Viewing the problem from imaginative perspectives
- Concentrating on anomalies
- Focusing on byproducts
- Interrogating imaginary experts
- Viewing the problem from the perspective of another discipline

Do not expect any dramatic ideas to emerge until some time in the future, when your mind has had time to mull things over.

◉ DISCUSSION OF ACTIVITY

You may like to look ahead to Box 19.1 in Chapter 19. It gives some examples of how creative thinking has helped research students.

Creativity and routine work

In research, having a good idea is not enough on its own. You must work on it to turn it into an approach, tool, model, theory, etc. that is convincingly tested and is justified according to the academic rigour of the subject. Such work is likely to be fairly routine, but it is none the less crucial.

Creativity and planning

Creativity cannot be done to command or to deadlines. Yet it is an essential part of good research. This can and will sabotage plans about where you would like your work to be by a particular time, and is one reason why planning has to be an ongoing process of revision. Plan in detail in the short term and in outline over the long term.

19 DEALING WITH FLAGGING

Don't give up when the pace seems slow.
You might succeed with another blow.
Stick to the fight when you're hardest hit.
It's when things seem worst that you mustn't quit.

(Anon.)

Understanding and coping with flagging

Research can be a long undertaking. For PhD students, in particular, it can take a number of years. These are years of having to maintain enthusiasm and commitment in the face of working independently to produce original and high quality work in an environment in which plans do not always work out as hoped or expected. In addition, there may be family matters, health matters, employment matters and financial matters which keep emerging to detract from the research. It is hardly surprising that students go through periods of doubting whether it is worth continuing.

Self-doubt and flagging are quite normal, and you need to understand that this is so. Nevertheless, they are debilitating. Their effects can be minimized in three ways. The first is by talking things through with others – and Chapter 5 highlighted the need to put effort into finding suitable people as early as possible in a research programme. The second is by maintaining a balanced outlook through a healthy lifestyle of sensible eating and drinking, and appropriate exercise; and the third is to find out about common causes of flagging and how best to deal with them. It is with the last of these that this chapter is primarily concerned. It is particularly directed to students on long research programmes such as the PhD, although other students may also find it useful.

The examples in Box 19.1 illustrate how real students have managed to salvage work when they felt like giving up. All are practical manifestations of the archery analogy of Figure 6.1 in Chapter 6.

Box 19.1   Creative ways in which research students have salvaged work that was not looking viable

The following examples are based on real anecdotes supplied by supervisors and students. They have been simplified and anonymized.

Example 1: Michael was some way into a project on wave power. Then the funding was unexpectedly cut off and all development work had to come to an abrupt halt. Michael was sure that this meant the end of his PhD. However, his supervisor advised him to look at what he had been doing so far and see whether any of it could be used as a basis for continued work with a different focus. Michael found that he could capitalize on the measurements that he had already made on winds, tides and grades of sand and pebbles at various points along a beach. He completed his PhD with little or no loss of time.

Example 2: Jill was exploring styles of teaching, for which she spent a considerable time developing a set of questionnaires. It then looked as if enough data to draw valid conclusions on teaching would take too long to collect. So she focused instead on the development and evaluation of the questionnaires, thus finishing her PhD much more quickly.

Example 3: Tara's PhD was on a particular author. Her intention was to work systematically through all of his works and so arrive at his view of the purpose of literature. She worked very hard on this, but the answer eluded her. She read more and analysed more deeply, but still the answer eluded her. There seemed no alternative but to give up the search and abandon the PhD. When she eventually plucked up the courage to confide in her supervisor, he pointed out that her work was indeed viable, and that all she needed to do was to justify a claim that the author did not have a particular view of what literature ought to be: that he wrote in different modes at different times, depending on the situation and how he was feeling. This is what Tara did, and she completed her PhD successfully.

Example 4: Simon's research was to use established theory to calculate a parameter which would make it possible to predict what happens when subatomic particles of a particular energy are scattered in certain circumstances. He spent considerable time on this. Then he found that another student elsewhere had already calculated the parameter. Simon's first reaction was that his own claim for original work had been snatched from under his nose. However he was able to extend his calculation to a range of energies, which enabled him to use what he had done so far, yet to claim that his work was, in fact, original.

Example 5: Angela was looking at a rather unpleasant historical episode. Her hunch was that money would turn out to be the root of all the evil. However her reading turned up contradictory findings. She just couldn't make a sound case, and she panicked. Her supervisor, however, pointed out that there is a great deal in research that 'won't go tidy'; that the model needed would have to be much more complex than originally envisaged; and that there is virtue in students recognizing such a fact. Angela went on to develop and justify a relatively complex model for the influences of money during the historical episode, incorporating the positive and energizing aspects as well as the negative ones. This earned her a PhD.

Example 6: Adam's research problem was to develop a conceptual software model and a prototype application for a particular type of electronic messaging library. After a year he had identified the key parameters of the problem and the weaknesses of related work. However, computing moves on quickly and he found to his dismay that a software giant was producing its own application. This meant that his own envisaged development would no longer have any claim to be original. His supervisor advised him to focus instead on the techniques that he had identified (which had not been published by the software giant), to develop them further and to make them his focus for original work. Adam was greatly relieved at this advice and successfully followed it.

Example 7: Sarah was looking for the expression (non-dormancy) of a particular gene in a human tissue. However, the result came back negative. She refined her procedures and tried again, but still the result was negative. This kept happening and she became increasingly despondent that a substantial body of work had been wasted. Then it suddenly dawned on her that the negative result might be meaningful. She re-examined the literature in the light of the negative result and developed an alternative theory for the possible role of the tissue being examined. Her existing data thus provided the foundations of a new PhD.

Example 8: Judy, Anthea, Andreas and Peter were ecology students who went together on an extended field trip to gather specimens from a particular location. All four were full of enthusiasm and they each made large collections. However, back in the laboratory, they found themselves overwhelmed by the months of work ahead: to sort, count and identify what they had collected. Morale fell progressively lower, and they were on the point of giving up. However, a new supervisor took a firm line. He stressed that they only had to do enough to get their PhDs and that the rest of the specimens could be shelved or discarded. He then worked with Judy, Anthea, Andreas and Peter, both individually and together, to help them to develop their own specific questions to guide their treatments of just a selection of their specimens. In consequence, morale picked up and the work progressed well. (Normally supervisors would provide such guidance in advance of a field trip.)

Example 9: Melanie was an MPhil student developing a manual of training materials for which she was collecting contributions from a number of experienced professionals. When she wanted to transfer her registration to PhD, her supervisor told her that the next stage of her work would need to be much more scholarly, with theoretical underpinning; and he advised her to complete the manual, run the training and then evaluate it in terms of learning theories. Melanie was appalled at how much extra time this would need. So she looked for an alternative and quicker way forward. What she eventually did was to use (and build on) the records that she had kept for administrative purposes to test theories about attitudes to change and innovation. She completed her PhD within her four-year period of part-time registration.

Lacking a sense of direction

Any piece of research can develop in a number of different ways, all of which could be viable. If you feel that you haven't got a firm direction, just look back on what you have done and see if you can consolidate your work around a focus of some sort. Read or reread Chapter 6 and think particularly about the message of Figure 6.1. Then use Chapters 17 and 18 to take your thinking forward.

A related problem is that students who think they do have a sense of direction suddenly find it undermined. Perhaps this is due to conflicting advice from different supervisors; or a colleague or visitor may point out different expectations of what the research ought to be about (e.g. who it ought to be helping, or how). The different approach may have some appeal, but your task is to complete just one programme of research – and the chances are that the one that you already have is entirely viable. If you like, in the final chapter of your thesis, you can always point out how you might have done things differently if starting again. This in no way detracts from the fact that you will already have produced a consolidated piece of research in its own right. In fact it shows your development as a scholar and researcher.

Students may feel that their lack of direction is due to lack of support from their supervisors, possibly because the supervisors lack interest or the necessary academic expertise. The truth may be very different. A supervisor's task is not to lead every step of the way. Postgraduates are expected to act independently, following their own ideas, under, of course, the watchful eyes of supervisors to advise and warn. If you think that the problem may be that you have not appreciated your supervisor's role, the answer is to start taking responsibility for yourself. If, after sufficient thought, you really do think that another supervisor would help, be resolute, and set about making it happen. Chapter 7 outlines possible ways forward.

Feeling overwhelmed by the quantity of work ahead

Students can find themselves overwhelmed by what they see as the immensity of what lies before them. If this is your problem, glance back to Box 10.3 in Chapter 10. Essentially it is your task, in conjunction with your supervisor, to limit the scope of your work so that it can be fitted into the time available. The process may require some creative thinking to 'tweak' research problems, foci or themes, so that what can be achieved in the time does in fact address them and also forms a consolidated piece of research in its own right. Chapters 17 and 18 should provide some ideas.

Another aspect of feeling overwhelmed is the huge bulk of the literature. It isn't possible to read it all. For practical purposes you have to treat a literature survey in terms of diminishing returns on your time. When you find that whatever you read seems to reference works that you have already consulted, it is time to regard the survey as finished for all practical purposes. It can, after all, still be added to later if anything else relevant happens to come to light. If something crucial should come to your attention after the thesis is ready but before you are examined, few examiners would hold this against you.

It is always possible for every researcher to do more. If you have identified further work and are depressed that you don't have the time to do it (and your supervisor thinks that you have already done enough for the award for which you are registered), you can actually capitalize on the situation. Simply express your hopes in the final chapter of your thesis that other workers may undertake the work. Remember that you will be judged on the scholarly way in which you make your case in the thesis, not on the quantity of work alone. So be ruthless about cutting down the scope of work that seems too large.

Aiming for perfection

Students ought to be vigilant to ensure that their work is good enough for the award for which they are registered. However, it is not necessary to aim for perfection, which is unattainable anyway.

Research needs to convince by conforming to the normal research practices of the discipline. If you need to be reminded of these, Chapter 6 should help, although a more detailed understanding needs to be developed over time through reading the literature in your subject, discussions with your supervisor and attending departmental seminars or other training. Your aims should be to reach a stage where you feel confident about monitoring your own standards.

Research at PhD level needs to be original, independent and significant. Chapter 17 considers the various manifestations and configurations of originality, and Chapter 18 presents techniques to help develop it. Independence could be a problem where a team project is concerned, but with care and attention to the boundaries of individual contributions, and goodwill and professionalism all round, it seldom is. There is a view that all new knowledge must be significant, but the nature of acceptable significance does depend on the norms of the discipline. Discussion and reading are the means to identify these.

It is natural at times for students to feel that their work is rather trivial and to strive for a perfectionism that is not only time-consuming but also unobtainable. Be guided by your supervisor on this. If you would appreciate the reassurance of other people who are experienced in standards of research, you could give a departmental seminar so that other students and academic staff can give their opinions on your work. Bear in mind, too, that fine-tuning to your work, over and beyond what is required for the thesis, can always, later, go into a journal article or book.

Worrying about being pipped at the post

Students, particularly PhD students, can feel like giving up when they learn that someone, somewhere is working on the same problem and is likely to finish sooner. This is something that they must discuss with their supervisors, because supervisors know the work, the general field and the regulations of the institution.

In practice, the matter may not be particularly serious. Even if the other work is identical, which is most likely to occur in science-based subjects, it normally takes some months for research findings to reach the market-place or be published in a journal, and most institutional regulations allow a breathing space for a thesis to go forward provided that this is sufficiently short to guarantee that the work is the student's own.

The chances are, though, that the work is only broadly similar, particularly in the humanities and social sciences. Then the thing to do is to contact the other researchers to find out precisely what they have done. It is bound to be different in some way: perhaps in the research design, or the sample, or the precision of the result. You would merely need to build a new section into your thesis to compare and contrast the work with your own, drawing some meaningful conclusions. See also some of the examples in Box 19.1.

Feeling disorganized

The independence which students have during lengthy research programmes can mean that it is all too easy to let time run away in talking to people, drinking coffee, spending time at the bar or popping out to the shops. Students need to plan their work and manage themselves and their time. If this is your problem, Chapters 9, 10 and 11 should be helpful. Nevertheless, knowing what to do is not the same as doing it. Students have to learn self-discipline.

Your problem may be that you are working so hard that you cannot think straight. Then you must take a break or even a short holiday, so as to refresh yourself. Not only is there nothing at all wrong in doing this, it is probably essential if you are to continue the programme effectively and efficiently.

Losing interest, becoming bored and getting depressed

Research should be intellectually fascinating because it involves discovering or developing something new in an area that should have considerable personal appeal. Nevertheless, it is natural to lose interest or become bored at times. It is often helpful to have several themes on the go at once, so that there is more likely to be something tempting to work on.

You may be at a stage where your work really is excessively routine and monotonous. Some people find that it helps to listen to light music during tasks which do not require much concentration. Monotonous stages in research should pass. If they look unlikely to do so, a solution could be to take up an alternative direction or approach (see Chapter 17).

Some reasons for getting depressed and feeling unable to cope are intensely personal. This is where the support of others is so important, as they can often recognize and diagnose the cause of the problem before you can yourself. Listen to them and allow them to support you. Also, if it seems appropriate, make use of institutional counselling services. Most are excellent as well as confidential. There are few personal problems that professional counsellors have not seen before, and they can often point to sources of help.

For short-term depression, many people find that certain pieces of music can be mood-enhancing. For longer-term or more serious depression, do not make quick decisions about giving up. Find and use the support you need. Then you may feel differently before too long. If after a time you still feel like giving up, take a holiday. If, even then, you still feel like giving up, this may be the right decision for you. Before you do give up, though, talk with your supervisor. This may be difficult because you may feel that you are letting him or her down, but there is little that upsets a good supervisor more than a student just disappearing.

Interacting ineffectually with associates

It is self-evident that students need to be able to interact effectively with other people. Chapters 7 and 12 respectively consider the specifics of interacting with a supervisor and more generally with other people. Further advice and counselling on effective interaction need to come from someone who knows and cares about you or is a professional counsellor.

Everything seeming to go wrong

It is a fundamental feature of research that it seldom goes according to plan (see Box 19.2). No one is responsible, although it is the research student who has to find a way of compensating.

> **Box 19.2**   The rational model of how research should operate
>
> *The rational model for the conduct of research is perhaps an idealised guide to how research ought to be conducted. [It] does not attempt to provide an accurate description of the process whereby research actually is conducted. At the present time, to my knowledge, a commonly accepted descriptive model of the research process is not available.*
>
> (Martin 1982: 19)

Also, research invariably goes more slowly than anticipated. So the feeling of getting nowhere is to be expected, provided that it doesn't last too long. It is not that a jinx is on an individual; neither is it an indication that the individual is not up to the job. Small problems can normally be sorted out quite easily by keeping on good terms with others in the department: other students, academics, secretaries, technicians, etc. Then supervisors do not have to be disturbed unnecessarily.

Students' worries that they are getting nowhere can be simply because they are so close to what they are doing that they cannot spot where a slight change of direction or emphasis could provide the security of a fall-back position. Spotting such changes in direction or emphasis requires creative thinking and an understanding of what else would be acceptable at the level of the award concerned (see Chapters 17 and 18). Some of the examples in Box 19.1 illustrate the idea.

Frustrated at the difficulties of part-time study

Students usually register part-time because they have commitments elsewhere, and these invariably produce conflicting demands on their time and attention. It is particularly difficult having to do research work in the evenings, at weekends and on odd days. You are tired; you miss out on social activities with family and friends; and essential resources, such as specialist libraries or laboratories, may not be accessible at suitable times. Various parts of this book should help with such concerns, in particular Chapters 4, 5, 10, 11, 12 and 18. Remember that committed people in your situation do, in sizeable numbers, successfully complete their research programmes.

Facing a time-consuming emergency

If you are going through an emergency which needs a great deal of time and energy to handle, such as illness, you may find it helpful to take time out, rather than try to cope ineffectively with too many things at the same time. Most institutions have a category of registration for students who are forced to interrupt their studies, but who intend to continue at a later date. A fee is seldom levied for this category, and the time out does not count towards the required period of registration. Funding bodies may not be as sympathetic as institutions, so the position does need to be explored with them.

A common alternative is to switch from full-time to part-time study. There are also other categories of registration, and it is important for your finances as well as your time management that you are registered in the most appropriate category. Changes of registration should, if possible, be discussed with supervisors well in advance of when the change is to take place, and approval must then be given by the institution.

Feeling stressed and unable to cope

Everyone goes through phases of feeling emotionally wound up or drained and unable to cope. Students are no exception. If the reason is not one of those already mentioned, it is probably because the students are overworked or need regular exercise, a break or a holiday. Or they may need to see a counsellor or doctor.

Box 19.3 gives some common and quite general reasons for feeling stressed. You may like to compare them with what you are experiencing.

Wanting to get on with the next stage of life

Wanting to get on with the next stage of one's life is a common cause, not just of flagging, but of dropping out completely.

A good job offer may come along, and it may seem a good idea to take it on the assumption that the thesis can be written up in the evenings and at weekends. In fact, this is an extremely difficult thing to do, and it is one of the most common reasons for not completing a PhD. So think carefully before taking any action in this respect that you may later regret.

In some fields of study, a reason for giving up may be that the qualification or research training seems unlikely to help employment

---

Box 19.3 Causes of stress at work

Fontana (1993) lists *general* causes of stress under the following headings:

- Organizational problems
- Insufficient backup
- Long or unsociable hours
- Poor status, pay and promotion prospects
- Unnecessary rituals and procedures
- Uncertainty and insecurity

For *specific* causes of stress at work, Fontana lists the following:

- Unclear role specifications
- Role conflict
- Unrealistically high expectations (perfectionism)
- Inability to influence decision-making (powerlessness)
- Frequent clashes with supervisors
- Isolation from colleagues' support
- Overwork and time pressures
- Lack of variety
- Poor communication
- Inadequate leadership
- Conflicts with colleagues
- Inability to finish a job
- Fighting unnecessary battles

---

prospects. This is by no means necessarily so (see Box 15.3 in Chapter 15) and it is quite common, even for PhD graduates, to go into careers which are unrelated to their PhD topics. There are a range of skills which students of research degrees can offer employers and which go far beyond those of graduates with first degrees. What matters is to be aware of them so as to be able to impress at interview (see Chapter 15).

Not wanting to get on with the next stage of life

Being a student does offer a form of security: belonging to a community, being cared for by a professional, etc. This can make some students not want to get on with the next stage of their lives. The problem has to be recognized and faced up to. It cannot be allowed to go on for ever. The best solution is to talk it through with someone responsible and caring, perhaps the institutional counsellor.

Other reasons

There can be many reasons for a thesis being delayed or never completed. Box 19.4 gives some identified by a research council.

Box 19.4 Research council identifies reasons for delay and non-completion

It is worth looking at some of the reasons for long completion times or failure to complete . . . One quite common reason for late completion [is] a slow start . . . If insufficient effort is put into the formulation of the problem, to making a literature survey where appropriate, or such other initial activities as are desirable, the result is that the remaining portion of . . . activities is always a scramble and the programme inevitably slips.

A second common cause of delay is the student who is never satisfied. He can always think of a way of improving his results. In short, he cannot bring anything to a conclusion. Perfectionism can be a virtue, but if only a student would write up what he had achieved, he would almost certainly see more clearly whether any improvement was actually necessary, the amount of effort required if it was desirable, or whether it was sensible to attempt that amount of work in the time available . . .

A third common cause of delay is distraction from the main line of enquiry. These days a common distraction is for a student to get 'hooked on' computing with the result that he over analyses his experimental data, largely because of the sheer pleasure he gets out of manipulating the computer; but with inevitable delays, leading to a delayed thesis . . .

When the work has gone well and opened up prospects for future research, the supervisor may in some subjects suggest that the student might like to consider a two or three year continuation as a post-doctoral research assistant. Experience shows that if the student accepts, and is appointed before handing in his thesis, in the vast majority of cases the progress on the thesis slows dramatically.

(Science and Engineering Research Council 1992: 7–9)

The *further reading* section references a book on ten students' experiences of the PhD process which is essential reading for all research students who think that their problems are unique, and who want some encouragement.

 ACTIVITY

If you feel yourself flagging, where, in view of this chapter, do you think the problem lies, and what can you do about it?

From your experience or from the advice of others, what pieces of music are most likely to improve your mood?

Should you take more exercise or eat more healthily?

Should you take some time off as a break or to interact with others socially?

20 PRODUCING YOUR THESIS

Many research students believe that the quality of a thesis necessarily improves with the amount of time taken to prepare it and the number of words it contains. This is not true.
(Economic and Social Research Council 1986: 13)

The importance of the thesis

The thesis is the culmination of a student's research programme, and it is on the thesis that he or she will be examined and judged, possibly in conjunction with an oral examination or viva. So it is in your best interests to make your thesis good, and give yourself enough preparation time to do yourself justice. A thesis must demonstrate that you are worthy of the award for which you are registered, and this has implications for its quality. Box 20.1 summarizes the points that most examiners will be looking for, and it is on these that the book has concentrated so far. This chapter goes further by giving advice on producing the thesis. Most of the advice should be useful for producing all theses, but the chapter is primarily designed for students registered for PhDs in the United Kingdom system where the examination is in two parts: a thesis and an oral examination or viva. If you will not be having an oral examination, your thesis needs to pay particular attention to the sorts of points that examiners normally probe in such examinations. So scan Chapter 21 before finalizing your thesis.

The suggestions in this chapter will not be totally appropriate for all fields of study, as there is no consistent view across disciplines about what constitutes an acceptable thesis, either for a degree entirely by research or for an award with a research component. Nevertheless, the chapter should stimulate your thinking and indicate topics for discussion and clarification with your supervisor.

The chapter builds on the chapter on report writing (Chapter 13), and you should scan that chapter as revision before reading further.

Box 20.1 Some things that examiners may be looking for

- The case for the research problem, focus or theme, etc. (or problems, foci or themes etc.)
- The knowledge of the general field in which the work is being set
- The case for appropriateness of the research design (and all that this entails)
- The case for the appropriateness of the solutions to the research problem(s) (or conclusions, or outcomes, etc.)
- The originality of the work
- The significance of the work
- The independence of the work
- Critical ability and personal development
- The coherence of arguments
- The balance of quality to quantity
- General competence

Orientating yourself for the task ahead

As an orientation for producing a thesis, it is useful to return to the analogy of Chapter 17, where the research programme is a major expedition of discovery and the student is its leader (both student and leader were, for ease of reading, taken to be male).

Knowing that he will be telling his story when he gets home from the expedition, the leader will keep careful and detailed records while away. These are analogous to the students' logs, diaries, draft theses, etc. The leader may start writing his story while still on the expedition – just as students may find that it aids their thinking to write draft thesis chapters and have a thesis outline as they go along. However, the leader will appreciate that how he eventually tells the story will, with hindsight, be different in sequence, scope and emphasis, depending on who he tells it to and the time slot available for telling it. So it is with a thesis.

There are a number of points that the leader will bear in mind when he comes to tell his story afterwards. He will certainly want to stress the novelty and value of the outcomes. Although he will probably include what he hoped at the outset that the general outcomes might be, he will give most attention to features of special importance that may or may not have been predicted in advance, such as finding hidden treasure, or special procedures developed for successfully tracking a certain animal, etc. So he will not necessarily tell the story in the order in which things happened. Neither will he give every period of the expedition an equal slot of story time or length, although he may mention chronological development as a justification or explanation in connection with something else. Similarly, the final version of a thesis should be written with hindsight, to make best sense of what has happened. It should take the reader naturally and convincingly to the major outcomes, which may or may not have been anticipated at the outset. So, for your own thesis, although you should draft the introduction early to orientate yourself for the writing to follow, you must finalize it much later to orientate the reader for how the thesis eventually turns out, after all the redrafts.

The leader of the expedition will vary his way of telling his story according to the audience. The crucially important audience for theses are the examiners, and in particular external examiners. In fact, theses seldom reach wider audiences, which is why journal articles, conferences and books are the places for disseminating research. Think of examiners as individuals who are exceptionally busy and grossly underpaid, and who therefore have to read theses quickly. They will expect a thesis to be well structured and to be argued coherently to make the case for the solutions, conclusions or outcomes, etc. Irrelevancies will irritate, as will having to cope with loose style and typing errors, and having to tease out meaning that students should have extracted themselves.

Examiners are very able and experienced in the general area, which means that background material should be as concise as is consistent with showing that it is known. However, no examiner can be an expert in a student's particular niche of work. By the time you finalize your thesis, you and you alone are the world's expert in what it contains. Your task is to convince others of its value, by marshalling evidence and arguing with it, rather as a barrister makes a case in a court of law (see the roles in which students have to operate in Box 6.2 in Chapter 6). The features that make your work significant, original and worthy of the PhD (or other award) need to be argued cogently: each step needs to be spelt out; the solutions, conclusions or outcomes must be stated unambiguously; and all their implications identified and discussed in depth.

Developing a framework of chapters

A good way to start developing a framework for a thesis is to draft out the case (or cases) on which the thesis is based. The chances are that this (or these) can be thought of as 'building blocks' of various sizes, linked by streams of argument. The following, to set you think-ing, are examples of what could be some of the rather larger build-ing blocks:

- The general research area and how the research problem, topic, theme or focus was identified and refined
- Discussion leading to statements of the research methodology
- Reports on work done
- The emerging data
- The analysis of the data
- The solutions, conclusions or outcomes to the work
- A discussion of their applicability and limitations, and the scope for further work

The emphasis placed on a literature survey chapter in its own right depends on the field of study. Where it is usual to define a research problem early on, and to keep it relatively unchanged, a separate literature survey chapter is often the norm. In fields where it is usual for the direction of each stage of the research to rely on findings of an earlier stage, new literature may need to be incorpor-ated at each stage. Most theses will require some, at least minimal, reference to literature to run throughout. Running throughout any thesis should be the identification of difficulties and constraints, and how they were handled.

 ACTIVITY

In your field of study, how normal is it for almost all the literature survey material to be in a single chapter?

How useful do the major building blocks, as given above, seem to be for your thesis?

● DISCUSSION OF ACTIVITY

Irrespective of whether a literature survey is considered worthy of a chapter in its own right, do continually bear in mind, as pointed out in Chapter 13, that literature should be used to substantiate and carry forward arguments and to help deal with counter-arguments. A literature survey should not read as a catalogue of vaguely relevant material, even though it is wise to find a way of bringing in all the important works in the field.

Developing the content of a chapter

When developing the material to go into any chapter, the following checklist may be a useful starting point to stimulate further thinking:

- Purposes of the chapter
- Links with other knowledge (e.g. earlier or later chapters or the works of other people)
- Constraints (if any, under which the work described had to operate)
- Work carried out
- Outcomes of that work
- Where next?

It may be that much of the substance of chapters can be obtained by lifting sections directly out of earlier reports. The chances are, however, that these will need editing to reflect a more recently emerging coherence.

If you like to work with mind maps (see Chapter 18), a useful technique is to use one for developing ideas for the content of a chapter. It will enable your creativity to have full rein. The above bullet points can serve as spokes.

● ACTIVITY

Look back at Chapter 18 and the section on mind maps. Then get a feel for using a mind map to develop the content of a thesis chapter. Label the spokes with the bullet points above, and see where this takes your thinking. (If you are not ready to do a chapter, experience the technique with a report or essay.) The purpose is merely to set your mind thinking about this use of mind maps, and not, at this stage, to develop any lasting content.

(■) DISCUSSION OF ACTIVITY

Developing content is a separate task from putting that content into a logical order. This is considered in the next section.

Sequencing the content of a chapter

There is no single right way of sequencing material within a chapter, although some students waste considerable time searching for it. What matters is that the sequencing should be acceptable, irrespective of whether it could be done differently. There needs to be an internal logic, which should be stated explicitly so as to guide readers. If the chapter contains more than one stream of argument, all the streams need to be linked by careful structuring and cross-referencing. Much of the advice in Chapter 13 on structuring a report can be adapted for structuring a thesis chapter.

As you write, amendments to content and structure will suggest themselves – often as a result of the highly productive exercise of arguing with yourself as you write.

Linking chapters into a storyline

Chapters of a thesis should link together to make a unified whole with one or more storylines. The technique of developing and demonstrating a storyline was introduced in Chapter 13, but for a thesis, being so much longer and almost certainly having several themes, it is even more useful. So it is always worth wording the headings of chapters and sections so that they convey as comprehensively as possible what is in them. Then it is helpful to keep an up-to-date contents list, as you work, to be able to see the developing storyline at a glance. It is here that any lack of coherence is likely to show up first; so the technique can save hours of writing that would later have to be discarded. (As Chapter 13 pointed out, the 'outline' and/ or 'document map' features of modern word processors can enable one to view a working contents list quickly and easily without having to go to the trouble of constructing it.)

It should be made clear to a reader from the first paragraph of a chapter where that chapter fits into the rest of the thesis. A good technique to accomplish this is to write a few keywords or some notes under each of the following headings:

- Setting the scene for the chapter, i.e. the general area(s) that the chapter considers.
- The gap in knowledge or understanding which the chapter addresses – usually as identified as an issue in (an) earlier chapter(s).
- How the chapter fills the gap.
- A brief overview of what is in the chapter.

Then edit the notes together to form the introduction to the chapter. Figure 20.1 illustrates the technique.

The concluding paragraph of a chapter (except for the final chapter) should show how its theme is carried on elsewhere in the thesis. The technique for doing this consists of writing a few keywords or some notes under each of the following headings:

- What the chapter has done.
- What new questions the chapter has identified.
- Where these questions are dealt with.

Then edit the notes together. Figure 20.2 illustrates the technique.

Write notes under each of the following:

1 Setting the scene for the chapter, i.e. the general area(s) that the chapter considers, e.g.:

Self-instruction, universities, Sierra Leone

2 The gap in knowledge or understanding which the chapter addresses – usually as identified as an issue in (an) earlier chapter(s), e.g.:

Self-instruction is not used in universities in Sierra Leone. Could it be - since Chapter 3 shows that self-instruction has proved useful in other countries?

3 How the chapter fills the gap, e.g.:

Suggests ways in which self-instruction might be used for teaching English as a foreign language in the national university of Sierra Leone.

4 A brief overview of what is in the chapter, e.g.:

Surveys and draws conclusions from the very limited use of self-instruction over the last twenty years in other subject areas and at various educational levels in Sierra Leone.

Edit the notes together to form the introductory paragraph, e.g.:

Self-instruction for teaching undergraduates is little used in Sierra Leone, even though the evidence from Chapter 3 shows that it has proved useful in other countries. The present chapter suggests ways in which self-instruction might be used as a means of teaching English as a foreign language in the national university of Sierra Leone. The chapter does so on the basis of surveying and discussing the very limited use of self-instruction over the last twenty years in other subject areas and at various educational levels in Sierra Leone.

Figure 20.1 A technique for developing the introductory paragraph of a thesis chapter

Write notes under each of the following:

1 What the chapter has done, e.g.:

> *Concluded that self-instruction could work well for teaching English as a foreign language in the national university of Sierra Leone.*

2 What new questions the chapter has identified, e.g.:

> *How should the self-instructional materials be developed? How should they be produced? How should the teachers be trained to use them?*

3 Where these questions are dealt with, e.g.:

> *In Chapters 7 and 8.*

Edit the notes together to form a concluding paragraph, e.g.:

> *This chapter has concluded that self-instruction could be usefully employed to teach English as a foreign language in the national university of Sierra Leone. The chapter has raised questions about how the self-instructional materials should be developed and produced, and how the teachers should be trained to use them. These questions are addressed in Chapters 7 and 8 respectively.*

Figure 20.2 A technique for developing the concluding paragraph of a thesis chapter

 ACTIVITY

Assume that you are about to write the introduction to a chapter of your thesis. If you are not ready to do this yet, practise the technique on any other piece of writing, such as an essay or report. Write a few keywords or some notes under each of the above headings and then edit them together into an introduction.

Imagine that you are about to write the concluding paragraph to a chapter of your thesis. Write a few keywords or some notes under each of the above headings and then edit them together into a concluding paragraph.

Cross-referencing in the thesis

A document as large as a thesis will inevitably require cross-references between sections and chapters, but during the drafting stage it is not possible to know what the page or section of the cross-reference will be. In principle, modern word processors can automate cross-referencing, but that would require working with a single, extremely large document. A more manageable alternative, at least in the early stages, is to work with separate documents (files) for each chapter. A low-tech technique is to call the cross-reference 'page ##' or 'section ##' to signify that a number (or something else) is to be put in later. The double symbol is less ambiguous than a single one because it is less likely to have a meaning of its own. When finalizing the thesis, all that is necessary is to use the 'find' command to locate all the ## symbols and replace them with a number (or the something else) which is now known. This is much easier than having to read through to locate all instances where a reference number is needed. The same technique can be used, along with a message to yourself, to indicate anywhere where you need to return for further work, although word processing 'comment' and 'bookmark' tools do the same job.

The writing process

Writing a thesis is generally a matter of progressively refining chapters in the light of their internal consistency and their relationship to other chapters. This cannot be done quickly, and most students underestimate the time it requires.

It is not usually worth trying to write the chapters of a thesis in sequence. Start with a chapter or several chapters that are currently fascinating you or that you have already come to grips with in your mind. Then develop them in whatever way is easiest for you, be it text on a computer, or scribble on blank sheets of paper, or as a mind map. The emphasis should be on producing a coherent structure, rather than on grammar or style. When you come to do the actual composition, it is most straightforward to do your own typing and then use the 'drawer treatment' as described in Chapter 13.

Ask your supervisor at what stage he or she would like to see the drafts. A common procedure is for students to write a chapter of a thesis, submit it to their supervisors and then rewrite to accommodate comments, but it is a mistake then to believe that the revised chapter is completely finished, never to need further modification. The 'storyline' of a thesis can never be clear from a single chapter. The full thesis is required, at least in draft. No supervisor will finally 'approve' a chapter in isolation. The scene-setting chapters are most likely to remain unchanged, but the analytical and interpretative ones depend too much on one another. According to most institutional regulations, the decision that a thesis is ready to submit is the student's, not the supervisor's. That is why 'approve' is in inverted commas, and it applies to the entire thesis as well as to any single chapter.

Updating drafts is so easy on a word processor that some students produce them copiously. So negotiate with your supervisor how many drafts he or she is prepared to comment on and in what detail. Most supervisors have to set some limits.

Your supervisor and you will have been very close indeed to your work for a considerable time. You, in particular, will know it inside out and back to front. So the links between its components may be clear to you both, while not being as clear to those who have met your work only recently. It is important to minimize misunderstandings and to find out as early as possible where you are not making yourself clear. Giving departmental seminars will have helped; as will giving conference presentations and writing journal articles. If you have not done any of these recently, then try to find someone new to your work who will listen to you explaining it or will read the draft thesis and tell you where they have trouble following it.

You must work through the final draft of the thesis in an editorial mode. Finalizing a thesis is always much more time-consuming than expected. The style must be academic; the text must be written to make a case; chapters have to be linked into a storyline; cross-references and 'pointers' need to be inserted to keep the reader orientated to what is where and why; there should be no typing or stylistic errors; and tables, figures and references should be complete, accurate and presented in whatever format has been agreed with the supervisor. Pay particular attention to the abstract, contents list, beginning and ends of chapters and the final chapter, as it is these which examiners tend to study first, and it is on these that they may form their impressions – and first impressions count.

There may be departmental or institutional guidelines on maximum length. For example, many require a doctoral thesis not to exceed 100,000 words.

Throughout the writing and editing process, be meticulous about keeping backups. Chapter 13 makes suggestions in this connection.

Most students, having word-processed drafts of their theses, choose to prepare the final versions themselves. Professional copy-editors and typists can, however, support to varying extents. If you need help, make enquiries well in advance of your deadline, because such individuals inevitably find that certain times of the year are busier than others. The departmental secretary or the students' union should be able to make recommendations.

Although most students underestimate the time that a thesis takes, it is also worth pointing out that many students spend longer than necessary, either conducting extra work to include or toying with refinements to the writing. The assertion of Box 20.2 should thus be regarded as highly pertinent advice.

Box 20.2   Finding an acceptable end-point for a thesis

A dissertation is never finished, it is just abandoned at the least damaging point.

(Race 1999: 121)

Presenting the thesis in accordance with institutional requirements

Institutions differ in their requirements for the presentation of a thesis. Normal practice is still for a thesis to be printed on paper rather than submitted electronically. There needs to be a title page which normally gives the officially approved thesis title, full name of candidate, title of degree and name of institution. This should normally be followed by an abstract of less than 300 words, a contents page and possibly also a list of diagrams, plates, maps, plans and tables. The normal regulations are that the text should be word-processed or typed using double or $1^1/2$ line spacing (except for indented quotations and footnotes, which should be single spaced) on one side only of A4 paper with $1^1/2$ inch or 300mm margins, and pages should be numbered continuously from the title page to the end, including all appendices and illustrations. Layout requirements should be easy to accommodate if you have used your word processor's 'styles' in the development of the thesis, as advised in Chapter 13. Copyright is normally retained by the student.

Institutions and possibly departments usually require a specified number of copies for their own records. Decide how many extra copies you will want for yourself and to give to people who have helped you. It is common politeness to give a copy to your supervisor, and to acknowledge him or her formally in the thesis, along with others who have helped, and it is a nice gesture to include a handwritten note of appreciation in the copy that you give your supervisor.

Theses are not cheap to bind, and professional binding takes time. So it is worth finding out early on whether or not the institution requires theses to be hard-bound at the time of any oral examination. Practices vary on this. If regulations allow theses to be unbound or soft-bound, so much the better, as examiners normally require at least a few amendments to be inserted into the final bound copies. Institutions normally insist on their own binding house style and nominate official binders. If there should be more than one, it is worth checking their prices, as costs of binding can vary considerably.

Use the following activity as a checklist of the salient presentational requirements of your institution.

 ACTIVITY

What are the requirements of your institution for thesis presentation in terms of the following?

• Number of copies

• Paper size, colour and weight

• Fonts and/or typefaces

• Methods of reproduction

- Layout (e.g. margin sizes and line spacing)

- Pagination (e.g. of front material as well as of main text)

- Style of title page

- Abstract

- Table of contents

- Illustrations, audio and video recordings, etc.

- Binding

- Style of print on binding

- Corrigenda – i.e. how errors may be corrected without retyping and rebinding

Do your institutional regulations require a thesis to be unbound or soft bound for the examination?

How long needs to be allowed for a thesis to be bound, who does the institution allow to do it, and how much does it cost?

21 PREPARING FOR THE EXAMINATION AND CONDUCTING YOURSELF IN THE ORAL/VIVA

> *Postgraduate research can be seen as a period of uncertainty, ambiguity and lack of structure. The task is not really complete until the oral examination is over.*
>
> (Mathias and Gale 1991: 10)

The importance of the examination

For the PhD and MPhil degrees in the United Kingdom, the examination is normally in two parts: first, the submission and preliminary assessment of the thesis; and second, its defence by oral examination, also called a viva. In some countries there is no oral examination for the PhD, while in others it is a very formal public occasion. This chapter is primarily for PhD and MPhil students who will be experiencing an oral examination of the sort which is standard practice in the United Kingdom. Candidates for other qualifications with a research component may also like to scan the chapter as it may suggest additional points to make in the thesis or be useful if a face-to-face examination should be required for purposes of quality control.

The decision as to whether or not the thesis is up to the required standard is tentatively taken before the oral examination. However, a poor performance in the oral may lead the examiners to question their decision, while a good performance can boost an unfavourable one into a pass. This is the main reason why it is in students' best interests to present themselves as well as they can. Other reasons are that the oral examination can be enjoyable, stimulating and useful.

Entering for the examination

With good working relationships between supervisors and students there will be a mutual agreement about when a student is ready to enter for the examination, although institutional legislation normally lays down that the responsibility belongs to the students. Clearly it would not be sensible to go against a supervisor's advice except in very special circumstances.

It is normally students, not their supervisors, who are responsible for obtaining, completing and delivering entry forms for the examination. So these need to be thought about several months ahead of time. If the thesis is not submitted within a specified time afterwards, the whole entry procedure has to be repeated.

Some months before your thesis is ready, your supervisor will nominate an external examiner to propose to the appropriate institutional committee. That person will have expertise in your field and be from another institution. While few supervisors would be naive enough to suggest a politically or methodologically incompatible examiner, it is in your own interests, where possible, to involve yourself in the selection. You will know the literature in your field, so your supervisor's suggestions should not come as a surprise, and you may even be able to suggest some possibilities yourself. Many supervisors would expect you to, although regulations in some institutions prevent students from even knowing the names of their examiners in advance.

There will almost certainly also be an internal examiner. The number and status of examiners depends on the regulations of the institution.

How orals/vivas are conducted

It is normal for oral examinations to take place at students' home institutions, which the external examiners visit. However, some institutions are considering cutting down on the time and costs of travel by arranging the contacts through video link.

There is no such thing as a typical oral examination (see Box 21.1). However, it is likely to last between one and three hours, although it seldom seems this long because everyone gets so involved in the discussion. The external examiner normally chairs and takes the lead. Being an expert in the topic, he or she is concerned primarily with that topic and with ensuring that standards are as near uniform as possible across institutions. The internal examiner's role is normally more one of organizing and administering the

Box 21.1 Some general points about orals/vivas

There is no such thing as a standard viva, but a few general points should be borne in mind. A candidate will not be expected to answer questions from memory and examiners will specify pages or passages in the thesis and allow time to look at them. Usually an examiner will give a general indication of how he or she feels about the thesis including areas of approval or of possible concern. Questions about what worries an examiner should not be taken as a sign that the candidate will be failed, but it is important that they should be answered directly and backed by references to the text of the thesis itself. Finally a candidate should always be prepared to discuss how the work presented by the thesis might be developed further, especially for publication.

(Smith 1991: 56)

examination, ensuring that it is conducted fairly and that appropriate institutional standards are set and maintained. The internal examiner is also likely to be concerned with the student's general knowledge of the wider field and with how the work being examined fits into that field. In some countries the examination is open to the public, and/or candidates may be expected to give seminars on their work.

Many students prefer not to have their supervisors with them at the oral examination because it can be inhibiting to explain their work in front of someone who knows it so thoroughly already. Supervisors can, however, be present in certain circumstances, depending on institutional regulations. So you should think about whether there are good reasons for this to happen in your case, and then discuss possibilities with your supervisor.

 ACTIVITY

It is sensible to find out as much as possible in advance about what is likely to happen in your oral examination. Ask around to find some answers to the following questions.

• Where will your oral examination take place?

- How long is the examination likely to last?

- How is the examination likely to be conducted?

- Can your supervisor attend, and would you want this to happen?

Preparing yourself for your oral/viva

Once you know who your examiners will be, it is sensible to find out what you can about them. You should certainly familiarize yourself with their work and find links between it and your own. If at all possible, ask around to find out their examination style.

Since the date of the oral may be several months after completion of your work, you will have to reread your thesis some days before, so that it is at your fingertips. An oral examination is often called a 'thesis defence', which may help you to prepare better. Reread your thesis as if trying to find fault. If possible, solicit the aid of a friend. Then prepare suitable defences. Defending is not the same as being defensive. If criticisms seem valid, prepare responses to show that you recognize this by saying, for example, what you would have liked to be able to do about them if there were more resources or if you had thought about them at the right time, or what you hope that other workers may still do about them. Box 21.2 suggests some questions to prepare for. It may be helpful to annotate your thesis, using 'Post-it' style stickers, so that you can find key areas quickly.

Common early questions are likely to be 'What did you enjoy most about your work?' or 'What would you do differently if you were starting out all over again?' These questions may appear to be simple pleasantries to put you at your ease, but they may mask skilful probing into how well you can appraise your own work and your personal development as a researcher and scholar. Unless you prepare for them, they may throw you and affect how you conduct yourself in the rest of the examination.

Examiners may ask you to present parts of your work orally. They often do this to check that a thesis is a student's own work and to gauge his or her understanding of it. Come prepared to talk through – and possibly also sketch out – the major 'route maps' through your work. This may mean repeating what is already written.

Box 21.2 Some questions to prepare for

(a) The 'context' of your research – which debates, issues, problems it is addressing.
(b) The 'red thread' of your research – the idea that binds it together.
(c) Its main findings, i.e. your (major) contribution(s) to knowledge.

It is one of the classic opening gambits of external examiners, after an initial question to set the candidate at ease, to ask a question along these lines.

(Clark 1991: 45)

You may also like to prepare some questions for the examiners, although whether or not you use them should be a matter of judgement at the time. You will certainly want to impress with the quality of your thinking, but it would be unwise to raise issues which could seem peripheral and to which examiners might not be able to respond readily. Suitable questions might concern information which examiners might have on recent related work elsewhere or advice on how to go about publishing your work.

You will want to be in good form for the examination. Do not think that drugs or alcohol or chewing gum will relax the tension. They will not. There is some evidence that they make performance worse, and they will probably lower the examiners' view of you. A clean handkerchief or box of tissues is good insurance, to wipe sweaty palms and even tears, although any tension should disappear rapidly once discussion gets under way.

 ACTIVITY

What can you find out about your external examiner's examining style?

What can you find out about your external examiner's own work?

What can you usefully find out about your internal examiner?

With the aid of staff and other students, develop a set of simple questions that examiners are likely to use to open the proceedings.

Prepare responses to these questions, orientated towards giving the impression that you are thoughtful and honest and that you appreciate what a research degree ought to be about.

Read through your thesis as if you were an examiner trying to criticize aspects of it, and develop a defence. Check this out, preferably with your supervisor, to make sure that it is reasonable and not defensive.

Prepare – with due sensitivity – some questions to ask or issues to raise with the examiners.

Setting up tokens of appreciation

In some departments it may be a normal courtesy to give some small token of appreciation to a supervisor, or to put on a celebration for other students. These may have to be set up in advance of the examination, even at the risk of tempting fate.

 ACTIVITY

You will probably already know the normal practice in the department for showing appreciation to examiners, the supervisor and other staff and students. If not, find out, and then adapt it to suit your own situation.

Dressing for the oral/viva

You would be well advised to choose clothes that are smart and businesslike, to show that you appreciate the importance of the occasion. The exception is where the external examiner is likely to be scruffy – effectively a form of 'uniform' in some areas of academia and with certain academics. Be guided by what is known about the way the examiners tend to dress, and do not upstage them. Whatever style of dress you eventually think appropriate, choose your outfit with care and make sure that it is both comfortable and reasonably cool to wear.

It may help to ask a friend to check over your outfit with you and spend time discussing options. If you have nothing suitable, consider buying or borrowing. Think about whether you would give a better impression if you did your hair differently – which applies to both sexes!

Conducting yourself in the oral/viva

Although it is understandable that you may be nervous at the prospect of the oral examination, most students find that they enjoy the experience of discussing their work with able and informed individuals. Remember, you are the world's expert on your work, and your supervisor and the resources of your department should have provided you with sound support throughout your period as a research student; if you are not considered ready to be examined, you should have been told – and if you are considered ready, everything should go smoothly.

There are, however, a few guidelines on conducting yourself:

- Take a pen and paper into the examination, along with your thesis.
- Act with composure. Say good morning or good afternoon when you enter the room, but do not speak again until you are spoken to, or until the discussion reaches the stage of exhilarated debate. The examiners will want you to be pleasant but they will not be impressed by gregariousness.
- Sit squarely on the chair, not poised on the edge. If there is anything about the room arrangement that disturbs you, ask politely for it to be changed.
- Show that you are listening attentively to the examiners' questions. They will expect you to argue, but try to do so without emotion, on the basis of evidence and keeping personalities out of it, showing that you take others' points of view seriously, even if you do not agree with them. If you are in doubt about what examiners mean or whether you have answered a question in the way they are expecting, ask for clarification. Don't defend every point; be prepared to concede some, but not too many.
- Don't hesitate to jot points down on paper if this helps you think.

Preparing for the result

It is not unknown for examiners to say at the beginning of the oral examination that the candidate has passed. Many examiners, however, would never consider doing so, in that it would invalidate the whole purpose of the examination. Normally, if everything goes smoothly, you will be told shortly afterwards that you have passed, subject as always to ratification by the institution.

In even the best theses, examiners often want small amendments. The supervisor, in conjunction with one of the examiners, is usually given the responsibility of ensuring that this work is carried out satisfactorily, without further formal examination.

If more substantial changes are required, or additional work needs to be done, the revised thesis has to be examined again at a later date. The student is given a specified time to conduct the further work and write it up, normally about 18 months – but it is advisable to start as soon as possible while the work is still fresh in one's mind.

The examiners have a number of other options, depending on the regulations of the institution. These include failing the thesis completely or awarding an MPhil instead of a PhD, if they feel that the thesis does not merit the award of a PhD.

22 AFTERWARDS!

There is no security on this earth; there is only opportunity.
(Douglas MacArthur, quoted in Tripp 1976: 447)

Handling the outcome of the examination

Having stuck with a postgraduate programme through to completion, it is normal to pass the final examination. However, in the case of a full research degree such as a PhD, the examiners generally require some amendments to the thesis. They may be so trivial for congratulations to be in order immediately. Or they may take some time to implement. Either way, it is best not to delay dealing with them, because the work is still fresh in your mind. If the examiners award an MPhil instead of a PhD or if anything should have gone seriously wrong, you will want to discuss the matter with your supervisor. If necessary, students' unions can normally supply professionals to advise on appeals.

You may expect to feel elated at your success. Other emotions, however, are not unusual, because the emotional build-up has been so great. A common emotion is detachment, as if this great thing has not really happened. Another is lack of purpose because a driving force of your life over a long period has been severed. After a while, though, your main emotion should be pride and a sense of personal confidence at having become uniquely knowledgeable in your chosen area.

It is a good idea, if you can, to take a short holiday to mark the end of your time as a student and to refresh yourself for getting on with the next stage of your life. If you would like this next stage to include publishing your research, either as a book or as journal articles, your supervisor will doubtless help, as will an interested publisher. Useful guides are referenced in the *further reading* section.

Into the rest of your life

The skills developed during your research programme will prove invaluable in the rest of your professional life. This is not only true where they relate directly to your discipline area. The so-called personal transferable skills considered in Chapter 15 are equally important and will prove their worth whether your career develops

---

Box 22.1 Skills for succeeding in your career

The following comment is from the co-author of *Skills for Graduates in the 21st Century*, a report by the Association of Graduate Recruiters.

Will graduates need IT skills? Of course they will. Will they need foreign language skills? Of course they will. But will those skills be the defining skills of the 21st century? I don't think so. The skills for the future include self-promotion, action planning, networking, coping with uncertainty and 'political awareness' – or an understanding of the hidden tensions and power struggles within organisations.

(Jonathan Winter, as reported by Targett 1995: 5)

Box 22.2 Recognizing the obstacles to career advancement

The first step in dealing with obstacles to career advancement is to recognize them, for which the following list is revealing. It was written for women, but minor adaptation can make it useful, either generally or for specific disadvantaged groups.

- *Old-school tie network*
- *People staying in positions a long time*
- *Barriers in larger traditional, male-dominated organizations*
- *Less mentoring (formal and informal) for women*
- *Lack of confidence*
- *Dislike of playing office politics*
- *False assumption that competence and ability are enough*

(Bogan 1999: 9)

Box 22.3 Planning the direction of a career path

Career planning for those in the fast lane is not scientific. It is mostly to do with spotting and taking advantage of opportunities.
(Mileham 1995: 32)

There is no such thing as a career path – it's crazy paving, and you have to lay it yourself.
(Robin Linnecar, quoted in
Association for Graduate Recruiters 1995: 12)

---

inside or outside the field of your postgraduate study. It is crucial, though, to appreciate that you will, like everyone else, need to keep on learning. Professional skills rapidly need to be updated as new practices overtake existing ones. So much is generally appreciated. Perhaps less appreciated, though, is the ongoing need to reappraise and improve how you are interacting with the people and situations around you, to discern and handle internal politics and to recognize and grasp opportunities which may arrive unexpectedly and last only fleetingly. Boxes 22.1, 22.2 and 22.3 make these points well.

In general terms, perhaps the two most important skills for your future are those of identifying what your next learning requirement is and then finding a way to accommodate it. The term 'lifelong learning' encapsulates the idea.

USEFUL WEBSITES

There is a considerable amount of information on the worldwide web which is likely to be very useful indeed to research students. There is also a great deal more which could be useful to some research students some of the time, and there is more still which looks appealing at first sight, but turns out to be of questionable value. This is one reason why it has been difficult to decide which sites to reference here and which ones to leave out. A second reason is that sites link to one another, which means, in theory at least, that it would be reasonable to omit certain potentially useful sites on the assumption that users would find them anyway from the sites that are referenced.

These problems have been resolved, at least in part, as follows. The *general interest* section lists the home pages of organizations which are likely to be particularly useful to research students. It is assumed that you will use the links in these sites to explore other sites, according to your own interests and needs. Sites are next suggested (where applicable) according to the chapter topics in the book. Where a site in the *general interest* section is particularly pertinent, it is again referenced, along with other sites that are also pertinent. Sites which are effectively lecture notes on aspects of research are not included because, for students who are not on the programmes for which the notes were written, the sites are generally inferior to textbooks.

Some cautions are in order for using the web:

- Information can be put onto the web without any external control whatsoever. So it may be experimental, it may not come from a reputable source, and it may be inaccurate or out of date.
- Websites which are readily accessible on one day may no longer be so the next. Perhaps whoever mounted the site is no longer maintaining it, or the address has changed, or the site has been put onto a subscription basis.

So it is safest to consider the following sites as no more than *samples* to illustrate the scope and type of information and support which may be available on the web. Use the list to stimulate your thinking about what else to search for and follow the links to visit other sites which may turn out to be more useful for your purpose. If the accuracy of the information on any site is crucial for you, don't act on it without checking on the actual position with your supervisor, or the office dealing with postgraduate matters (or its equivalent) in your institution, or other sources of professional advice. They may also be able to help where sites are accessible on a subscription basis.

All the following websites were accessible at the time of going to press, but that does not guarantee that they will still be when you read this. In all probability, some sites will certainly not be, which is a frustrating and time-wasting fact of life. However, you can find renamed sites or alternative sites by searching for words or phrases using an up-to-date search engine. Your institution should be able to advise you on current options. Box 3.2 in Chapter 3 should get you started, although you should expect to be presented with sites that you don't ask for along with those that you do.

General interest

The (UK) National Postgraduate Committee
Also for links to the national postgraduate associations of various countries and to institutional postgraduate associations within the UK: www.npc.org.uk

Universities UK (formerly the Committee of Vice-Chancellors and Principals of the Universities of the United Kingdom)
www.universitiesUK.ac.uk

The web gateway on research supervision for all fields of study
For a search facility useful to research students:
www.iah.bbsrc.ac.uk/supervisor-training

Prospects – set up by Higher Education Careers Services Unit
www.prospects.csu.ac.uk

The Research Councils of the United Kingdom:
Arts and Humanities Research Board: www.ahrb.ac.uk
Biotechnology and Biological Sciences Research Council: www.bbsrc.ac.uk
Economic and Social Research Council: www.esrc.ac.uk
  In particular the link to postgraduate training and the studentship holder's handbook: www.esrc.ac.uk/postgrad.html
Engineering and Physical Sciences Research Council: www.epsrc.ac.uk
Medical Research Council: www.mrc.ac.uk
Natural Environment Research Council: www.nerc.ac.uk
Particle Physics and Astronomy Research Council: www.pparc.ac.uk

The Council for International Education (UKCOSA)
www.ukcosa.org.uk

The UK Council for Graduate Education
www.ukcge.ac.uk

The British Council
www.britcoun.org

Mailbase lists (covering a range of topics from a range of viewpoints)
www.jiscmail.ac.uk

By chapter

Where no website is suggested, it is always worth conducting a search on a specific or related aspect.

1 Introduction

Learning styles:
Links from: www.namss.org.uk/lstyles.htm
Links from: www2.ncsu.edu/unity/lockers/users/f/felder/public/Learning_Styles.html

2 Exploring the opportunities for postgraduate study and research

General opportunities:
Links from: www.scit.wlv.ac.uk/ukinfo/uk.map.html
Links from: www.prospects.csu.ac.uk

Opportunities by distance learning:
Links from: www-icdl.open.ac.uk

Web searching tools:
www.cln.org/searching_faqs.html
www.jisc.ac.uk/services/index.html

3 Liaising with institutions

The websites of the institutions concerned.

Funding issues:
Links from: www.prospects.csu.ac.uk

4 Setting yourself up in a supportive way of life

Being a part-time student/working during the postgraduate programme:
Links from: www.prospects.csu.ac.uk

Coping with isolation:
Links from: www.jiscmail.ac.uk

Coping with disabilities:
www.student.city.ac.uk/~cx639/pgdis.htm

5 Settling in as a new student

Opportunities for induction and general training
The website of your own institution and possibly also, for comparison purposes, the websites of other institutions.

Courses on IT skills for the UK Higher Education Community:
www.netskills.ac.uk

On-line tutorials on IT packages:
www.lgta.org

On-line citation index:
www.bids.com

Other types of on-line information:
www.mcb.co.uk/forums.htm
www.tucows.com

Sources of downloadable software:
www.microsoft.com

6 Towards recognizing quality in research

Opportunities for general (non-discipline-specific) training:
The website of your own institution and possibly also, for comparison purposes, the websites of other institutions.

Training in the social sciences (mounted by the Economic and Social Research Council (ESRC) and the Joint Information Systems Committee (JISC) of the United Kingdom):
www.jisc.ac.uk/subject/socsci

Training and information geared towards the needs of students in art, design, media and related fields of study:
www.biad.uce.ac.uk/research/guides/index.html

7 Interacting with your supervisor(s)

Interacting with people generally:
www.keirsey.com

Complaints procedures:
www.npc.org.uk

Aspects of supervision (primarily for supervisors and academic managers, but also of interest to students):
Links to the SRHE Postgraduate Issues Network from: cryer.freeserve.co.uk
and www.srhe.ac.uk
Links from: www.ukcge.ac.uk and www.iah.bbsrc.ac.uk/supervisor-training

8 Keeping records

9 Planning ahead

10 Managing yourself and your time

Understanding yourself and how you interact with others:
www.keirsey.com
www2.ncsu.edu/unity/lockers/users/f/felder/public/Learning_Styles.html
www.srg.co.uk
www.shlgroup.com/direct

11 Taking responsibility for your own progress

Taking paid work during the postgraduate programme:
Links from: www.prospects.csu.ac.uk

Intellectual property and copyright laws:
www.cla.co.uk
www.nla.co.uk
www.european-patent-office.org
www.patent.gov.uk
www.european-patent-office.org/espacenet/info
www.patents.ibm.com/
See also Box 11.3

12 Cooperating with others for mutual help and support

Interacting with people generally:
www.keirsey.com
www.mailbase.ac.uk

Interacting with other postgraduates:
www.npc.org.uk
www.mailbase.ac.uk

Contacting people:
www.bt.com/phonenetuk
www.lookupuk.com/index.html
www.teldir.com

Locating postal addresses:
www.streetmap.co.uk

13 Producing reports

14 Giving presentations on your work

On-line tutorials on PowerPoint:
www.lgta.org

15 Using the research programme as preparation for employment

The website of your own institution and, for non-local local employment opportunities, the websites of other institutions.

Links from: www.namss.org.uk

Opportunities for training in skills-development and support in preparing for and finding employment
www.crac.org.uk

Employment opportunities generally:
Links from www.careers.lon.ac.uk/jobseek
Links from www.hobsons.com

Links from www.jobs.ac.uk
Links from www.nesta.org.uk
Links from www.npc.org.uk
Links from www.phdjobs.com
Links from www.prospects.csu.ac.uk
Links from www.shlgroup.com/direct

16 Progress checks and hurdles – and the transfer from MPhil to PhD

The website of your own institution and possibly also, for comparison purposes, the websites of other institutions.

17 Coming to terms with originality in research

18 Developing skills for creative thinking

19 Dealing with flagging

20 Producing your thesis

The website of your own institution, and possibly also, for comparison purposes, the websites of other institutions.

21 Preparing for the examination and conducting yourself in the oral/viva

The website of your own institution, and possibly also, for comparison purposes, the websites of other institutions.

Dealing with people assertively:
www.keirsey.com

22 Afterwards!

Appeals procedures:
www.npc.org.uk

FURTHER READING

If I have seen further, it is by standing on the shoulders of giants.
(Sir Isaac Newton, letter to Robert Hooke)

This section lists some tried and tested print-based material which is likely to be useful to research students across all fields of study. Where the title implies orientation towards a specific discipline the usefulness is, in fact, more general.

The list cannot be comprehensive because new material is constantly becoming available. So a good approach is to identify the location/classification numbers of items in the list and then browse along titles which are adjacent to them, either on the shelves in a library or in an on-line catalogue. You may also find it useful to refer to the lists in the following sections of the book: the *select bibliography* gives the major works consulted in the preparation of the book; the *references* section gives full bibliographical references for all the quotations in the book; and the *websites* section lists potentially useful sites on the worldwide web.

No general reading list can ever be a substitute for the advice of supervisors and other researchers in your field and for literature in that field. You need to seek out both. You may also find it worthwhile to explore what is available through the learned society or professional body for your subject.

Of general interest

CSU (Careers Service Unit) (ongoing) *The Prospects Postgraduate Series*. Manchester: Careers Service Unit. Available from institutional careers offices and on-line (see *websites* section).

National Postgraduate Committee (1995) *The Postgraduate Book*, 2nd edn. Brandon House, Troon, Ayrshire, KA10 6HX.

Phillips, E. and Pugh, D. (2000) *How to get a PhD*, 3rd edn. Buckingham: Open University Press.

Rudestam, K. and Newton, R. (1992) *Surviving your Dissertation*. London: Sage.

Salmon, P. (1992) *Achieving a PhD – Ten Students' Experiences*. Stoke-on-Trent: Trentham Books.

1 Introduction

On study skills at undergraduate and taught aspects of masters-level work:
Freeman, R. and Meed, J. (1993) *How to Study Effectively*. Hammersmith: CollinsEducational.
Marshall, L. and Rowland, F. (1999) *A Guide to Learning Independently*, 3rd edn. Buckingham: Open University Press.
Race, P. (1999) *How to get a Good Degree*. Buckingham: Open University Press.

2 Exploring the opportunities for postgraduate study and research

3 Liaising with an institution

See publications from individual institutions.

4 Setting yourself up in a supportive way of life

On being a part-time student:
Bourner, T. and Race, P. (1990) *How to Win as a Part-time Student*. London: Kogan Page.

On being a woman student:
Vartuli, S. (ed.) (1982) *The PhD Experience: A Woman's Point of View*. New York: Praeger.

On handling cultural differences (a booklet primarily for supervisors, but it is also enlightening for students):
Okorocha, O. (1997) *Supervising Overseas Research Students: Issues in Postgraduate Supervision, Teaching and Management, Guide no 1*. London: Society for Research into Higher Education/*Times Higher Education Supplement*.

On handling research based in or for an outside organization (booklets primarily for supervisors, but it is also enlightening for students):
Denicolo, P. (1999) *Supervising Students from Public Sector Organisations: Issues in Postgraduate Supervision, Teaching and Management, Guide no 5*. London: Society for Research into Higher Education/*Times Higher Education Supplement*.
Smith, A. and Gilby, J. (1999) *Supervising Students on Industrial-based Projects: Issues in Postgraduate Supervision, Teaching and Management, Guide no 4*. London: Society for Research into Higher Education/*Times Higher Education Supplement*.

5 Settling in as a new student

On office accommodation:
Gross, B. (1994) Accommodation of research students. *Journal of Graduate Education*, 1(1): 21–4.
National Postgraduate Committee (1995) *Guidelines on Accommodation and Facilities for Postgraduate Research*. For availability see http://www.npc.org.uk

6 Towards recognizing quality in research

On the nature of the PhD in different disciplines (this is for interest only – be guided by your supervisor for research in your discipline area):
Advisory Board for the Research Councils (1993) *The Nature of the PhD*, London: ABRC.

On different approaches to research and research methodology:
Denzin, N. and Lincoln, Y. (eds) (1994) *Handbook of Qualitative Research*. Beverly Hills, CA: Sage.
Guba, E. and Lincoln, Y. (1988) Do inquiry paradigms imply inquiry methodologies? in D. Fetterman (ed.) *Qualitative Approaches to Evaluation in Education*. New York: Praeger.
Robson, C. (1993) *Real World Research*. Oxford: Blackwell.
Saloman, G. (1991) Transcending the qualitative-quantitative debate: the anatomy of systematic approaches to educational research. *Educational Researcher*, 20(6): 10–18.

On research design:
Bell, J. (1999) *Doing Your Research Project*, 3rd edn. Buckingham: Open University Press.
Blaxter, L., Hughes, G. and Tight, M. (1996) *How to Research*. Buckingham: Open University Press.
Howard, K. and Sharp, J. (1983) *The Management of a Student Research Project*. Aldershot: Gower.
Leedy, P. (1997) *Practical Research – Planning and Design*. Upper Saddle River, NJ: Merrill (Prentice Hall).
Madsen, D. (1983) *Successful Dissertations and Theses: A Guide to Graduate Student Research from Proposal to Completion*. San Francisco: Jossey Bass.
Sharp, J. (1996) *The Management of a Student Research Project*, 2nd edn. Aldershot: Gower.

On conducting a literature review:
Hart, C. (1998) *Doing a Literature Review*. London: Sage.

On compiling arguments, counter-arguments and discussion:
Fairbairn, G. and Winch, C. (1996) *Reading, Writing and Reasoning*, 2nd edn. Buckingham: Society for Research into Higher Education and Open University Press.
Pirie, D. (1991) *How to Write Critical Essays*. London: Routledge.

On procedures for style and documentation in writing up research:
Turabian, K. (1993) *A Manual for Writers of Research Papers, Theses and Dissertations*, rev ed edn. Cambridge: Cambridge University Press.

7 Interacting with your supervisor(s)

On being assertive when dealing with people:
Back, K. and Bac K. (1982) *Assertiveness at Work*. London: McGraw-Hill.

On supervisory practices:
HEFCE (Higher Education Funding Council for England) (1996) *HEFCE/CVCP/SCOP Review of Postgraduate Education*. London: HEFCE.

Quality Assurance Agency (1999) *Code of Practice for the Assurance of Academic Quality and Standards in Higher Education: Postgraduate Research Programmes.* Gloucester: QAA.

National Postgraduate Committee (1995) *Guidelines for Codes of Practice for Postgraduate Research* (for availability see NPC website in the *websites* section).

On support for supervisors:

Cryer, P. (1997) *Handling Common Dilemmas in Supervision: Issues in Postgraduate Supervision, Teaching and Management, Guide no 2.* London: Society for Research into Higher Education/*Times Higher Education Supplement.*

Cryer, P. (ed.) (1998) *Developing Postgraduates' Key Skills: Issues in Postgraduate Supervision, Teaching and Management, Guide no 3.* London: Society for Research into Higher Education/*Times Higher Education Supplement.*

Delamont, S., Atkinson, P. and Parry, O. (1997) *Supervising the PhD: A Guide to Success.* Buckingham: Society for Research into Higher Education and Open University Press.

Denicolo, P. (1999) *Supervising Students from Public Sector Organisations: Issues in Postgraduate Supervision, Teaching and Management, Guide no 5.* London: Society for Research into Higher Education/*Times Higher Education Supplement.*

Okorocha, O. (1997) *Supervising Overseas Research Students: Issues in Postgraduate Supervision, Teaching and Management, Guide no 1.* London: Society for Research into Higher Education/*Times Higher Education Supplement.*

Smith, A. and Gilby, J. (1999) *Supervising Students on Industrial-based Projects: Issues in Postgraduate Supervision, Teaching and Management, Guide no 4.* London: Society for Research into Higher Education/*Times Higher Education Supplement.*

On complaints procedures:

National Postgraduate Committee (1995) *Guidelines for the Conduct of Research Degree Appeals* (for availability see http://www.npc.org.uk).

Staniford, D. (1998) 'Complaints in practice: complaints in crisis. A complaints survey carried out by the National Postgraduate Committee and the Union of UEA students.' Unpublished report (contact don.staniford@virgin.net).

8 Keeping records

The books in the 'Of general interest' section also give some advice on keeping records.

9 Planning ahead

Meredith, J. and Mantel, S. (1995) *Project Management, a Managerial Approach,* 3rd edn. New York and Chichester: Wiley.

10 Managing yourself and your time

The books in the 'Of general interest' section also give advice on managing time. In addition, there is no shortage of books on time management generally, but these need to be adapted for the particular circumstances of research students.

On taking on teaching work:
Many institutions have their own support materials on this topic.

National Postgraduate Committee (1994) *Guidelines for Employment of Postgraduate Students as Teachers* (for availability see http://www.npc.org.uk).

11 Taking responsibility for your own progress

The books in the 'Of general interest' section also give advice on managing your own progress.

12 Cooperating with others for mutual help and support

On asserting oneself with others:
Back, K. and Back, K. (1982) *Assertiveness at Work*. London: McGraw-Hill.

On intellectual property rights:
The law on intellectual property is constantly changing, and there is always a fear that written information may not be current. Note the recommended reading in Box 11.3, and then seek expert advice. Note also the websites listed in the *websites* section

13 Producing reports

Blicq, R.S. (1987) *Writing Reports to Get Results: Guidelines for the Computer Age*. New York: Electrical and Electronic Engineers Press.
Booth, V. (1985) *Communicating in Science: Writing and Speaking*. Cambridge: Cambridge University Press.
Collinson, D., Kirkup, G., Kyd, R. and Slocombe, L. (1992) *Plain English*. Buckingham: Open University Press.

14 Giving presentations on your work

On general presentational techniques:
Hamlin, D. (1989) *How to Talk So People Listen*. Wellingborough: Thorsons.
Tufte, E.R. (1983) *The Visual Display of Quantitative Information*. Cheshire, CT: Graphics Press.

On computer-aided presentations:
See any of the wide range of manuals and textbooks on computing, in particular those on PowerPoint.

15 Using the research programme as preparation for employment

See publications from individual institutions and in particular the 'Prospects' and 'AGCAS' series which should be available from institutional careers offices.

On skills development, skills for employment and lifelong learning:
Association of Graduate Recruiters (1995) *Skills for Graduates in the 21st Century*. Cambridge: Association of Graduate Recruiters.
Belbin, R.M. (1996) *Management Teams – Why They Succeed or Fail*. Oxford: Butterworth-Heinemann.
Purcell, K. and Pitcher, J. (1997) *Great Expectations: the New Diversity of Graduate Skills and Aspirations*. Manchester: Central Services Higher Education Unit, Institute for Employment Research and Association of Graduate Careers Advisory Services.

16 Progress checks and hurdles – and the transfer from MPhil to PhD

On the nature of the landmarks and institutional procedures:
See publications from individual institutions.

On writing and structuring reports:
Barrass, R. (1991) *Scientists Must Write*. London: Chapman & Hall.
Becker, H. (1986) *Writing for Social Scientists*. Chicago: University of Chicago Press.
Blicq, R.S. (1987) *Writing Reports to Get Results: Guidelines for the Computer Age*. New York: Electrical and Electronic Engineers Press.
Booth, V. (1985) *Communicating in Science: Writing and Speaking*. Cambridge: Cambridge University Press.
Day, R.A. (1988) *How to Write and Publish a Scientific Paper*, 3rd edn. Cambridge: Cambridge University Press.

On compiling arguments, counter-arguments and discussion:
Fairbairn, G. and Winch, C. (1996) *Reading, Writing and Reasoning*, 2nd edn. Buckingham: Society for Research into Higher Education and Open University Press.
Pirie, D. (1991) *How to Write Critical Essays*. London: Routledge.

On procedures for style and documentation in writing up research:
Turabian, K. (1993) *A Manual for Writers of Research Papers, Theses and Dissertations*, revised edn. Cambridge: Cambridge University Press.

17 Coming to terms with originality in research

Phillips, E. and Pugh, D. (2000) *How to get a PhD*, 3rd edn. Buckingham: Open University Press.

18 Developing skills for creative thinking

Buzan, T. (1989) *Use Your Head*, revised edn. London: BBC Publications.
De Bono, E. (1991) *Serious Creativity*. London: HarperCollins.
Kemp, R. and Race, P. (1992) Promoting the development of personal and professional skills, module 10 of P. Cryer (ed.) *Effective Learning and Teaching in Higher Education*. Sheffield: Universities' Staff Development Unit.

19 Dealing with flagging

Fontana, D. (1993) *Managing Stress*. Leicester: British Psychological Society and Routledge.
Salmon, P. (1992) *Achieving a PhD – Ten Students' Experiences*. Stoke-on-Trent: Trentham Books.

20 Producing your thesis

On writing and structuring reports:
Barrass, R. (1991) *Scientists Must Write*. London: Chapman & Hall.
Becker, H. (1986) *Writing for Social Scientists*. Chicago: University of Chicago Press.
Blicq, R.S. (1987) *Writing Reports to Get Results: Guidelines for the Computer Age*. New York: Electrical and Electronic Engineers Press.
Day, R.A. (1988) *How to Write and Publish a Scientific Paper*, 3rd edn. Cambridge: Cambridge University Press.

On compiling argument, counter-argument and discussion:
Fairbairn, G. and Winch, C. (1993) *Reading, Writing and Reasoning*. Buckingham: Society for Research into Higher Education and Open University Press.
Pirie, D. (1991) *How to Write Critical Essays*. London: Routledge.

On procedures for style and documentation in writing up research:
Turabian, K. (1993) *A Manual for Writers of Research Papers, Theses and Dissertations*, revised edn. Cambridge: Cambridge University Press.

On thesis writing:
Allison, K. (1997) *Student Guide for Preparing Dissertations*. London: Kogan Page.

21 Preparing for the examination and conducting yourself in the oral/viva

On the oral examination:
Burnham, P. (1994) 'Surviving the viva: unravelling the mysteries of the PhD oral'. *Journal of Graduate Education*, 1(1): 30 4.

On dealing with people assertively:
Back, K. and Back, K. (1982) *Assertiveness at Work*. London: McGraw-Hill.

22 Afterwards!

On turning the thesis into a book:
Delamont, S., Atkinson, P. and Parry, O. (1997) *Supervising the PhD: A Guide to Success*, 2nd edn. Society for Research into Higher Education and Open University Press.
Harman, E. and Montagnes, I. (eds) (1976) *The Thesis and the Book*. Toronto: Toronto University Press.

On appeals procedures:

National Postgraduate Committee (1995) *Guidelines for the Conduct of Research Degree Appeals* (for availability see http://www.npc.org.uk).

On career development:

See under 15 above.

SELECT BIBLIOGRAPHY

This select bibliography contains those more significant works consulted during the preparation of this book which are not listed in the *references* section.

Advisory Board for the Research Councils (1993) *The Nature of the PhD.* London: ABRC.

Allan, G. and Skinner, C. (eds) (1991) *Handbook for Research Students in the Social Sciences.* Brighton: Falmer Press.

Back, K. and Back, K. (1982) *Assertiveness at Work.* London: McGraw-Hill.

Barrass, R. (1991) *Scientists Must Write.* London: Chapman & Hall.

Becher, T., Henkel, M. and Kogan, M. (1994) *Graduate Education in Britain.* London: Jessica Kingsley.

Becker, H. (1986) *Writing for Social Scientists.* Chicago: University of Chicago Press.

Bell, J. (1999) *Doing Your Research Project*, 3rd edn. Buckingham: Open University Press.

Bennect, R. and Knubbs, J. (1986) Researching for a higher degree: the role(s) of the supervisor, *Management Education and Development*, 17(2): 137–45.

Blicq, R.S. (1987) *Writing Reports to Get Results: Guidelines for the Computer Age.* New York: Electrical and Electronic Engineers Press.

Bourner, T. and Hughes, M. (1991) Joint supervision of research degrees, *Higher Education Review*, 24: 21–34.

Bourner, T. and Race, P. (1990) *How to Win as a Part-time Student.* London: Kogan Page.

Bowen, W. and Rudenstine, N. (1992) *In Pursuit of the PhD.* Princeton, NJ: Princeton University Press.

Brown, S., McDowell, L. and Race, P. (1996) *500 Tips for Research Students.* London: Kogan Page.

Bruce, S. (1994) Research students' early experiences of the dissertation literature review, *Studies in Higher Education*, 19(2): 217–29.

Burgess, R. (ed.) (1994) *Postgraduate Education and Training in the Social Sciences: Processes and Products.* London: Jessica Kingsley.

Burgess, R. (ed.) (1997) *Beyond the First Degree*. Buckingham: Society for Research into Higher Education and Open University Press.

Burnham, P. (1994) Surviving the viva: unravelling the mysteries of the PhD oral, *Journal of Graduate Education*, 1(1): 30–4.

Buzan, T. (1989) *Use Your Head*, revised edn. London: BBC Publications.

Committee of Vice-Chancellors and Principals/Committee of Directors of Polytechnics (1992) *The Management of Higher Degrees Undertaken by Overseas Students*. London: CVCP/CDP.

Cryer, P. (1988) Transferable skills, marketability and lifelong learning: the particular case of postgraduate research students, *Studies in Higher Education*, 23(2): 207–16.

Cryer, P. (1996) Training research students and supporting supervisors through self-study materials customised for the research student, *Journal of Graduate Education*, 2(2): 44–52.

Cryer, P. (ed.) (1998) *Guide 3: Developing Postgraduates' Key Skills*. London: Society for Research into Higher Education/*Times Higher Education Supplement*.

Day, R.A. (1988) *How to Write and Publish a Scientific Paper*, 3rd edn. Cambridge: Cambridge University Press.

Delamont, S., Atkinson, P. and Parry, O. (1997) *Supervising the PhD: A Guide to Success*, 2nd edn. Buckingham: Society for Research into Higher Education and Open University Press.

Denicolo, P., Entwistle, N. and Hounsell, D. (1992) What is active learning? module 1 of P. Cryer (ed.) *Effective Learning and Teaching in Higher Education*. Sheffield: Universities' Staff Development Unit.

Economic and Social Research Council (undated) *Postgraduate Training*. Swindon: Economic and Social Research Council.

Elton, L. and Pope, M. (1989) Research supervision: the value of collegiality, *Cambridge Journal of Education*, 19: 267–76.

Freeman, R. and Meed, J. (1993) *How to Study Effectively*. Hammersmith: CollinsEducational.

Goleman, D. (1996) *Emotional Intelligence*. London: Bloomsbury.

Goleman, D. (1998) *Working with Emotional Intelligence*. London: Bloomsbury.

Graham, A. and Grant, B. (1997) *Managing More Postgraduate Research Students*. Oxford: The Oxford Centre for Staff Development.

Guba, E. (1978) *Towards a Methodology of Naturalistic Enquiry*. Los Angeles: Center for the Study of Education.

Guba, E. and Lincoln, Y. (1988) Do inquiry paradigms imply inquiry methodologies? in D. Fetterman (ed.) *Qualitative Approaches to Evaluation in Education*. New York: Praeger.

Hamilton, J. (ed.) (1990) *They Made Our World*. London: BBC Publications.

Hamlin, D. (1989) *How To Talk So People Listen*. Wellingborough: Thorsons.

Hampson, L. (1994) *How's Your Dissertation Going?* Lancaster: Unit for Innovation in Higher Education.

Harman, E. and Montagnes, I. (eds) (1976) *The Thesis and the Book*. Toronto: Toronto University Press.

Hector Taylor, M. and Bonsall, M. (eds) (1993) *Successful Study*. Sheffield: Hallamshire Press.

HMSO (1976) *British Standard 1629: Recommendations for Bibliographical References*. London: HMSO.

HMSO (1978) *British Standard 5605: Recommendations for Citing Publications by Bibliographical References*. London: HMSO.

HMSO (1990) *British Standard 4821: Recommendations for the Presentation of Theses*. London: HMSO.

Howard, K. and Sharp, J. (1983) *The Management of a Student Research Project*. Aldershot: Gower.

Jankowicz, A. (1995) *Business Research Projects*. London: International Thomson Business Press.

Katz, J. and Hartnett, R. (eds) (1976) *Scholars in the Making*. Cambridge, MA: Ballinger.

Kemp, R. and Race, P. (1992) Promoting the development of personal and professional skills, module 10 of P. Cryer (ed.) *Effective Learning and Teaching in Higher Education*. Sheffield: Universities' Staff Development Unit.

Kirkman, J. (1975) That pernicious passive voice, *Physics in Technology*, September: 197–200.

Knight, P. (ed.) (1997) *Materclass: Learning, Teaching and Curriculum in Taught Master's Degrees*. London: Cassell.

Leedy, P. (1997) *Practical Research – Planning and Design*, Upper Saddle River, NJ: Merrill.

Lewis, V. and Habeshaw, S. (1997) *53 Interesting Ways to Supervise Student Projects, Dissertations and Theses*. Bristol: Technical and Educational Services Ltd.

Maddox, H. (1988) *How to Study*. London: Pan.

Madsen, D. (1983) *Successful Dissertations and Theses: A Guide to Graduate Student Research from Proposal to Completion*. San Francisco: Jossey-Bass.

Meredith, J. and Mantel, S. (1995) *Project Management: A Managerial Approach*, 3rd edn. New York and Chichester: Wiley.

Moses, I. (1984) Supervision of higher degree students – problem areas and possible solutions, *Higher Education Research and Development*, 3(2): 153–65.

Moses, I. (1985) *Supervising Postgraduates*. Kensington, NSW: Higher Education Research and Development Society of Australasia.

National Postgraduate Committee (1993) *The Postgraduate Book*. For availability see http://www.npc.org.uk

National Postgraduate Committee (1994a) *Annual Report 1993–1994*. Brandon House, Troon, Ayrshire, KA10 6HX.

National Postgraduate Committee (1994b) *Guidelines for Employment of Postgraduate Students as Teachers*. Brandon House, Troon, Ayrshire, KA10 6HX.

National Postgraduate Committee (1995a) *Guidelines for the Conduct of Research Degree Appeals*. Brandon House, Troon, Ayrshire, KA10 6HX.

National Postgraduate Committee (1995b) *Guidelines on Accommodation and Facilities for Postgraduate Research*. Brandon House, Troon, Ayrshire, KA10 6HX.

Noble, K. (1994) *Changing Doctoral Degrees: An International Perspective.* Buckingham: Society for Research into Higher Education and Open University Press.

Office of Science and Technology (1994) *Consultative Document: A New Structure for Postgraduate Research Training Supported by the Research Councils.* London: HMSO.

Open University Course Team (1999) *Doing Academic Research.* Milton Keynes: The Open University.

Patton, M.Q. (1990) *Qualitative Evaluation and Research Methods.* Beverly Hills, CA: Sage.

Phillips, E. (1991) Learning to do research, in N. Smith and D. Dainty (eds) *The Management Research Handbook.* London: Routledge.

Phillips, E. (1994) Avoiding communication breakdown, in O. Zuber-Skerritt and Y. Ryan (eds) *Quality in Postgraduate Education.* London: Kogan Page.

Phillips, E. and Pugh, D. (2000) *How to get a PhD,* 3rd edn. Buckingham: Open University Press.

Pirie, D. (1991) *How to Write Critical Essays.* London: Routledge.

Pratt, J.M. (1984) Writing your thesis, *Chemistry in Britain,* 20: 1114–15.

Quality Assurance Agency (1999) *Code of Practice for the Assurance of Academic Quality and Standards in Higher Education: Postgraduate Research Programmes.* Gloucester: QAA.

Rist, R. (1977) On the relations among educational paradigms: from distain to detente, *Anthropology and Education Quarterly,* 8: 42–9.

Robson, C. (1993) *Real World Research.* Oxford: Blackwell.

Rowntree, D. (1988) *Learn How to Study.* London: Warner.

Rudestam, K. and Newton, R. (1992) *Surviving Your Dissertation.* London: Sage.

Ryan, Y. and Zuber-Skerritt, O. (eds) (1999) *Supervising Postgraduates from Non-English Speaking Backgrounds.* Buckingham: Society for Research into Higher Education and Open University Press.

Stephenson, B. (ed.) (1967) *Home Book of Quotations: Classical and Modern.* New York: Dood, Mead.

Tripp, R. (1976) *The International Thesaurus of Quotations.* Harmondsworth: Penguin.

Tufte, E.R. (1983) *The Visual Display of Quantitative Information.* Cheshire, CT: Graphics Press.

Turabian, K. (1993) *A Manual for Writers of Research Papers, Theses and Dissertations,* revised edn. Cambridge: Cambridge University Press.

UKCGE (UK Council for Graduate Education) (1995) *Graduate Schools.* Coventry: UKCGE.

UKCGE (UK Council for Graduate Education) (1996a) *Quality and Standards of Postgraduate Research Degrees.* Coventry: UKCGE.

UKCGE (UK Council for Graduate Education) (1996b) *The Award of PhD on the Basis of Published Work in the UK.* Coventry: UKCGE.

UKCGE (UK Council for Graduate Education) (1997) *Practice-based Doctorates in the Creative and Performing Arts.* Coventry: UKCGE.

UKCGE (UK Council for Graduate Education) (1998a) *PhD by Published Work in Mainland Europe.* Coventry: UKCGE.

UKCGE (UK Council for Graduate Education) (1998b) *Inter-institutional Collaboration*. Coventry: UKCGE.

UKCGE (UK Council for Graduate Education) (1999a) *Preparing Postgraduates to Teach in Higher Education*. Coventry: UKCGE.

UKCGE (UK Council for Graduate Education) (1999b) *International Students*. Coventry: UKCGE.

Vartuli, S. (ed.) (1982) *The PhD Experience: A Woman's Point of View*. New York: Praeger.

Watson, G. (1970) *The Literary Thesis: a Guide to Research*. London: Longman.

Welsh, J.M. (1979) *The First Year of Postgraduate Study*. Guildford: Society for Research into Higher Education.

Williams, K. (1989) *Study Skills*. Basingstoke: Macmillan.

Wisker, G. and Sutcliffe, N. (eds) (1999) *Good Practice in Postgraduate Supervision*. Birmingham: Staff and Educational Development Association.

Wright, J. and Lodwick, R. (1989) The process of the PhD: a study of the first year of doctoral study, *Research Papers in Education*, 4: 22–56.

Youngman, M.B. (1989) *Role Expectations of Research Supervisors and Students: Final Report R231786*. Swindon: Economic and Social Research Council.

Zuber-Skerritt, O. and Ryan, Y. (eds) (1994) *Quality in Postgraduate Education*. London: Kogan Page.

REFERENCES

Association of Graduate Recruiters (1995) *Skills for Graduates in the 21st Century*. Cambridge: Association of Graduate Recruiters.

Australian Vice-Chancellors' Committee (1990) *Guidelines for Responsible Practice in Research and Dealing with Problems of Research Misconduct*. Deakin, Vic.: Australian Vice-Chancellors' Committee.

Bargar, R. and Duncan, J. (1982) Cultivating creative endeavour in doctoral research, *Journal of Higher Education*, 53(1): 1–31.

Becher, T., Henkel, M. and Kogan, M. (1995) *Graduate Education and Staffing: Report of a Research Seminar*. London: Committee of Vice-Chancellors and Principals/Society for Reseach into Higher Education.

Berry, R. (1986) *How to Write a Research Paper*. Oxford: Pergamon.

Bogan, M. (1999) Is the workplace a level playing field?, in S. Tyler (ed.) *Career Women Casebook 2000*. London: Hobsons.

Bowrick, P. (1995) Blowing the whistle on referees, *Times Higher Education Supplement*, 10 February: 11.

Bristow, J. (1995) Teachers and petting do not mix, *Times Higher Education Supplement*, 2 June: 12.

British Academy (1992) *Postgraduate Research in the Humanities*. London: British Academy.

Clark, D. (1995) Foreword, *Journal of Graduate Education*, 1(4): 101–2.

Clark, J. (1991) Personal views, in G. Allan and C. Skinner (eds) *Handbook for Research Students in the Social Sciences*. Brighton: Falmer Press.

Cryer, P. (1997) How to get ahead with a PhD, *Times Higher Education Supplement: Research Opportunities*, 16 May: i.

Denicolo, P. (1999) Discussion document used in training supervisors of postgraduate research students at the University of Reading. Unpublished.

Denzin, N. and Lincoln, Y. (eds) (1994) *Handbook of Qualitative Research*. Beverly Hills, CA: Sage.

Economic and Social Research Council (1986) *The Preparation and Supervision of Research Theses in the Social Sciences*. Swindon: Economic and Social Research Council.

Ehrenberg, A. (1982) Writing technical papers or reports, *The American Statistician*, 36(4): 326–9.

Elton, L. (1999) Personal communication.

Engineering and Physical Sciences Research Council (1995) *Postgraduate Research: A Guide to Good Supervisory Practice, Consultative Document*. Swindon: Engineering and Physical Sciences Research Council.

Eysenck, H. (1994) Past masters: Hans Eysenck describes his unsympathetic mentor, Sir Cyril Burt, *Times Higher Education Supplement*, 14 October: 17.

Fairbairn, G. and Winch, C. (1996) *Reading, Writing and Reasoning*, 2nd edn. Buckingham: Society for Research into Higher Education and Open University Press.

Fontana, D. (1993) *Managing Stress*. Leicester: British Psychological Society and Routledge.

Gross, B. (1994) The accommodation of research students, *Journal of Graduate Education*, 1(1): 21–4.

HEFCE (Higher Education Funding Council for England) (1996) *HEFCE/CVCP/SCOP Review of Postgraduate Education*. London: HEFCE.

Heisenberg, W. (1971) *Physics and Beyond: Encounters and Conversations*, trans. A.J. Pomerans. New York: Harper & Row.

HEQC (Higher Education Quality Council) (1996) *Guidelines on Quality Assurance of Research Degrees*. London: HEQC.

Jackson, R. (1997) Postgraduate typology and awards. *National Postgraduate Committee Newsletter*, July.

MacAleese, M. (1998) Keynote address at the International Postgraduate Students Conference, Dublin, 20 November.

McArthur, T. (1992) *The Oxford Companion to the English Language*. Oxford: Oxford University Press.

Martin, J. (1982) A garbage can model of the research process, in M. McGrath *et al.* (eds) *Judgment Calls in Research*. Beverly Hills, CA: Sage.

Mathews, E.H. and Taylor, P.B. (1998) *Making the Researcher's Life Easier with Research Toolbox* – the manual for Research Toolbox Software. Contact http//:www.research toolbox.com

Mathias, H. and Gale, T. (1991) Undertaking a research degree, in G. Allen and C. Skinner (eds) *Handbook for Research Students in the Social Sciences*. Brighton: Falmer Press.

Medawar, P. (1981) *Advice to a Young Scientist*. London: Pan.

Mileham, P. (1995) Executive cases in brief, *Times Higher Education Supplement*, 24 November: 32.

National Committee of Inquiry into Higher Education (1997) *Higher Education in the Learning Society* (the Dearing Report). Norwich: HMSO.

National Postgraduate Committee (1995) *Guidelines for Codes of Practice for Postgraduate Research*, 2nd edn. For availability see http://www.npc.org.uk

Ochert, A. (1999) A time and emotion study, *Times Higher Education Supplement*, 4 June: 20.

Parry, S. and Hayden, M. (1994) *Supervising Higher Degree Research Students: An Investigation of Practices across a Range of Academic Departments*. Canberra: Australian Government Publishing Service.

Prima Magazine (1994) October: 57.

Purcell, K. and Pitcher, J. (1997) *Great Expectations: The New Diversity of Graduate Skills and Aspirations*. Manchester: Central Services Higher

Education Unit, Institute for Employment Research and Association of Graduate Careers Advisory Services.

Race, P. (1999) *How to get a Good Degree*. Buckingham: Open University Press.

Salmon, P. (1992) *Achieving a PhD – Ten Students' Experiences*. Stoke-on-Trent: Trentham Books.

Science and Engineering Research Council (1992) *Research Student and Supervisor: An Approach to Good Supervisory Practice*. Swindon: Science and Engineering Research Council.

Shatner, W. (1993) *Star Trek Memories*. London: HarperCollins.

Smith, J. (1991) What are examiners looking for? in G. Allan and C. Skinner (eds) *Handbook for Research Students in the Social Sciences*. Brighton: Falmer Press.

Taaffe, O. (1998) Labours of love, *Guardian Higher*, 29 September: vi.

Targett, S. (1995) More money than job skills, *Times Higher Education Supplement*, 13 October: 5.

Temple, P. (1999) So much to see, so little time, *Financial Times Weekend Money*, June, 26/7: 26.

Times Higher Education Supplement (1995) Lecturers told to dampen ardour, 2 June: 4.

Times Higher Education Supplement (1998) Employability courses attract cash, 6 March: 6.

Times Higher Education Supplement (1999) Explicit ideas on sex, 27 August: 11.

Tripp, R. (1976) *The International Thesaurus of Quotations*. Harmondsworth: Penguin.

UK Council for Graduate Education (1999) Preparing postgraduates for teaching, *UK Council for Graduate Education Newsletter*, August: 2.

University College London Graduate School (1994) What to do when the money runs out, *Graduate Society Newsletter*, Issue 1.

INDEX